G

CHRISTOPHER ANDERSEN

These Few Precious Days

The Final Year of Jack with Jackie

G

Gallery Books

New York   London   Toronto   Sydney   New Delhi

Gallery Books
A Division of Simon & Schuster, Inc.
1230 Avenue of the Americas
New York, NY 10020

First Gallery Books hardcover edition August 2013

GALLERY BOOKS and colophon are registered trademarks of Simon & Schuster, Inc.

For information about special discounts for bulk purchases, please contact Simon & Schuster Special Sales at 1-866-506-1949 or business@simonandschuster.com.

The Simon & Schuster Speakers Bureau can bring authors to your live event. For more information or to book an event contact the Simon & Schuster Speakers Bureau at 1-866-248-3049 or visit our website at www.simonspeakers.com.

Designed by Ruth Lee-Mui

PHOTO CREDITS:
John F. Kennedy Presidential Library and Museum: 2, 6, 10, 12, 15, 17, 18, 19, 20, 21, 22, 23, 24, 25, 26, 27, 28, 29, 30, 32, 34, 37, 38, 39, 40
Bettmann/Corbis: 3, 4, 5, 7, 9, 11, 31, 35, 36
Corbis: 8
Henry Burroughs/AP/Corbis: 1
John Rous/AP/Corbis: 13
Globe Photos: 14, 16, 33

Library of Congress Cataloging-in-Publication Data

Andersen, Christopher P.
These few precious days : the final year of Jack with Jackie / Christopher Andersen. — 1st Gallery Books hardcover edition.
pages   cm
Includes bibliographical references and index.   1. Kennedy, John F. (John Fitzgerald), 1917–1963.   2. Onassis, Jacqueline Kennedy, 1929–1994.   3. Presidents — United States — Biography.   4. Presidents' spouses — United States — Biography.   I. Title.
E841.A538   2013
973.922092'2 — dc23
[B]   2013013676

ISBN 978-1-4767-3232-9
ISBN 978-1-4767-3234-3 (ebook)

Manufactured in the United States of America

1   3   5   7   9   10   8   6   4   2

For my grandson,

Graham Andersen Brower

Contents

Contents

Preface

‿

THEY WERE, BY ANY DEFINITION, one of history's most remarkable couples: he the handsome, dynamic young president whose
wit, charm, and idealistic fervor captured the world's imagina-
tion; she the young wife and mother whose beauty, style, and
elegance made her one of the most admired first ladies in American history. By the time it all ended with gunshots in Texas on
November 22, 1963, Jack and Jackie Kennedy were irrefutably the
First Couple of the World.

In the immediate aftermath of Dallas, Jackie's quiet strength
and natural dignity—her *gallantry*, historian Arthur Schlesinger Jr.
called it—were the glue that held the nation together. What did
not endure, however, was the glittering fairy tale conjured up by
Jackie as a way to preserve her husband's legacy. By the turn of the
new century, the flood of revelations concerning JFK's reckless
private life washed away what little remained of the Camelot myth.

The ultimate question remains: *On that day in Dallas fifty years
ago when Jack was shot to death with Jackie at his side, did they truly
love each other?* After the affairs, the humiliations, the triumphs,
and tragedies both known and unknown to the public, had they
finally come together?

Together, they had survived his life-threatening illnesses, his unfettered infidelity, the death of one parent and the crippling stroke of another, a miscarriage, a stillbirth, a difficult delivery that nearly killed both mother and child, and the loss of their son Patrick. Incredibly, over the course of their marriage, either the president or his first lady were administered the last rites at least six times—a little-known statistic that spoke volumes about what they had suffered through, and triumphed over, in private.

It is no wonder we are still fascinated by them. They were impossibly attractive, outlandishly rich, brilliant, passionate, *exciting*—and deliciously complicated. Power, sex, mystique, money, and glamour—not to mention the dreams and aspirations of an entire generation—were embodied in the charismatic young couple who occupied the White House for a thousand days. Yet it is the bittersweet account of how they came together in their final year as a couple that really makes theirs a love story for the ages.

IT WAS A SCENE REPLAYED on more than a dozen occasions—at Hyannis Port, in the White House, wherever President Kennedy gathered with family and friends to unwind.

"Red," he asked his old Navy buddy Paul "Red" Fay, "sing 'Hooray for Hollywood.' "

And with that, Fay burst into a slightly off-key, window-rattling version of the song while the boisterous crowd laughed and clapped. Afterward, Jack's youngest brother, Ted, led everyone in singing "Heart of My Heart."

Until that moment, the president had been silent. "Do you know 'September Song'?" JFK asked Ted's wife, Joan, who was at the piano. She played the chorus twice, and then Jack began to sing the melancholy standard that tells the bittersweet story of a middle-aged man facing his own mortality.

This night, the normally boisterous crowd fell silent as Jack looked over at Jackie with tears welling in his eyes and sang the final lines:

> *Oh, the days dwindle down to a precious few.*
> *September, November!*
> *And these few precious days I'll spend with you . . .*

Jack was the love of my life. No one will ever know a big part of me died with him.

—JACKIE

❧

Of all the women I've ever known, there was only one I could have married—and I married her.

—JACK

1

⤸

"Jack, Jack, Jack!
Can You Hear Me?"

DALLAS

NOVEMBER 22, 1963

12:30 P.M.

*S*he would always remember the roses. Three times that day before they got to Dallas, she feigned delight as someone presented her with the yellow roses for which Texas was so famous. "Only in Dallas," Jackie said, "I was given *red* roses. How funny, I thought—red roses for me." Soon, the backseat of their car would be strewn with blood-soaked rose petals—a surreal image she would never be able to erase from her mind. But for now, as they basked in the noonday sunlight and cheers from the crowds that lined the streets, Jack and Jackie seemed happier—and closer—than they had ever been.

The forty-six-year-old president and his thirty-four-year-old first lady exchanged one final glance. And then, in an instant, it all ended.

The look on Jack's still-boyish face the moment the first bullet struck him in the back of the neck, severing his windpipe and exiting his throat, would haunt Jackie's dreams for the rest of her life. "He looked puzzled," she later said. "I remember he looked as if he just had a slight headache."

For a split second, Jackie thought the crack she had heard was the sound of a motorcycle backfiring—until she realized she was watching, as if in slow motion, the president's head begin to pull apart. "I could see a piece of his skull coming off," she recalled. "It was flesh-colored, not white. I can see this perfectly clean piece detaching itself from his head. Then he slumped in my lap."

Texas governor John Connally, riding in the jumpseat in front of the president, had also been seriously wounded. "Oh no, no, no," he yelled, "they're going to kill us all!" Connally's wife, Nellie, who with her husband was now covered with blood and bits of brain matter from JFK's head wound, looked back at the first lady. "I have his brains," Jackie said as she sat staring for a full seven seconds, "in my hands!"

The driver of the presidential limousine floored the accelerator, and the "sensation of enormous speed" gave Jackie a sudden jolt of adrenaline. It also nearly dislodged Secret Service agent Clint Hill from his tenuous perch on the rear step; ever since the first shot rang out, Hill, who had been riding in the backup car, had sprinted to catch up. He finally reached the president's Lincoln just as the third shot struck, spraying Hill as well with bits of bone and brain matter.

What Hill then witnessed along with a breathless nation was

something Jackie herself would not remember. Numb with shock and panic, Jackie clambered onto the slippery trunk of the Lincoln. To many, it appeared that she was trying to reach out to Agent Hill and pull him onto the car. In fact, she was grasping for a large chunk of the president's skull. Terrified that the first lady would now tumble off the back of the speeding vehicle, Hill pushed her back into her seat as the shard from JFK's skull flew into the street.

With the 190-pound Hill now sprawled over her, trying to act as a human shield for both the president and the first lady, Jackie cradled her husband's shattered head in her lap. She pressed down on the top with her white-gloved hands, she said later, "to keep the brains in."

Jackie's head was down, her face only inches from the president's. She was struck by the "pink-rose ridges" inside his broken skull, she later said, and the fact that despite everything, from the hairline down, "his head was so beautiful. I tried to hold the top of his head down, maybe I could keep it in . . . but I knew he was dead." So did the crowds that lined the street. "He's dead! He's dead!" she could hear people shouting as the motorcade sped to Parkland Memorial Hospital.

Jackie clung to the slimmest hope that maybe there was life there still, a latent if quickly ebbing consciousness. "Jack, Jack, Jack! Can you hear me?" she whispered over and over into his ear. The president's blue eyes were wide open in a fixed stare. "I love you, Jack," Jackie said. "I love you."

Although she later said it "seemed like an eternity," it took just seven minutes before the car screeched to a halt outside the emergency room entrance at Parkland. Hill, a fellow Secret Service agent named Roy Kellerman, and JFK's longtime aide Dave

Powers were about to lift the president onto a waiting stretcher, but Jackie, still cradling Jack's head, refused.

"Please, Mrs. Kennedy," Hill said. "We must get the president to a doctor."

"I'm not letting him go, Mr. Hill," she said. "You know he's dead. Leave me alone." Hill understood what was happening: Jackie did not want the world to see the gaping crater in her husband's skull. Struggling to control his own emotions, Hill whipped off the jacket of his black suit and wrapped it around the president's head.

Jackie ran alongside the gurney as her husband was wheeled into the hospital; she held Hill's jacket in place so that it wouldn't slip to reveal the gruesome truth. "It wasn't repulsive to me for one moment," she said. "Nothing was repulsive to me, and I was running behind with the coat covering it . . ."

Incredibly, Jack had a faint pulse and was still breathing when he was admitted to Parkland Hospital, simply as "Case 24740, white male, gunshot wound." Inside Trauma Room 1 a team of doctors, soon joined by White House physician Admiral George Burkley, immediately began administering massive blood transfusions.

Suddenly two burly men in scrubs blocked Jackie's path and began trying to pull her away. "Mrs. Kennedy," one of them said, "you come with us." But Jackie had other ideas. Nine years earlier, she had been kept away from Jack when he nearly died following one of his back surgeries. "They're never going to keep me away from him again," she told herself then.

This time, Jackie was standing her ground. The "big Texas interns wanted to take me away from him," she later said. "They kept trying to get me, they kept trying to grab me." This time things would be different. "I'm not leaving him," she declared, softly at first. Then she raised her voice only slightly—but just enough to make the interns back away. "I am *not* leaving," she told them.

No one seemed to notice that during all this time, Jackie had her left hand cupped over something she held in her right. As Parkland's chief anesthesiologist, Dr. Marion Jenkins, stood outside Trauma Room 1, the first lady nudged him with her left elbow. Then, carefully, she handed Jenkins what the doctor could only describe as "a good-sized chunk of the president's brain. She didn't say a word. I handed it to the nurse."

One of the uniformed Dallas police officers who had escorted the motorcade offered Jackie a cigarette. She had always managed to conceal her heavy smoking habit from the press and never smoked in public, but none of that mattered now.

Ten minutes later, the same patrolman fetched folding chairs for the first lady and Nellie Connally, whose husband was being treated for his nonfatal bullet wounds in Trauma Room 2. The two women sat in total silence while Powers and White House Chief of Staff Kenneth P. O'Donnell paced the floor.

The night before as they were going to bed, Jackie had told her husband that she "hated" John Connally because he had been bragging about how he was more popular in Texas than the president. "I just can't bear his soft, weak mouth and his sitting there saying all these great things about himself," she complained. "It seems so rude. I really hate him." But Jack, who unlike Jackie never held a grudge, rubbed her back and tried to calm her down. "You mustn't say that," he told her. "If you start to say or think that you hate someone, then the next day you'll act as if you hate him. You mustn't say that about people." What struck Jackie about that moment, she recalled, was that he "said it so kindly . . . Jack never stayed mad at someone. Never!"

Powers, "too numb" to say anything himself, choked back tears at the sight of Jackie sitting in her gore-splattered pink wool suit. Staring straight ahead, she periodically brought the cigarette to her mouth, revealing that the president's blood had stained her white kid gloves a deep crimson.

Suddenly she was gripped by the possibility that Jack might survive. "Maybe he isn't dead," she thought. "He's going to live!" After all, Jack had cheated death at least three times during their marriage. Of course, if he survived this time, he would be severely brain-damaged. When a stroke left his father, Joseph P. Kennedy, partially paralyzed and unable to speak, Jack let Jackie know in no uncertain terms where he stood. "Don't ever," he told her, "let that happen to me." Now faced with options that were far worse, Jackie began bargaining with the Almighty: "Please, don't let him die. I'll take care of him every day of his life. I'll make him happy."

The moment of self-delusion passed as swiftly as it came. She didn't want to be sitting in a corridor waiting; Jackie wanted to be at her husband's side. She got up and headed for Trauma 1, only to encounter the hulking presence of head nurse Doris Nelson standing in the doorway. Nelson grabbed Jackie by both shoulders. "You can't come in here," she said.

"I'm going to get in that room," Jackie replied firmly. Admiral Burkley came out of the room and offered her a sedative. "No," she said without hesitation. "I want to be in there when he dies."

Burkley relented. As they pushed through the swinging door into the trauma room, Jackie witnessed the medical team's final, futile effort to revive the president. The floor was covered with

Jack's blood. Looking up from the operating table, chief surgeon Dr. Malcolm Perry shouted, "Get her out of here!"

"It's her prerogative," Burkley argued. "It's her prerogative."

"No," Perry shot back. "She has got to leave. Mrs. Kennedy, you must leave."

For the first time that day, the preternaturally cool Mrs. Kennedy lost her temper. "I will *not* leave," she said. "It's my husband. His blood, his brains, are all over me." Then, as Perry returned to his work, Jackie dropped down on one knee and said a brief, silent prayer. When she got back up, the front of her skirt was drenched with blood from the floor.

At 1 p.m., Dr. Jenkins pulled a white sheet over Jack's face while another member of the medical team, Dr. Kemp Clark, was given the onerous task of informing Jackie that the president was dead. "Your husband," he told her, "has sustained a fatal wound."

Unable to speak, Jackie mouthed two words in response: "I *know*."

The room fell silent as Jackie walked up to Jack's body. She scanned the length of the operating table, and noticed one of his feet was sticking out, looking "whiter than the sheet." Instinctively, she took the exposed foot in her hand, knelt down, and gently kissed it.

What happened next stunned everyone. Jackie pulled the sheet back to expose Jack's face and shoulders. His eyes were open, she later said, "and his mouth was so *beautiful*." According to Dr. Jenkins, Jackie then began kissing Jack again—starting with his exposed foot and then, through the sheet, slowly, deliberately, working her way up. "She kissed his foot, his leg, thigh, chest, and then his lips." During this entire process, Jenkins recalled, "she didn't say a word." The process had left everyone in the room "feeling as if the wind had been knocked out of us. It was the most moving thing," Jenkins said, "any of us had ever seen."

Father Oscar Huber had rushed to the hospital from nearby Holy Trinity Church and now feared he might pass out at any moment. Steeling himself, Huber stepped up to perform the last rites. Another physician guided Jackie's hand to her husband's under the sheet, and she held it while Father Huber annointed the slain president's forehead with holy oil and bestowed the Apostolic Blessing in Latin. When he was finished, the priest dabbed the oil with cotton, then tried to conceal it from Jackie when he realized the swab was drenched in the president's blood.

She returned to the hallway and settled back into her little folding chair with a cigarette while orderlies washed Jack's body so it could be placed in a bronze coffin for the trip back to Washington, D.C. aboard Air Force One. A nurse materialized with a cold towel, and Jackie held it to her forehead to keep from passing out. "You must make sure," she told O'Donnell, "that I get in there before they close the coffin. I must see him."

O'Donnell led Jackie back into Trauma Room 1 just a few minutes later. There was still blood on the floor, but Jack's pale skin had been wiped completely clean. Four orderlies carefully lifted the president's naked body off the table and slowly lowered it into the coffin lined with white satin.

She was struck by how Jack, who had always seemed so much larger than life, now seemed "so small and fragile." She also noticed that, as one of his longtime physicians had pointed out, the left side of his body was smaller than the right. "The left side of his face was smaller," said back specialist Dr. Janet Travell. "His left shoulder was lower, and his left leg appreciably shorter"—a congenital condition that may have been the root cause of his lifelong back trouble.

Jackie's eyes widened as she began tugging at the white kid gloves that were now caked with her husband's blood. Finally, one of the policemen there stepped forward to help her pull them off. JFK never wore a wedding ring, so Jackie slipped hers over the bare finger on his left hand. The ring was also smeared with blood, and a nurse stepped forward to quickly sponge off the ring and the president's hand. "It's the right thing to do," O'Donnell reassured her. (Almost immediately Jackie began doubting whether she could bear parting with the simple gold band she had worn for a decade. Later that night at Bethesda Naval Hospital, O'Donnell instructed Admiral Burkley to remove the ring from Jack's finger and return it to Jackie.)

Before the casket was closed, Burkley handed Jackie two blood-soaked red roses that had fallen inside the president's shirt after the bullets struck. She handed one of the bloody stems back to Burkley. "This," he told her as he held up the rose, "is the greatest treasure of my life."

It would not be until Air Force One was winging its way back to Washington with Lyndon Baines Johnson sworn in as the new president that she finally began to unravel. She was seated next to Kenny O'Donnell at the rear of the plane, just opposite the casket, when Burkley came back and asked yet again if Jackie didn't want to change out of her bloody clothes.

"No!" she insisted. "I want them to see what they've done. I want them to see what they've done."

Once Burkley had slunk back to the front of the cabin, Jackie and O'Donnell looked at each other and, O'Donnell said, "she finally lost it. For the very first time that day, she allowed herself to cry."

Jackie sobbed for a full ten minutes, her poignant cries audible to the other passengers over the whine of the jet engines. Regaining her composure, she turned to O'Donnell. "Oh, it's happened," Jackie said.

"It's happened," answered O'Donnell, who with Powers was a leading member of Kennedy's fabled "Irish Mafia" of political cronies. Powers had already broken down several times in front of Jackie, but O'Donnell, whose eyes were red-rimmed from crying in private, struggled to hold it together.

"Oh, Kenny," Jackie said, choking back her tears, "what's going to happen?"

"You want to know something, Jackie?" O'Donnell answered. "I don't give a damn."

"Oh, you're right, you know," she said. "You're right. Just nothing matters but what you've lost."

"Well, I know what I'm going to do," O'Donnell said. "I'm having a Scotch, and I think you would have one, too."

Jackie's drink of choice was champagne; as the daughter of an alcoholic with a special fondness for hard drink, she had always been wary of whiskey. She remembered that Jack preferred beer—Heineken—but when he did drink Scotch he always asked for Ballantine's. "I've never even tasted Scotch before," she told O'Donnell. "Now," she added, "is as good a time as any to start." Staring at what she later described as "that long, long coffin," Jackie and O'Donnell both downed one triple, then another. "A lot of people were drinking," LBJ aide Jack Valenti recalled. "But honestly, everyone on that plane was in such a state of profound shock and disbelief the alcohol seemed to have no effect."

Attorney General Robert F. Kennedy was having lunch with guests at Hickory Hill, his Virginia estate, when FBI director J. Edgar Hoover called with the news that the president had been shot. Thirty minutes later, Clint Hill telephoned Bobby to confirm that his brother was dead. "Those poor children!" Bobby's wife Ethel cried when he told her that Jack and Jackie's children, Caroline and John, were now fatherless.

That afternoon five-year-old "Lyric" (Caroline's code name; the president was "Lancer," Jackie "Lace," and John, "Lark") sat beaming in the backseat of a family friend's station wagon, headed for her very first sleepover. Behind the wheel was the mother of Caroline's best friend. As soon as the terrible news blared over the radio she pulled to the side of the road. "We have a news bulletin," the announcer said. "This just in—President Kennedy has been shot." The driver switched off the radio and checked out her daughter and Caroline in the rearview mirror.

Caroline, her small suitcase at her feet and her favorite pink teddy bear in her lap, was still chatting excitedly with her friend. Maybe she hadn't heard, the driver thought. But she had.

A black Ford sedan driven by a member of the Secret Service "Kiddie Detail"—those agents assigned to protect the president's children—pulled up behind the station wagon, and soon Caroline was heading back to the White House (code name "Chateau") in their car. The little girl gave the agent a quizzical look, grabbed her suitcase, and said goodbye to her bewildered friend. As the Secret Service car headed for 1600 Pennsylvania Avenue, a passing driver spotted Caroline in the unmarked car and, having heard what had happened in Dallas, apparently assumed JFK's daughter was being abducted. After a wild chase through congested rush hour traffic, Caroline arrived safely back at the White House.

Neither she nor her brother would be there for long. As soon as Bobby called Janet Auchincloss with the horrible news, Jackie's famously meddlesome mother (Jack thought it hilarious that Janet's children called her, or anyone, "Mummy") made the unilateral decision to have Caroline and John brought to the Auchincloss house in Georgetown to spend the night.

Joined by their British nanny, Maud Shaw, John and Caroline were playing in the living room of their grandmother's house when Jackie's sixteen-year-old half brother, Jamie Auchincloss, bounded in. "Uncle Jamie! Uncle Jamie!" John yelled as he dashed about the room playing with his toy helicopter. Jamie assumed his mother or *someone* had told them what had happened, but it quickly became obvious no one had. "I thought, 'Why tell her now?' " recalled Jamie, who got down on the floor and began playing with his niece and nephew. "Why not let her have a few more hours of blissful innocence?"

At one point, Caroline leapt to her feet and dashed into the kitchen for a cookie. What she saw was several Secret Service agents glued to the television set in the kitchen. One of the agents blocked the screen, but too late. When she came back into the living room, said Jamie, "Caroline's mood had changed. She turned very quiet."

On the ground at Andrews Air Force Base, Jackie was met by Jack's brother Bobby. It had been up to Bobby to break the news to all the family members, with the exception of Caroline and John. Jackie, overwhelmed with the day's events and obviously still in a state of shock, had said nothing about the children yet.

Right now she was focused on staying at her husband's side. After Jack's coffin was loaded into a waiting hearse, she and Bobby slid in the back.

During the forty-minute ride from Andrews to Bethesda, Jackie recounted in vivid detail the events of the day. Once they arrived, she repeated the story for the small group that had come to offer her comfort: old friends Nancy Tuckerman, Martha and Charlie Bartlett and Tony and Ben Bradlee, Secretary of Defense Robert McNamara, Jackie's mother, and her stepfather, Hugh D. ("Uncle Hughdie") Auchincloss II.

Making what Ben Bradlee called a "strangely graceful arc" with her right hand as she described how "that part of the president's head had been blown away by one bullet," Jackie moved trance-like from one stunned person to the next. All the while, Bradlee said, Jackie's eyes were "still wide open with horror." All listened in numb shock as Jackie, still "amazingly calm," as Bradlee put it, relived the day's events over and over again. "Even if you didn't want to hear it," Charlie Bartlett said, "you knew she had to tell it."

Perhaps even more startling was the manner in which Jackie turned the tables on those who had come to console her. Instead, she insisted on comforting *them.* "Oh Dave, you have been with Jack all these years," she had already told Powers on the plane. "What will you do now?" She asked the same question of her secretary, Pamela Turnure, the Jackie look-alike who had once been her husband's lover. And to her girlhood chum Nancy Tuckerman, just hired to be Jackie's social secretary: "Poor Tucky. You came all the way down from New York to take this job and now it's all over. It's so sad."

All the while, Jackie resisted any effort to get her to change out of her blood-spattered suit. She had often joked with her friends about her compulsive need to change out of her clothes if she saw even the tiniest spot. Now she wore her stained Chanel proudly. Martha Bartlett took her husband aside. "It's as though," she told him as they watched Jackie talk, "she doesn't want the day to end."

Janet Auchincloss was surprised, then, when her daughter suddenly turned to her and asked, "Where are the children?"

"They are with Jamie at our house," she answered.

"What," Jackie wanted to know, "are they doing there?"

Janet, who was used to making executive decisions on her own, nevertheless claimed Jackie had sent her a message from Air Force One saying she wanted the children taken to their grandparents' home.

There was no question in Jackie's mind that her mother was making it all up. "But," she said, "I never sent such a message." In fact, Jackie was anything but pleased that her mother had interfered with the children's normal routine.

"The best thing for them," Jackie said, "would be to stay in their own rooms with their own things so their lives can be as normal as possible." Janet realized she had made a terrible mistake. "Mummy, my God," Jackie added, her voice rising in anger, "those poor children. Their lives shouldn't be disrupted now, of all times!"

Jackie's remarks sent Janet scurrying for the nearest phone. Within minutes, Maud Shaw was bundling Caroline and John into a White House limousine for the ride back home. "I knew their lives had changed forever," said Uncle Jamie, who waved goodbye as the car pulled away from the Auchincloss mansion. "But then so had everyone's."

✑

WHAT JACKIE WANTED FOR HER children that one last fateful
night was something that she had struggled against formidable
odds to achieve throughout her marriage: a happy, normal family
life—or at least a convincing imitation of it.

This was not something either Jack or Jackie had known they
were capable of achieving, or even wanted. In his scramble to the
summit of power, Jack had scarcely proven himself to be a model
husband. Jackie, living out her girlhood desire to be "part of a
great man's life," had been willing to put up with Jack's faithless-
ness so long as she was not the object of public humiliation—and
in the abiding belief that she was the only woman he really loved.

When she first set foot in the White House as America's first
lady, Jackie could not have dreamed that this would be where she
and Jack would come closest to fulfilling her dream of a happy
marriage. "I said to myself, 'It will be such a goldfish bowl. With
the Secret Service and everybody here, I'll never see my husband.
It will ruin our marriage.' "

Soon she realized the opposite was true. "I remember thinking,
'What was the matter with me?' It was when we were the closest,"
she said. "I hadn't realized the physical closeness of having his
office in the same building and seeing him so many times a day."
For all the soaring triumphs, soul-testing trials, and crushing tragedies that would befall them during this historic time, Jack and
Jackie would finally bridge the yawning emotional chasm between
them only within the walls of the White House.

"It was," Jackie said without hesitation, "the happiest time of
my life."

When they got to the White House, they fell in love all over again.

—OLEG CASSINI, LONGTIME FRIEND OF
BOTH JACK AND JACKIE

⚘

Jackie loved him. Jack loved her. Maybe for different reasons . . .

—JACQUES LOWE, JFK'S PERSONAL
PHOTOGRAPHER AND FRIEND

2

ೣ

"The President Says if You Don't Hurry, He'll Fall Asleep"

THE WHITE HOUSE

ALMOST ANY DAY JACK AND JACKIE

WERE IN RESIDENCE

"*O*kay, George," the president said as his longtime valet George Thomas rapped four times on the door of the first lady's bedroom. Jackie stirred beside him. "We hear you. We're awake." And so their day began with the soft-spoken, gray-haired Thomas waking the president promptly at 7:45 a.m. It was a routine the family quickly settled into, and it seldom varied during their thousand days in the White House.

Although Jack and Jackie slept together in her bedroom most nights, the president maintained his own quarters as well—a particularly practical arrangement in the Kennedys' case, since Jack's persistent back problems often made it necessary for him to sleep on a special rock-hard mattress prescribed by his physician. An electric heating pad was never far from reach on the nightstand.

The first couple's bedrooms said much about their personalities—and the nature of their relationship. Jackie's chandeliered French provincial bedroom was decorated in hues of powder blue and green, with a leopard-skin throw tossed in for drama. A couch upholstered in beige silk faced the fireplace, and large windows draped in silk framed the South Lawn. The first lady's king-sized canopy bed was actually two beds pushed together—a soft mattress for Jackie and a firm one better suited to Jack's problematic back.

Separated from the first lady's boudoir by a walk-in closet that also contained their stereo system—"the old Victrola" they brought with them from their first home in Georgetown—the president's white-walled bedroom was dominated by Harry Truman's immense mahogany four-poster. Jackie selected a simple blue-and-white design for the linens and drapes, and picked a single painting to adorn the wall: Childe Hassam's iconic *Flag Day*. Tucked off in one corner of the room was Jack's favorite Carolina rocker, which the first lady had padded and upholstered for maximum comfort.

While Jackie remained curled up under the blankets, her husband crawled out of bed, shed his pajamas, wrapped a towel around his waist, and ambled across the hall toward his bedroom and the warm bath that Thomas was already drawing for him. "He was the most unselfconscious man I've ever seen," Jackie once said of her husband's penchant for walking around in various states of undress within the confines of home. "He would walk around with just a towel on, and if it fell off or something, he'd just put it back on. So Jack was just always so natural. . . . Poor Nixon," Jackie would then add about the nervous tics that plagued her husband's presidential rival. "He had such a disadvantage, you know, he would sweat and everything."

Oddly, in the morning hours Jack and Jackie rarely saw each other. His first conversation of the day was always with his valet. "Good Morning, George," Jack said as he began rifling through the four morning newspapers Thomas always spread out at the foot of his bed.

A native of Berryville, Virginia, and a grandson of slaves, Thomas was still in his thirties and working for Pulitzer Prize–winning *New York Times* columnist Arthur Krock when Jack first ran for Congress in 1946. Krock's longtime friend, Joseph P. Kennedy, casually remarked to the esteemed journalist that his bachelor son was accustomed to being cared for by family servants and probably could use one of his own. Krock, who also owed Joe a not unsubstantial sum of money, jumped at the chance to repay his debt to the powerful patriarch by "giving" his valet to the young Kennedy. For the next sixteen years, George Thomas was a constant presence in Jack's life—and an eyewitness to some of the most intimate moments in the Kennedy marriage.

For the next half hour, the president shaved in the tub to save time, then settled back in the soapy water and pored over the morning newspapers and classified documents. "It was not at all unusual," said White House Press Secretary Pierre Salinger, "to get a sheet of paper from him that was soaking wet."

THOMAS, MEANWHILE, LAID OUT JACK'S first suit of the day. Over the course of an average day, JFK would change all of his clothes—from underwear on out—at least four times, often wearing as many as six shirts in a single twenty-four-hour period. Jack owned eighteen suits, all purchased by his father from Brooks Brothers. His underwear—JFK preferred white boxers—was also from Brooks Brothers, made exclusively for the store by D. & G. Anderson of Scotland. Jack's shirts were custom-made by Charles Dillon shirtmakers of 444 Park Avenue, New York, his ties by Christian Dior and Givenchy, his hand-sewn size-ten-and-a-half shoes and his size-thirty-four belts by Farnsworth-Reed. Thomas placed the president's gold Cartier watch with black leather band on the nightstand, alongside the three-foot-long custom-made shoehorn that enabled JFK to slip into his shoes—without having to bend down.

From the first day he went to work for Jack, then a first-time candidate for Massachusetts's Eleventh Congressional District, Thomas realized his duties would far transcend those of an ordinary valet. Suffering from the second in what would be a long series of botched back surgeries, Jack was emaciated and drawn as he hobbled from one campaign event to another. After a particularly grueling day, he collapsed—but only after he had managed to shake thousands of hands while marching in Boston's annual Bunker Hill Day Parade.

One campaign worker, Robert Lee, remembered that Jack "turned yellow and blue. He appeared to me as a man who had probably had a heart attack." Lee and Thomas scooped Jack up, carried him to a second-floor apartment, stripped off his clothes, and sponged him down. An ambulance was called, and George Thomas rode with Jack to the hospital. There would be countless such incidents over the years, and there were still times when

Jack's pain was so intense that Thomas, now fifty-five, had to help the younger man—Jack was just forty-three when he became the youngest man ever elected president—into his clothes.

At 8:15 a.m., while the president still soaked in the tub, Maud Shaw knocked tentatively on the outer door to the president's bedroom. More Mrs. Doubtfire than Mary Poppins, the Kennedys' nanny had been caring for Caroline since she was eleven days old and still in the hospital. Breast-feeding, not particularly in vogue in the 1950s, was something that few society moms practiced, and Jackie was no exception. Like her mother before her, Jackie also felt that giving the baby her bottle or changing a diaper were tasks best left to the professionals. "If one of them was holding the baby and that smell began wafting up," recalled close Kennedy friend Chuck Spalding, "well, it was, 'Maud . . . oh, MAUD!' and they held that kid at arm's length until they could hand her over. But that was the way they'd been brought up— with servants always sort of appearing out of nowhere to clean things up. They weren't your average people, and they weren't your average parents either."

At least Jack tried. During Shaw's first week on the job, he told her he wanted to give Caroline her bottle. "He asked me to stand quite near him," she said, "in case he dropped her." Within five minutes, the president grew bored. "Miss Shaw," he said, handing the baby back to her nanny, "how have you got the patience to feed the child all this bottle?"

Yet no one, least of all Miss Shaw, doubted Jack's total devotion to Caroline. When the Kennedys lived in a narrow brick town-house on Georgetown's N Street, Jack wasted no time bounding upstairs to the nursery as soon as he came home. "That child always smiled for him when she never did for anybody else," the nanny said. "Right from the very beginning, he loved her and she adored him."

During the 1960 presidential campaign and long summer weekends spent at the Kennedy family compound in Hyannis Port, all Daddy had to do was clap his hands twice to summon his daughter. "As soon as Caroline heard that first clap," said presidential press secretary Pierre Salinger, "she took off like a rocket." The memory of her father's sharp hand clap would linger in Caroline's memory always, as would the sound of Jack's voice as he called out the pet name he and only he had for her: Buttons.

Of course, Caroline wasn't the only child in the Kennedy White House. Each morning Nanny Shaw awoke in her small room strategically situated between Caroline and the room occupied by John Jr., who was three years his sister's junior. The children's suite of rooms was just opposite the Yellow Oval Room, with its doors opening onto the Truman Balcony, and Jackie had gone to great pains to erase all traces of the drab, dated hotel décor favored by the Eisenhowers and the Trumans before them.

John's spacious nursery was white—like his father's bedroom— with blue crown molding, while Caroline's was done in white and pink, with matching rosebud drapes and linens, a white canopy bed, stuffed animals, rocking horses, an ornate dollhouse (a gift from French president Charles de Gaulle), and a Grandma Moses hanging on one wall. Their nanny's room had all the charm of a hall closet. "Maud Shaw won't need much," Jackie had written chief White House usher J. B. West before moving in. "Just find a wicker wastebasket for her banana peels and a little table for her false teeth at night."

Once she had made sure the children had brushed their teeth and were bathed and dressed, Shaw brought them over to say good morning to their father. After knocking on the president's door—by this time JFK had finished shaving—Shaw waited in the hallway while Caroline and John dashed past Harry Truman's four-poster and into the bathroom.

"Daddy! Daddy!" Caroline and John shouted in unison as they ran up to the tub. Jack exuberantly greeted each with a kiss, oblivious to the fact that ink from soaked State Department cables was running down his arm and into the bathwater.

In preparation for their arrival, Jack always kept a dozen yellow rubber duckies lined up on the edge of the tub. "Here you are, John," the president said, plucking a duck from the lineup and handing it to his wide-eyed son. "Let's see if this little guy floats upside down!"

Caroline, meantime, ran back into her father's room and turned the television on full blast. "You could hear it booming right down the hall," recalled Nanny Shaw, "and it always made the Secret Service agents laugh. The president grew up in the middle of a big, noisy family, and he just loved the commotion— you could see the delight on his face."

Ten minutes later, JFK, now wearing a dress shirt and boxer shorts, sat down in front of a tray and tore into his usual hearty breakfast: two soft-boiled eggs prepared to his specifications in a double boiler, bacon, toast, and orange juice. Thomas poured the president's coffee, which he took with cream and at least three teaspoons of sugar. "Nauseating," Jackie once said of the concoction, "but Jack had an enormous sweet tooth."

While their daddy went over his schedule for the day, Caroline and John were sprawled on the floor, transfixed by the morning cartoons—*Rocky and His Friends, Huckleberry Hound, Yogi Bear*—that blared from the bulky black-and-white television set.

At 9 a.m. they switched to TV exercise pioneer Jack LaLanne, and Jack would clap and count out the repetitions as Caroline and John imitated LaLanne's spirited repertoire of squats, push-ups, lunges, and jumping jacks. Depending on how bad his back was that day, the president would join John and Caroline in stretches and attempts to touch his toes, but for the most part he simply reveled in rolling around on the floor with his children.

On rare occasions Jackie, who seldom rose before nine, came over to watch. "He loved those children tumbling around with him," she said, "in this sort of—sensual is the only way I can think of it. . . . He needed that time with them, he was just so completely crazy about them."

The children were just winding down their exercise routine as Daddy slipped into one of the two-button, European-cut suits picked out for him by George Thomas. He then took Caroline and John by the hand and asked them to walk him to the Oval Office. On their way, they popped in to see Mommy, who by this time was usually eating her breakfast of white toast and coffee served on a tray in her bedroom.

Once the president was seated behind his desk, Miss Shaw whisked John away for a morning nap. Caroline, meanwhile, headed for the little school Jackie had set up in the third-floor solarium for her children as well as sixteen others—the offspring of White House staffers and several close friends. The invitation-only White House School boasted two teachers and a kindergarten and first-grade curriculum that included American history, hygiene, arithmetic, and French. Jackie had no trouble coming up with the colors for the school uniforms: red, white, and blue.

Ninety minutes later, the children were scampering about the White House grounds during morning recess—all under the watchful eye of two Secret Service agents, Nanny Shaw, and White House schoolteachers Alice Grimes and Elizabeth Boyd. As soon as he heard the sound of the children's voices, the president stopped whatever he was doing and stepped out into the garden. "He'd clap his hands," Jackie recalled, "and all the little things from school would come running."

Not even the president, however, could trump the teachers' authority. When JFK kept reaching into his pocket and doling out candy to Caroline and her best friend, Mary Warner, Grimes complained that he was being unfair to the other children. From that point on Kennedy's devoted secretary, Evelyn Lincoln, always kept a glass jar filled with pink and blue rock candy on her desk as well as an entire box of Barricini chocolates in a drawer. This was more than enough for all of Caroline's classmates and for John, who invariably toddled in with Miss Shaw to bang on Mrs. Lincoln's typewriter for a few minutes before heading off for lunch at 12:30.

For her part, Jackie chose to remain in her room for most of the morning, going over the newspapers before summoning her personal secretary, Mary Gallagher, to her bedside with steno pad in hand. For the next hour, Jackie dictated letters and memos in a no-nonsense, rapid-fire style that belied her breathy, ethereal persona.

Once she was finished with the day's correspondence, Jackie took a brisk hour-long stroll alone around the White House grounds before sitting down to work at what she described as her most prized possession: the Empire-style, ormolu-mounted, slant-front desk that had belonged to her late father, the flamboyant "Black Jack" Bouvier.

Sometimes, Jackie joined Caroline and John in the "High Chair Room"—the small informal dining area for the children she had set up off the kitchen—and watched while they gobbled hot dogs or hamburgers prepared by the White House chef and served to them by a butler on a silver tray.

Jack, in the meantime, headed for the White House pool promptly at 1:30. Once there, he usually stripped off his clothes poolside and eased himself into the 80-degree water. These brief, twice-daily swims were initially prescribed by Kennedy's doctors both as a form of low-impact exercise and as therapy for his back.

When he arrived at the White House, Jackie noted that Jack was in "the best physical condition he was ever in in his life"—the result of unwinding at La Guerida, Joe Kennedy's white-walled oceanfront villa in Palm Beach, Florida, between winning the 1960 presidential election and the inauguration nearly three months later.

"He never really needed to exercise," Jackie said. "The campaign—jumping in and out of cars, walking, you know, kept him fit." After the election, he swam in the ocean, walked on the beach, and played golf three times a week. "He had muscles and everything," Jackie marveled. "It was wonderful."

Landing at the White House, Jack "sat at his desk, without moving, for six weeks. He didn't walk around the driveway, he didn't swim, and suddenly his back went bad. He'd lost all the muscle tone."

Getting "pumped full of Novocain"—Jackie's words—by the physician who had always treated his back, Dr. Janet Travell, no longer worked. Instead, Jack managed to find at least some relief in the White House pool.

The president's daily swims served another purpose as well. He looked forward to this time in the water as a chance to unwind with friends and escape the pressures of office.

"He hated to swim alone," said the Kennedys' photographer and friend Jacques Lowe, "so he was always grabbing people by the collar to swim with him." Jack's longtime political aide and storytelling buddy, Dave Powers, could always be counted on to take the plunge—literally—with the president.

A half hour later, the president pulled on a terry-cloth robe and ducked out a back door through the White House flower shop and the exercise room to elevators that took him upstairs to the family living quarters. By this time, Maud Shaw had tucked the children in for their afternoon naps, and Jackie was waiting for Jack in the living room.

"Mrs. Kennedy dropped everything, no matter how important, to join her husband," chief White House usher J. B. West said. "If she had visitors in tow, they would be left for me to entertain." The next two hours were, in fact, sacrosanct for the first couple. All staff and visitors were barred from the second floor, and the White House switchboard was directed to hold all calls short of anything alerting the president to a national emergency.

Jack, still clad only in his robe, joined the first lady for lunch served on trays—always a grilled cheese sandwich for Jackie and usually a medium-rare hamburger for her husband, although at times the weight-conscious Jack opted for a glass of the diet drink Metrecal. Jackie was equally mindful of her weight. If she gained as little as one pound, she fasted for a day and stepped up her exercise regimen—walking ten times around the South Lawn, or bouncing on a canvas trampoline she ostensibly installed for the children. "It's not only terrific exercise," she told Pierre Salinger, "but a marvelous way to reduce stress."

Jack's vanity extended beyond his waistline and his wardrobe. Periodically, he would use part of his nap time to have Jackie massage a special tonic from a New York firm called Frances Fox into his hair. Later in the day, he would have someone—sometimes Jackie but just as often one of the attractive young female aides assigned to the West Wing—add a few drops of another Frances Fox concoction and then put the finishing touches on his famously tousled coif. Whoever was assigned this task knew that it must be done with a brush, never a comb. "My God, Jack, everyone keeps talking about copying my hairstyle," said Jackie, whose own bedtime routine involved sprinkling cologne on a brush and then stroking her hair one hundred times. "If they only knew the real expert about hair is you!"

(According to Jackie's half brother Jamie Auchincloss, what made JFK's hair so striking was its "odd color—or rather *colors*. Once I counted fifteen distinctly different colors in his hair, ranging from silver to orange." Although JFK's secret hair treatments may have also been at least partly responsible, Auchincloss learned that this was one of the peculiar symptoms of Jack's Addison's disease, a degeneration of the adrenal glands that destroys the immune system. Another symptom of Addison's: the deceptively healthy-looking orange glow that was often mistaken for a Palm Beach tan.)

When they were finished, Jackie, who joked that "the only song Jack really likes is 'Hail to the Chief,' " walked over to the stereo system between their two rooms and piled the turntable high with his favorite albums. Soon music—jazz, show tunes, songs by Peggy

Lee, Frank Sinatra, and even Elvis—was drifting through the eerily empty corridors. It was then that they each retired to their separate rooms.

Or not. George Thomas had been instructed to always wake the president precisely at 3:30 p.m., but there were many times when JFK's bed was empty. On those occasions, he quietly slipped into Jackie's bedroom and whispered into the president's ear so as not to wake the first lady, who was sleeping soundly beside him.

"They had a very close, very romantic relationship," Jackie's stepbrother Hugh "Yusha" Auchincloss observed. "Technically they had separate bedrooms, but they slept together. There was a lot of laughter. They enjoyed each other. They had *fun.*"

Indeed, one lunchtime Jackie got so wrapped up in her paperwork that she forgot her husband was waiting for her. At Jack's behest, Thomas tracked her down. "Miz Kennedy," the valet said, "the President says if you don't hurry, he'll fall asleep." Jackie put down her pen, jumped up from her desk, and headed straight for her bedroom.

The entire concept of taking a nap in the middle of the day struck Jackie as peculiar at first. "Jack never took a nap before," she said, "but in the White House I think he made up his mind he would because it was good for his health." Jack insisted that he was merely following the example of his idol, Winston Churchill. "It gave him so much more staying power, so much more stamina," Jack explained. "I need every ounce of strength to do this job."

Jack's habit of changing in and out of clothes several times a day also struck his wife as "extremely odd. I used to think," she later confided, "for a forty-five-minute nap, would you bother to take off all your clothes? It would take me forty-five minutes to just snuggle down and start to doze off." Again, Jack said it was necessary to copy Sir Winston's approach exactly. "If I'm going to do this," the president told Pierre Salinger when his press secretary asked why he felt it necessary for so many changes of wardrobe, "then I'm going to do it right. Otherwise, what's the point? Lying down and getting up in wrinkled clothes?"

Knowing how much he liked to sleep with fresh air blowing through the room, Jackie often closed the curtains and then threw open the large windows herself. Jackie did not share Jack's talent for napping ("I just can't shut my mind off like that"), so she often tiptoed into her room, read one of her magazines, then came back to wake him before Thomas "officially sounded the alarm."

Jack took his third shower of the day after his afternoon nap, put on a fresh suit, and returned to work. More than any other president, Jack had crammed the Oval Office with photographs and cherished mementos. His first week in office, JFK personally carried photos of Jackie and the children as well as a favorite watercolor painting over from the family quarters in the East Wing. As might have been expected, the room took on a seafaring motif as Jack decorated it with naval paintings and seascapes, ship models, pieces of scrimshaw, semaphore flags, and a plaque with an old fisherman's prayer: "O God, Thy sea is great and my boat is so small."

From the windows of the Oval Office, Jack could watch Jackie and the children in the play area she had specially designed for them. There was the small trampoline concealed by evergreens, a rabbit hutch, a leather swing, a barrel tunnel, and a tree house with a slide. When they first moved into the White House, Jackie often had to keep Caroline from trying to push her infant brother down the tree house slide, "carriage and all."

Soon Jackie returned to her mounting pile of correspondence, returning to the High Chair Room at 5:30 to sit with the children as they ate dinner. Caroline would later remember how her mother always made a point of asking them what they had learned in school that day.

"Caroline is already reading at three," Jackie boasted to family friend Chuck Spalding, "and over dinner she bubbles with excitement about what happened that day in her little class in the solarium." Able to properly pronounce the tongue-twisting names of such world leaders as Konrad Adenauer, Nikita Khrushchev, and Jawaharlal Nehru, Caroline had no use for baby talk. When Pierre Salinger pointed out a "moo cow" standing in a field, Caroline replied, "No, that's a Hereford." (Nor did she brook any misbehavior on the part of her little brother. When John spit out food or banged his spoon on the table, Caroline's reaction was swift. Rolling her eyes and shaking her head, she sighed, "There he goes again.")

Jack was seldom privy to his children's dinnertime chitchat. Out of the office by 5:30, he repeated his morning ritual—into the pool with Powers, O'Donnell, or whoever else happened to be around for a half-hour dip, then back upstairs to shave, shower, and change into yet another suit—his third full wardrobe change of the day. (Jack was dumbfounded when, during a visit to the White House, his longtime journalist-friend Ben Bradlee informed him that he and a lot of other men saw nothing wrong with wearing the same shirt two days in a row.)

There were times when some pressing matter kept Jack working in his office until 8 p.m. or later, but his day usually ended around six. It was then that Jackie, who always changed into a dress for dinner, met her husband for daiquiris in the Yellow Oval Room. In the absence of any formal functions requiring their presence downstairs, they usually dined alone or with close friends like Bradlee and his wife Tony, Kentucky senator John Sherman Cooper and his wife Lorraine, or the couple who actually introduced them, Charles and Martha Bartlett. At the time, Charles Bartlett was the Washington correspondent for the *Chattanooga Times* and Ben Bradlee wrote for *Newsweek*.

The next two hours or more were devoted to drinks and banter and, occasionally, board games. "We played Chinese checkers, Monopoly, bridge," recalled Charlie Bartlett. "Somebody said Jack played Monopoly like the property was real, and they were right. He loved winning, and he hated to lose even more. Jackie was the same way—very competitive, a born game-player. There was always a great deal of laughter, and everybody had a great time."

By way of after-dinner entertainment, they also screened new movies in the White House theater. Even though he regarded Jack as "the most urbane man I have ever met," Bradlee had to confess that the president's taste in movies was markedly middlebrow. "My mommy always watched cowboy movies with my daddy," Caroline later told her teachers, "because my daddy liked cowboy movies. My mommy doesn't like cowboy movies *at all*, but she watched them because she loves my daddy." She didn't have to watch for long; too restless to sit through an entire feature film, Jack usually excused himself after the first twenty minutes or so.

TO BE SURE, IT WAS Jackie—not the president—who spearheaded a cultural renaissance in the nation's capital by using the White House to showcase the arts. She invited stars of the Royal Ballet and the Metropolitan Opera, as well as Shakespearean actors and the world's greatest classical musicians, to perform for visiting heads of state in the East Room.

According to key Kennedy adviser Theodore Sorensen, JFK had "no interest in opera, dozed off at symphony concerts, and was bored by ballet." (Chubby Checker's "The Twist" was one of JFK's favorite records, and the president asked that it be played repeatedly at private White House functions.)

Still, Jack was immensely proud of his wife's efforts and usually did his best to mask his distaste for what he privately derided as "longhair crap." He certainly didn't fool Caroline, who shared her mother's love of ballet even as a child. "Daddy claps," she said at the time, "but I don't think he really likes it. He makes faces when he thinks no one is looking."

In fact, the high-spirited Kennedy kids were themselves often part of an evening's entertainment. Several dinner guests arrived just as Caroline raced past them stark naked, with Maud Shaw in hot pursuit. Caroline "practically knocked us over," one guest recalled. "Then she looked up with these huge eyes, looked back at the nanny, and shot off down the hall." Caroline's antics certainly kept Secret Service agents on their toes; members of the Kiddie Detail spent hours in hot pursuit of the first daughter as she ran from pillar to pillar firing off her cap pistol, or zipped down marble hallways on roller skates.

Jack delighted in their shenanigans, and made a point of spending time with Caroline and John just before bedtime. "No matter who we were having dinner with," Jackie later recalled. "No matter how important they were, Jack would turn to me and say, 'Go get the children!' And of course I'd have to bring them out in their underwear or their pajamas. . . . You know, the children were never bratty, but he liked to have them underfoot."

So did Jackie. While the president was more inclined to roughhouse—even at the risk of reinjuring his back—Jackie smothered them with hugs, kisses, and motherly concern no matter who was watching.

Yet for all the warmth they openly displayed as young parents, the president and first lady were often strangely formal around each other—even in front of staff members who saw them every day. In part, this was due to Jack's antipathy toward couples that were overly affectionate in public, and his deep-seated aversion to touching and being touched in a nonsexual way—an idiosyncrasy rooted in his childhood.

"He never would hold hands in public," Jackie conceded, "or put his arm around me—that was naturally just distasteful to him." Even when campaign aides asked Jack and Jackie to put their arms around each other for the cameras, JFK refused. "He wouldn't be fake in any way," Jackie said. "People just don't understand him."

Long before Jack and Jackie were a couple, Jack's friend and Senate colleague George Smathers of Florida noted that JFK "absolutely *hated* to be touched. If you put your hand on his shoulder, he would literally pull away. He just wasn't brought up in a family where there was a lot of hugging and that sort of thing. It just made him terribly uncomfortable. It wasn't like he could help himself. Jackie eventually broke through the wall, but it took her a long, long time."

Like Jack, Jackie grew up watching her parents treat each other with icy indifference. And, along with most members of her generation and her class, she viewed egregious displays of affection in public places as gauche.

"Jackie was a very self-contained person, especially in the White House," said Kennedy family photographer and close friend Jacques Lowe. "She very much lived her own life, as much as she was allowed to. Jack certainly wasn't jumping into bed with her every night. But when they were both there, they made time for each other."

White House social secretary Letitia "Tish" Baldrige, who had known Jackie since when they were both students at Miss Porter's School for Girls, in Farmington, Connecticut, insisted their day-to-day relationship was poignant. "Maybe they weren't always madly 'at' one another," Baldrige said, "but there were plenty of tender moments when I would catch him putting his arm around her waist, or she'd lean her head on his shoulder . . ."

Throughout the day, Jack would find wry memos Jackie had planted around the White House to lift his spirits. "He'd read one of these little notes," Baldrige said, "and burst out laughing. It was their private joke."

If Jack's back was preventing him from falling asleep, Jackie would walk into the closet between their rooms and put the cast recording of Lerner and Loewe's *Camelot* on the "old Victrola." In the role of King Arthur, Richard Burton belted out the president's favorite line at the very end of the album: "Don't let it be forgot, that once there was a spot, for one brief shining moment . . ."

Indeed, even as JFK coped with one domestic and international crisis after another, the public perception of life in the Kennedy White House was one of wit and charm wrapped in a glistening chrysalis of style.

From their first triumphant European tour, when Jack introduced himself as "the man who accompanied Jacqueline Kennedy to Paris," to the sixty-six glittering state occasions they presided over with regal aplomb, the vital young president and his queenly first lady were the closest thing America had to royalty. "When they appeared at the top of those stairs," veteran *Washington Star* reporter Betty Beale said of the Kennedys' entrances at state dinners and formal receptions, "they were a glorious-looking, stunning couple—almost beyond belief. It was more a royal court than an administration."

NO ONE OUTSIDE A HANDFUL of intimates knew about the drama that played out behind the scenes: about Jack's failing health and reckless womanizing, or how the very public loss of a child seemed to bring the president and the first lady closer than they had ever been before.

In reality, during their brief time at 1600 Pennsylvania Avenue, Jack and Jackie were working on clearing away the emotional obstacles in their path. Their afternoon naps—of which there were hundreds during the course of Kennedy's presidency—proved at least a desire for closeness, for true intimacy. So did the daiquiris in the Yellow Oval Room, the casual lunches on trays and the quiet dinners with friends, the time spent with the children—all part of a daily routine designed to bring some semblance of normalcy to two of the most extraordinary lives ever lived.

"Comparing their problems to another couple's," Jack's confidant Paul "Red" Fay said, "is like comparing a Duesenberg to a Chevy." Certainly, both John F. Kennedy and Jacqueline Bouvier had been born into lives of wealth and privilege. But both had also been deeply scarred growing up in wildly dysfunctional households—families in which power, money, sex, and social position eclipsed more traditional values.

Their ambition would, in the end, make them the most celebrated couple in the world. But a shared ambition was not what drew them together at first. "They were two lonely people," their friend Chuck Spalding said. "And they instantly recognized that in each other." In fact, Spalding went on to describe them as "emotionally the two most isolated, most *alone* people I ever met."

It was easy to see why. A casualty of her parents' bitter divorce, Jackie sought solace in solitary pursuits like horseback riding or reading. "She could be the belle of the ball when it was required," a friend said. "But that was just an act. Jack was the same way. Before entering a room, Jack would say 'Time to turn on the B.P.'— the Big Personality—but he hated glad-handers. It's ironic that these two people who personified charm and grace for millions of people around the world were really lone wolves."

What Jackie detected beneath Jack's gleaming breastplate of self-confidence was the sickly child who for years suffered fever, weight loss, stomach pains, hives, dizziness, and nausea—all while doctors tried in vain to diagnose what Jack himself called his "wasting disease." Looked after by a battalion of governesses and nurses, Jack was virtually ignored by his mother, who dealt with her husband Joe's rampant womanizing by taking expensive trips and lavishing gifts on herself. As a result, Jack, who grew up in a family of nine children, worshiped the boisterous, fun-loving family patriarch while resenting the emotionally unavailable Rose. "My mother never really held me and hugged me," Jack fumed after he had reached the White House. "Never, never!"

Spending weeks at a time in bed recuperating, young Jack lost himself in the works of Rudyard Kipling, Robert Louis Stevenson, and Sir Walter Scott. This was the little-known part of Jack's past that Jackie felt held the key to his personality. To her, the dazzling

Mr. Kennedy was "really this lonely sick little boy, in bed so much of the time reading history, devouring the Knights of the Round Table."

It was hard not to be reminded of that little boy when they got ready for bed. Throughout their marriage, Jack said his prayers every night just as he had since childhood. "He'd come in and kneel on the edge of the bed and say them, you know," Jackie recalled. "Take about three seconds. Then he'd cross himself. It was just a little childish mannerism, I suppose, like brushing your teeth. Just a habit," she said. "I thought it was so sweet. It used to amuse me so, standing there . . ."

It was the frail little boy hidden beneath the bravado, she reasoned, who emerged to connect with Caroline and John in a way she never thought possible. Jackie, thrilled that her husband had chosen to play such a hands-on role in their children's lives, reveled in the small things—the fact, for instance, that on some days in the White House Caroline and John would "even have lunch with him. If you told me that would happen, I'd never have believed it."

In the end, Jackie concluded that they might never have come together as a tight-knit family had her husband not been elected to the world's most powerful office. "You see," she explained, "the one thing that happens to a president is that his ties to the outside world are cut. And *then* all you really have," Jackie added with a smile, "is each other."

They both wanted desperately to connect, but hadn't the faintest idea how. That's what made their love story so achingly poignant. And it was, in every sense of the word, a love story.

—CHUCK SPALDING, LONGTIME FRIEND

⁂

They were so much alike. Even the names—Jack and Jackie: two halves of a single whole. They were both actors and they appreciated each other's performance.

—LEM BILLINGS, JFK'S FRIEND

Getting to know him intimately was not easy. There were many parts of him . . . that he never revealed to anybody.

—KENNETH O'DONNELL,
JFK AIDE AND CONFIDANT

&

Jack was no Boy Scout, but then a Boy Scout would have bored her senseless.

—CHUCK SPALDING

3

_ఎౣ_

"An Electrical Current Between Them"

"*H*ow can you live with a husband who is bound to be unfaithful?" Jacqueline Bouvier asked a friend in a rare un-
guarded moment shortly before marrying Jack on September 12,
1953. "Even if you love that person, how can you put up with that,
and not lose a large piece of yourself?"

Yet Jackie clearly saw in the young senator from Massachusetts
the same roguish qualities she admired in her own father, the
tall, tanned, rakishly handsome, devilishly charming, Ivy League–
educated John Vernou "Black Jack" Bouvier III. Like JFK, Jackie's
father remained a bachelor until his mid-thirties, when he decided to finally march down the aisle with a girl a dozen years his
junior. While he did not share Black Jack's penchant for boozing
and gambling, there seemed little doubt that Jack was more than
a match for Jackie's father in the philandering department.

As their romance heated up, several of Jack's friends went out of their way to caution Jackie that, at thirty-five, Kennedy was "set in his ways" and "not about to change." Chuck Spalding felt that "only made her *more* interested in him. Jackie had this thing about Black Jack. Dangerous men excited her. There was that element of danger in Jack Kennedy, without doubt."

"Jackie was always talking about her father," said Jack's pal and colleague in the Senate, Florida's George Smathers, "and it was pretty clear that they worshiped each other. Marrying Jack Kennedy was as close as she was ever going to get to marrying Black Jack Bouvier." Writer George Plimpton, whom she had met in 1949 during her junior year in Paris studying at the Sorbonne, concurred. "Jackie loved pirates," Plimpton said. "Her father was one. So was Jack."

It wasn't enough simply to be dangerous. "Jackie wanted to be the confidante of an important man," said John White, a State Department official who dated her for a time. "Power and charisma seemed to override all other qualities in her estimation of people."

Jack unquestionably had all the qualities she was looking for, and then some. His heroic exploits as the skipper of PT-109 in the Pacific during World War II were to become the stuff of legend.

The young Kennedy's wartime derring-do would also have unintended consequences for his family—and alter the course of history. Eager to outdo his little brother, Joe Kennedy Jr.—the Kennedy Joe Sr. intended to install in the White House—volunteered for what amounted to a suicide mission over German-controlled territory in France. On August 12, 1944, Joe Jr.'s plane exploded in midair, killing him and leaving Jack to pick up the torch for his martyred brother. Giving up plans to pursue a literary career—thanks to Joe buying up huge numbers of copies, he had already turned his Harvard thesis into a minor bestseller titled *Why England Slept*—Jack instead ran for and won a seat in Congress. After two terms in the House, Jack, again relying heavily on his father's clout, trounced popular Republican Henry Cabot Lodge to win a seat in the Senate.

What made these achievements all the more remarkable was the precarious state of Jack's health dating all the way back to early childhood. Nearly killed by scarlet fever at the age of two, Jack suffered chicken pox, German measles, whooping cough, mumps, diphtheria, bronchitis, anemia, tonsillitis, ear infections, and allergies (to dogs, cats, horses, dust, wool, and more) that quickly turned into severe asthma. While away at Canterbury, a Catholic boarding school in bucolic New Milford, Connecticut, thirteen-year-old Jack was rushed to the hospital in nearby Danbury with stabbing pains in his stomach. Hours later—and apparently just in the nick of time—Jack underwent an emergency appendectomy.

Transferring to a markedly more Waspy Connecticut institution, Choate, Jack was in and out of the school infirmary with severe dehydration, abdominal pains, fainting spells, rashes, and fevers. Doctors suspected hepatitis, then leukemia, even ulcers. None of these diagnoses proved correct. (Doctors would later discover that Jack was also lactose intolerant, suffered from an underactive thyroid, and had a high cholesterol count that would peak at a startling 350 when he reached adulthood.)

To further complicate matters, Jack was only twenty and a junior at Harvard when he suffered the crippling back injury that would plague him for the rest of his life. In October 1937, Jack and his brother Joe were getting ready to compete in Harvard-

Princeton football matchups—Joe as a varsity player, Jack as a junior varsity substitute—when Joe Sr. pulled up in his chauffeur-driven Buick ("Joe Kennedy was nuts about Buicks—that's all the Kennedys drove," said JFK campaign aide Patrick "Patsy" Mulkern). On Joe Sr.'s orders, the family driver announced their arrival by sneaking up on Jack and tackling him from behind.

Jack, who as a freshman somehow also managed to qualify for the Harvard swimming and boxing teams, never played college sports again. "Jack was always sick with one thing or another," said his roommate, Charlie Houghton. "But this was different. This time he couldn't just bounce back. He tried, but the poor guy couldn't hide that he was in real misery."

From that point on, Jack almost always wore a corset or brace beneath his shirt. Fearing the truth—that he was a rich boy who had been bested by the chauffeur—JFK also concocted a less embarrassing story to explain how he sustained the injury, claiming in interviews that no fewer than three burly linemen had piled onto him during practice. "I've never been free from pain," Jack said, "since that day in practice."

In his twenties, Jack stood over six feet tall and never weighed more than 145 pounds. If anything, his scrawny physique and sickly pallor made him more attractive to women. "Are you kidding?" said Kirk LeMoyne "Lem" Billings, arguably the closest friend JFK ever had. "He had looks, sympathy, *and* money!"

Taking his father's advice to "get laid as often as possible," Jack began by losing his virginity at seventeen to a prostitute in Harlem. According to Jack's Choate buddy Rip Horton, Jack and Billings, who had also visited the prostitute, knocked on the door of his Manhattan apartment "in a total panic" over the possibility they may have contracted a sexually transmitted disease. Just to be safe, they rousted Joe Sr.'s personal physician out of a sound sleep so he could give them shots of penicillin.

Despite lingering fears that he would acquire a venereal disease, Jack went on to rack up an awe-inspiring string of sexual conquests during his four years at Harvard. "All he had to do," said his classmate James Rousmaniere, "was snap his fingers."

EVENTUALLY, JACK'S FEARS WERE REALIZED when doctors treated him for gonorrhea in 1940. JFK, who routinely referred to his penis as "JJ" or "the Implement" in wisecracking letters to his buddies, was stunned. Just two years earlier, he had been circumcised—a painful procedure for a twenty-one-year-old to undergo—on the advice of doctors who told him his level of sexual activity warranted it. "Gee," he told Billings, "I thought old JJ and I were in the clear."

According to JFK's urologist, Dr. William P. Herbst, sulfonamide drugs were used to successfully treat the disease. There were still to be long-term consequences, however. For the remainder of his life, Jack would suffer from persistent, drug-resistant urethritis, acute prostatitis, and recurring bladder infections. (Just before his marriage, Jack was concerned enough to ask Herbst if these problems would have an impact on his ability to father children.)

Had the women he encountered known his medical history, it's doubtful it would have made any difference. "I was utterly dumbfounded," said the actor Robert Stack, who shared an apartment with Jack for a time. "He'd just look at them and they'd tumble."

Jack owed at least some of his appeal to the fact that so many women "wanted to mother him," Patsy Mulkern said. "Every girl you met thought she was going to be Mrs. Kennedy."

Of course, there was something else that made Jack irresistible to women. Black Jack had squandered the Bouvier fortune—a fact Jackie's mother never tired of repeating—and Jackie and her younger sister, Lee, were left to play the poor relations following Janet's marriage into the wealthy Auchincloss clan. "She was brought up with a father who lost his money and a mother who had to marry for security," said Priscilla Johnson McMillan, who was working as a foreign policy researcher in JFK's Senate office when Jack and Jackie were engaged in the spring of 1953. "It was drummed into her that she had to go out and find a rich man of her own."

Pioneering NBC newswoman Nancy Dickerson, who dated JFK before he began seeing Jackie, agreed. "He was just so gosh-darn physically, animalistically attractive that it was hard to imagine," said Dickerson, who berated Jack when he honked his car horn instead of coming to her front door on their first date. "And of course power is the ultimate aphrodisiac and with that combination he was really something." But, Dickerson added, despite "that raw sexuality of his . . . there were plenty of other attractive, powerful men in Washington. There just weren't many with as much money as Jack."

Certainly not John Husted, the tall, handsome, Yale-educated investment banker Jackie was engaged to prior to JFK. "I thought she was heavenly looking," Husted recalled. "She was not aloof at all. She had a devastating, cutting wit, and an innate sense of style that was obvious even then. I fell totally, completely in love with her."

Not surprisingly, Husted, whose Wall Street salary was adequate but far from stellar, was "desperate" when Jackie jilted him amid rumors that she was dating JFK. Desperate, but not really surprised. "I knew he was a playboy, and so did she—but that was probably part of the appeal. Jack had to remind her of her father." Besides, Husted said, "Jackie was very ambitious. Socially, I was fine, but financially I was not a great catch."

"She was a very gracious, wonderful woman," Chuck Spalding said. "But she wouldn't have given Jack a second look if he hadn't had the money." JFK understood completely. "Jack grew up knowing that was part of his appeal to women. It didn't bother him a bit. He *enjoyed* being rich."

At the time Jack's personal fortune easily exceeded $10 million, not counting his share of $400 million in total Kennedy family assets. But he never picked up the check if he could help it. When they took a cab, Jack would turn to Jackie and say, "Could you take care of that?" She paid for their popcorn at the movies, fished around in her purse for cash to pay for dinner and drinks, and when they went to church it was left to Jackie to dig up a few dollars for the collection plate.

"Jack never carried cash, and I mean *never*," said George Smathers, another lady-killer who accompanied JFK on many of his skirt-chasing adventures. "One day I told Joe that people were getting pretty fed up picking up lunch tabs and the like, so he just told me to send him the bill and he'd take care of it."

In sizing Jack up as marriage material, nothing was of more concern to Jackie than his reputation as a ladies' man. Since his days at Choate, the exclusive prep school in Connecticut, Jack had cut a wide sexual swath through the worlds of high society and Hollywood—with countless coeds, waitresses, nightclub chorines, and cigarette girls thrown in for good measure.

Commissioned as an ensign in September 1941, Jack was assigned to the Office of Naval Intelligence in Washington and wasted no time trying to bed half the capital city's population. "He was a typical Don Juan," said JFK's friend Frank Waldrop, then editor of the Washington *Times-Herald.* "You could almost imagine him checking off names in a book."

One of Ensign Kennedy's affairs during the period had the potential of ending his political career before it began. In 1942, Jack fell for Danish beauty Inga Arvad, unaware that she was a friend of Herman Goering and Adolf Hitler. She was also under surveillance by the FBI, which suspected her of being a Nazi spy.

Jack called Arvad "the Scandalous Scandinavian," "Inga Binga," and "Bingo," and no one took more delight in listening to recordings of their steamy encounters ("If he wanted to make love, you'd make love—now," Arvad later told her son) than FBI director J. Edgar Hoover. Most important, the young naval officer's indiscretion gave the Machiavellian Hoover leverage in his future dealings with the Kennedys. The affair ended only after Joe succeeded in getting Jack reassigned to active duty in the Pacific.

Returning from the war, Jack took full advantage of his father's status as a force in the motion picture industry—one of many sectors of the economy where the enterprising Joe, whose torrid affair with silent screen star Gloria Swanson had tongues wagging on both coasts, had found a way to make a killing. In the late 1940s, Jack dated Joan Crawford, Lana Turner, Hedy Lamarr, Susan Hayward, and Zsa Zsa Gabor. (Years later, when she bumped into Jack and his fiancée in New York, Zsa Zsa joked, "She's a lovely girl. Don't dare corrupt her, Jack." Jackie's dead-serious reply: "But he already has.")

The most serious of Jack's Hollywood dalliances was with

Gene Tierney, who shot to fame in the 1940s whodunit *Laura*. "I turned," she recalled of meeting Jack on the set of her 1949 Gothic melodrama *Dragonwyck*, "and found myself staring into the most perfect blue eyes I had ever seen on a man. . . . Literally, my heart skipped."

When she divorced her then-husband Oleg Cassini, the noted fashion designer warned Tierney that Jack would never marry her. "His family won't stand for it," Cassini told her. "Gene, be sure you know what you are doing." Cassini was right. After Kennedy broke up with her, Tierney suffered a series of nervous breakdowns that led to her being institutionalized.

Scores of stunning women managed to seize Jack's attention; none managed to hold it. "He liked women," said Henry James, a friend he met during postgraduate studies at Stanford. "He needed women, but he didn't want a commitment to a relationship." As far as James could tell, Jack "was never in love."

THERE WERE THOSE, EVEN IN his own family, who doubted if Jack was even capable of falling in love. His sister Kathleen "Kick" Kennedy, who died with her married lover in a 1948 airplane crash, once declared coldly, "The thing about me you ought to know is that I'm like Jack, incapable of deep affection."

This seemed even more true after Kick's sudden death and the loss of their brother Joe. Add to these tragedies Jack's own Job-like suffering from a host of medical problems, and Joe's second son was left with an impending sense of doom. "He was very fatalistic," Smathers said. "When I first knew him, sometimes it seemed that women and death were all he talked about." During one of those conversations, the two men discussed what they felt was the best way to die. Given a choice of shooting, freezing, fire, drowning, and poison, Jack picked poison. "The point is," Jack concluded, "you've got to live every day like it's your last day on earth. That's what I'm doing."

Jack was, according to Spalding, "obsessed with the idea that he only had a short time on the planet." That conviction only intensified when, in 1947 at age thirty, he collapsed during a congressional fact-finding trip to London and was rushed to the hospital.

This time, doctors had finally landed on the correct diagnosis. The "wasting disease" that had brought him to the brink of death so many times was Addison's, a condition that destroys the adrenal glands and the immune system, leaving its victim defenseless against infection.

The initial prognosis was grim. Pamela Churchill, who later married Averell Harriman and would go on to serve as U.S. ambassador to France, looked in on Jack when he was hospitalized in London. She was told by doctors that Jack had less than a year to live.

Although Addison's is considered incurable and at that time often proved fatal, it was treatable in the late 1940s. At first, Jack was given daily injections of the synthetic hormone desoxycorticosterone acetate (DOCA). Later, to eliminate the need for daily shots, time-release pellets containing DOCA were surgically implanted in his thighs.

Still, doctors held out little hope for survival beyond a few years. There was almost no chance, the Kennedys were told, that Jack would ever make it to thirty-five—the constitutionally mandated minimum age for a president. The fact that Jack might never live to become president was a "crushing blow," Arthur

Krock said. "Joe started planning for Jack to win the White House the day after Joe Jr. died."

Not that Jack or anyone in his camp ever admitted that he had Addison's disease. As far as the world was concerned, young Kennedy was suffering a recurrence of the malaria he purportedly contracted in the Pacific. On the way home from London aboard the *Queen Mary*, Jack was given absolution but once again pulled through.

He was not out of the woods yet, though—far from it. Spirited off the ship on a stretcher, Jack was then transferred to a chartered plane and flown to Boston, where he spent weeks convalescing at the prestigious Lahey Clinic. Once he'd returned to work in Washington, Jack was surprised at how many people in his inner circle seemed to have bought the malaria yarn. "Yeah, he had malaria," Patsy Mulkern insisted. "His skin was yellow, almost green, and he had these terrible chills where you'd have to wrap him up in a blanket. Hell of a thing."

Despite the legions of women who were eager to care for him, Jack was in no hurry to marry. Each time he learned that yet another Navy buddy or college roommate was getting hitched, Jack shook his head and glowered. "Jesus Christ," he would invariably say to Red Fay or Lem Billings or whoever happened to be around, "another one bites the dust."

Given the miserable example set by his parents—in particular the way Joe's flagrant infidelity had destroyed his mother's spirit—Jack didn't see much reason for women to get married, either. Priscilla Johnson McMillan had expected Jack to congratulate her when she told him she was getting married. Instead, he shook his head. "Why?" he asked. "There are so many unhappy marriages."

In the end, it was made clear to Jack that if he ever wanted to win the White House, he would have to settle down and start a family. If he didn't, his father pointed out bluntly, he ran the risk of letting people jump to the wrong conclusions. "Old Joe told him he'd better get married," Jack's longtime secretary Evelyn Lincoln recalled, "or people would think he was gay."

NANCY DICKERSON WONDERED IF, BEFORE he met Jackie, Jack had ever really made an emotional connection with a woman. "All his life," she observed, "he was trained to view women as objects to be conquered, possessed. Jack really had no respect for women. You can hardly blame him. After all," she added with a nod to the lecherous Joe Sr., "Jack learned at the foot of the master." As for JFK's boundless appetites: "But to Jack sex *was* just like a cup of coffee—no more or less important than that." Another onetime girlfriend, Gloria Emerson, vouched for JFK's "Speedy Gonzales" approach. "It was strictly 'Up against the wall, Signora, if you have five minutes.' That sort of thing."

Even the most cynical of Jack's friends conceded that the thirty-five-year-old Senate candidate was captivated by the twenty-three-year-old Vassar graduate with the breathy voice and wide-set eyes from the moment he met her. It was easy to see why.

"To meet her was never to forget her," said Tish Baldrige, a classmate of Jackie's at Miss Porter's and then at Vassar. "She was a natural beauty, no globs of neon purple lipstick, no thick layer of Pan-Cake makeup." Even more important, Baldrige said, was her voice—"unforgettable in its soft, breathy tones. It was a sound that forced you to draw close and listen well."

Vassar classmate Selwa "Lucky" Roosevelt, later chief of protocol in the Reagan administration, was equally impressed by Jackie's curious mystique. "She had this almost starlike quality— when she entered a room you couldn't help but notice her, she was such an exquisite creature." At the same time, said Roosevelt, "she seemed so very private."

Perhaps, but Jackie had clearly enjoyed riding the avalanche of publicity when, at nineteen, she was crowned "Queen Deb of the Year" by Cholly Knickerbocker. (At the time the "Cholly Knickerbocker" column was written by Igor Cassini, designer Oleg's younger brother.) Miss Bouvier, wrote the society columnist, was a "regal brunette" with "classic features and the daintiness of Dresden porcelain." Even Walter Winchell, easily the most powerful and widely read columnist of the age, chimed in. "What a gal!" he gushed, adding that Jackie was "blessed with the looks of a fairytale princess."

Socially, Jackie's credentials were impeccable. With its implied connections to European aristocracy, the Bouvier name still carried a certain cachet, giving Jackie standing with the New York Social Register types whose estates dotted Long Island's north shore. As the stepdaughter of Hugh Auchincloss from the age of twelve, Jackie divided her time between two lavish properties: Hammersmith Farm, the twenty-eight-room shingled "cottage" with its sweeping views of Newport's Narragansett Bay, and Merrywood, an imposing Georgian mansion set on forty-six rolling acres in Virginia's hunt country. (At Merrywood, she moved into the third-floor room previously occupied by her stepbrother Gore Vidal. The writer's mother had been married to Hugh Auchincloss II before "Uncle Hughdie" married Jackie's mother, Janet.)

Yet Jackie had also proved she wasn't afraid of work—not even when the job paid just eleven dollars a day. Hired as the Washington *Times-Herald*'s "Inquiring Camera Girl," Jackie headed out each day armed with a bulky Graflex Speed Graphic camera and a reporter's notebook. Her man-in-the-street interviews, high-lighting a single "Question of the Day," quickly became one of the paper's most popular features. "Do the rich enjoy life more than the poor?" she asked one day. "Should men wear wedding rings?" the next. Many of the questions, asked well before she began dating JFK, could not have been more prescient: "Which first lady would you most like to have been?" "If you had a date with Marilyn Monroe, what would you talk about?" "What prominent person's death affected you most?"

As far as Charlie and Martha Bartlett were concerned, Jack Kennedy and Jacqueline Bouvier were a perfect match. Trouble was, the Bartletts never could seem to bring them together. JFK and Jackie had actually bumped into each other for the first time in 1948, on a train from Washington, D.C. to New York. Jackie seemed impressed enough to jot something down in her note-book about this brief encounter with a "tall, thin young congress-man with very long reddish hair."

Nevertheless, nothing came of it until the following year, when Charlie Bartlett pulled Jackie by the hand through a "giant crowd" at his brother's wedding—only to discover that by the time he got to the corner where Jack had been standing, "he'd vanished."

There would be another abortive try two years later, in June 1951, when Jack and Jackie hit it off at a small dinner party thrown by the Bartletts. Unfortunately, when JFK walked Jackie to her car that evening asking, "Shall we go somewhere for a drink?," John Husted popped up in the backseat to surprise her. Jack, un-derstandably, did not call to ask her out the next morning.

Despite these two false starts, Martha persisted; she simply chose to ignore the inconvenient fact that, at the time, Jackie was still very much engaged to another man. Since Husted was in New York and couldn't make it to the dinner party the Bartletts were hosting, Martha urged Jackie to invite Jack as a substitute. Although Jack would later claim he "leaned over the asparagus" and asked Jackie out that night, technically it was Jackie who, at the Bartletts' behest, had already invited Jack out on their first date.

Their ensuing courtship didn't keep Jack from seducing other women. Mary Gallagher, who was on Senator Kennedy's staff in the early 1950s and later worked as Jackie's private secretary, recalled another actress who sailed quickly in and out of Jack's life: Audrey Hepburn. The elegant, swanlike Hepburn was only twenty-three but had already made the film that would win her an Academy Award for Best Actress—the romantic comedy *Roman Holiday,* with Gregory Peck. Also a muse for Paris's top fashion designers and for photographers on both sides of the Atlantic, Hepburn was universally praised for her talent, charm, and unique sense of style.

YET THERE WAS SOMETHING ABOUT Jackie that set her apart from the others—even from Audrey Hepburn. "I have never met anyone like her. Do you want to see what she looks like?" Jack asked Dave Powers as he pulled out a strip of black-and-white photos taken in a photo booth. "She's different from any girl I know." The snapshots, Powers said, "clearly show two people in love."

It was only when Jack took him aside and asked him about the wisdom of marrying someone so much younger that Powers realized Jackie might be the one. Powers pointed out that he himself was twelve years older than his wife—exactly the difference in age between Jack and Jackie. "Apparently that wasn't enough," Powers recalled. Jack needed more reassurance than that. "Well," JFK continued, "you two get along fine, don't you?"

Powers wasn't the only friend who saw no problem with the age difference. "Jackie was wise beyond her years," George Plimpton said. "The way she looked and the way she sounded sometimes was at odds with her intellect, which was formidable. Jackie liked people to underestimate her, I think. That was how she survived in that rather rarefied world. Jackie was one very smart cookie even then, and Jack saw that in her."

But marriage? The Kennedys' Hyannis Port neighbor and longtime friend Larry Newman said he "didn't think Jack would ever get married. I think he did love Jackie, but it was never in his makeup to be monogamous."

George Smathers shared Newman's conviction and told Jack to be "damn sure that he was ready to give up his rather meandering ways and settle down to being a good husband." Jack's reaction? "He just laughed." Like most people who knew JFK, Smathers believed Jack was "a great politician, a great author, a great social guy, a great friend. But you never thought of him as a great husband or a great father."

The age difference was certainly of no consequence to their mutual friend Oleg Cassini, who had forgiven Jack for stealing Gene Tierney away from him. The designer pointed out to Jack that in Europe the formula for determining the ideal age for a bride was half the groom's age plus seven years. "They were perfectly matched in that sense," Cassini said, "although in some ways she was actually older than he was. She was a very well-read, cultured, charming person. . . . She had a devastatingly wicked sense of humor, and a kind of natural grace. Strangely, he was remarkably rough around the edges, especially for someone who grew up under such privileged circumstances and was so brilliant in other ways. They had much to offer each other."

Nevertheless, Jack's infirmities—particularly his incapacitating back trouble—at times made Jackie keenly aware of the age difference. "The year before we were married," she later said, "when he'd take me out, half the time it was on crutches. When I went to watch him campaign, he was on crutches. I remember him on crutches more than not." (Physician-pharmacologist Janet Travell, who treated JFK's back and became the first female White House physician, confirmed that for long stretches he averaged four days on crutches per week.)

If anything, Jackie was struck by the fact that, despite the intense pain he was in almost constantly, Jack never complained. "What's the exact opposite of a hypochondriac?" she once asked. "That was Jack." Dr. Travell agreed. "It was difficult," she said, "to get him to state his complaints."

Equally impressive was the way in which he managed to convey an image of strength that belied his significant medical issues. "It was so pathetic to see him go up the steps of a plane on crutches, because then he looked so vulnerable," Jackie said. "And once he was up there and standing at the podium, then he looked so in control of everything. . . . So tanned and fit and powerful."

Only a few of JFK's Senate colleagues were aware of his condition. When the bell rang for a Senate vote, it was up to George Smathers to literally pick Jack up and carry him down to the underground train that led to the Senate chamber. Once there,

Smathers recalled, Jack somehow managed to make it to the Senate floor on his own. Then JFK returned to his office, "where he was wiped out from the sheer pain and physical exertion. Complain? Not once."

Whatever the cost, Jack went to great lengths to dispel Capitol Hill gossip that he was, in Gore Vidal's unkind words, "decrepit—practically an invalid." Jack played golf, swam, and even played softball at a Georgetown park with his Senate colleagues. "And he always would play touch football," Jackie later recalled, "but he couldn't run—I mean, he could run enough, but he could never be the one to run for the touchdown. He would pass and catch and run around a little . . ."

Although Jackie often joked about his allergies ("Can you imagine *me* with someone who's allergic to horses?"), Jack tried to impress his fiancée by riding bareback with her across a field near Hammersmith Farm in Newport. "He was wheezing so badly when they returned," Jackie's mother recalled, "I thought he was going to pass out."

Not all of Jack's physical antics were designed to impress. Like all the Kennedys, he often exhibited a disregard for consequences that seemed unwise, even reckless. Jackie "held on for dear life," for instance, whenever Jack took the wheel of a car. Jack was "wicked, wicked, wicked" as a driver, Patsy Mulkern said. "Fast, very fast. Wild man."

Jack seemed in no particular hurry, however, to propose. Even after Jackie had broken off her engagement to John Husted, the senator from Massachusetts stalled for more than a year. To make matters worse, he was not exactly showering her with affection while she waited. "When he wanted to put his arm around her and kiss her," Red Fay said, "well, he didn't want to do it in front of me!"

Or in front of anyone else, for that matter. "Jackie was from a world where people greeted each other with hugs and kisses on the cheek—even if they hated each other," Cassini said. "It was difficult for her to put up with his inability to show affection in front of others. She knew it made him look cold, unfeeling toward her in the eyes of others, so she worked hard at getting him to warm up."

As for the usual romantic gestures and tokens: "Flowers? Candy? Valentine's cards? Forget it!" Jackie joked. "He doesn't even hold the door open for me. Jack did send me a postcard once, from Bermuda. It read: 'Wish you were here. Jack.'"

No one was more frustrated with Jack's foot-dragging than Joe, who was more convinced than ever that Jackie was perfect first lady material. The elder Kennedy had developed a fondness for Jackie, who, both in style and substance, contrasted sharply with the loud, boisterous, gung-ho Kennedy women—the "Rah-Rah Girls," Jackie dubbed them. "They fall all over each other," she reported back to her sister, Lee, "like a pack of gorillas." (The gorillas weren't about to go easy on the young woman who insisted her name be pronounced "Jock-*lean*." They even slammed into Jackie during one of their famous football matches, breaking her right foot. "They'll kill me before I ever get to marry him," she told her mother. "I know they will.")

Unlike the others who were cowed by the curmudgeonly patriarch, Jackie was not afraid to tease Joe. When Joe boasted at the dinner table that he had given each of his children $1 million when they turned twenty-one, Jackie piped up, "Do you know what I would tell you if you gave me a million dollars? I'd ask you to give me *another* million."

Jackie finally decided to take matters into her own hands by traveling to London to cover the coronation of Queen Elizabeth II for the *Times-Herald.* It was only then that Jack mustered the courage to propose to Jackie—over a crackling transatlantic phone line. Lem Billings thought it was the only way his friend could have done it, without having to actually look Jackie in the eye. "I couldn't visualize him actually saying 'I love you' to somebody and asking her to marry him," Billings said. "It was the sort of thing he would have liked to have happen without having to talk about it." When she returned, Jack sealed the deal with a two-carat diamond-and-emerald engagement ring.

Were they truly in love when Jack asked Jackie to marry him? Evelyn Lincoln thought not. "He was a politician who wanted to be president and for that he needed a wife. I am absolutely certain they were not in love. At least not at the time." (As the blindly loyal secretary who for years had fielded Jack's calls and made his excuses to the multitude of women he juggled at any given time, Lincoln was one of those key people Jack knew he could count on to do anything for him. "If I called her in here and told her that I had just cut off Jackie's head," Jack later joked, "and then said to her, 'Mrs. Lincoln, would you bring me a nice large box so I can put Jackie's head in it?' she would say to me, 'Oh, that's lovely, Mr. President, I'll get the box right away.' ")

Notwithstanding Evelyn Lincoln's view that Jack wasn't in love with Jackie when he married her, many of their friends believed that what they *did* have—what her half brother Jamie called "an intensity, an electrical current between them"—deepened over time. "If he was capable of loving any woman, and I believe he was," Dickerson conceded, "that woman was Jackie."

4

℘

"I Hate It, Hate It, Hate It!"

*I*t was a revealing moment the nation would not get to see. Jack was grateful for that. Wearing a tasteful triple strand of pearls and a blank expression, Jackie, nearly eight months pregnant, sat ramrod straight in the living room at Hickory Hill, the historic Virginia mansion they had bought for $125,000 ten months earlier. She was answering questions on the NBC prime-time TV news program *Outlook* about what it was like to be the wife of a rising star in the Democratic Party.

There was no hesitation when Jackie was asked if she wanted to be with her husband, who was making a dramatic eleventh-hour bid at the Democratic National Convention in Chicago to become presidential candidate Adlai Stevenson's running mate. The answer was an unequivocal, if thoroughly predictable, yes.

Then the interviewer interjected a casual observation of his own. "You're pretty much in love with him," the interviewer asked, "aren't you?"

"Oohh, *no*," she replied emphatically. For several excruciatingly awkward moments, Jackie stared into the camera, smiling inscrutably but totally aware that she had made a Freudian slip of epic proportions.

"I said 'no,' didn't I?" Jackie said calmly.

Clearly delighted, the reporter allowed that he was hoping Jackie wouldn't say anything. Her refreshingly unexpected, unblinking response was, he said, "wonderful."

Jackie knew, of course, that Jack wouldn't find her goof so wonderful. For another few unnerving moments, she continued to sit in total silence.

"Great," the interviewer continued. "You *are* pretty much in love with him, aren't you?"

Instead of rushing to set the record straight, Jackie hesitated *again* before finally murmuring a tepid response. "I suppose so . . . ," she said. Mercifully, the exchange was edited out of the final broadcast.

In the three years since their Newport, Rhode Island, wedding and the whirlwind Acapulco honeymoon that followed, their love had been tested many times. Jackie had nursed her husband through two disastrous back surgeries—operations that, doctors warned him from the beginning, were highly risky because of his Addison's disease.

As predicted, the first operation resulted in a massive staph infection that left Jack in a coma. As he drifted in and out of consciousness, Jackie could hear Jack call out her name, but doctors and nurses physically barred her from entering his hospital room.

A second operation months later was also a catastrophe, leaving Jack in even worse shape than before. In both instances, a priest was summoned to Jack's bedside and he was given last rites.

"He didn't even *need* the operations," Jackie fumed. "They said, 'We can't tell if it will help or not.' It just made me so mad how doctors just let people suffer . . . it's just criminal."

✂

HIS OWN UNCOMPLAINING NATURE ASIDE, Jack grew so dejected that for the first time Jackie saw "tears fill his eyes and roll down his cheeks." (She would only see him cry twice more, after they moved into the White House.)

In the wake of both failed back operations, Jackie seldom left Jack's side. She read to him, relayed messages from colleagues and well-wishers (most notably Vice President Richard Nixon, who had been one of Jack's closest friends in Congress), even arranged to have screen beauty Grace Kelly dress up in a nurse's uniform and pay Jack a surprise visit in the hospital.

Jackie also overlooked the fact that, to cheer himself up, Jack had taped a pinup of Marilyn Monroe to the back of his hospital room door. Priscilla Johnson McMillan, who visited Kennedy several times, recalled that the poster was especially suggestive because it was hung upside down and Marilyn's legs were "you know, up in the air."

The Monroe poster wasn't the only evidence of Jackie's forbearance during this period. In addition to the parade of attractive young female visitors he identified to hospital personnel as his "sisters" and "cousins," more than once Jack somehow mustered enough strength to slip out of his room for a night on the town sans Jackie.

"Jackie was confident that she was the only truly important woman in Jack's life, his one true love," Dickerson said. "But he was hard-wired to go after women, and she dealt with it. It added to the sexual tension between them." During her visits to Jack in the hospital, Jackie was "playful and kittenish—frolicking on Jack's bed, jumping up and down on her knees," Priscilla McMillan said. The objective, McMillan concluded, was "to keep him *interested*—and she did, even though he was unfaithful to her."

McMillan got a glimpse of this just before Jack underwent his first operation. At a dinner party in the legendary New York restaurant Le Pavillon, Jack was seated next to McMillan. Directly across from them sat Jackie with the host. "You know," Jack told McMillan without ever taking his eyes off Jackie, "I only got married because I was thirty-six and people would think I was queer if I wasn't."

McMillan was shocked, not only because Jack seemed to be making little effort to lower his voice, but because he never stopped staring at his wife, "literally drinking her in with his eyes. . . . He was obviously proud. In some incredible way he had assimilated her."

While her husband battled for his life in the hospital, Jackie had more to do than just boost the patient's morale. She finally decided to take matters into her own hands, striking out on her own to find a doctor who could end Jack's pain once and for all—without surgery.

She took Jack to see Janet Travell at Travell's offices on West Sixteenth Street in New York. When Dr. Travell said she could give Jack a shot that would end his pain permanently but leave him feeling nothing from the waist down, his response was hardly surprising. "Well," Jack scoffed, "we can't have that now, can we, Jackie?"

Travell offered another solution: Novocain, injected directly into Jack's back. These shots, which offered immediate relief, were only a stopgap measure; the effects wore off after a few hours. But that was enough. "Well, she could fix him," Jackie recalled. "I mean, life just changed then. Jack was being driven crazy by this pain. If it hadn't been for Dr. Travell . . ."

NOT THAT JACK WOULD EVER be entirely free of pain. Returning to a hero's welcome on Capitol Hill, Jack still came home each evening and climbed into a hospital bed. "But during the day he'd walk all around the Senate," she said, "looking wonderful and tan in his gray suit."

It was also during this time that Jack, growing bored during long stretches of confinement, began compiling material for an article on the lives of politicians who at some point risked everything to make the right choice. While he recuperated at the family's Palm Beach mansion, where Joe had transformed an entire wing into a hospital ward staffed with nurses and orderlies, Jackie helped her husband expand the article into a book. Soon they were joined in this effort by Jack's eager young assistant, Ted Sorensen.

Sorensen's contribution would always be a matter of debate. Jackie, knowing that Jack had written portions of the book in longhand on yellow legal pads while continuing his recovery at Merrywood, resented the fact that Sorensen did little to quell rumors that he had actually written *Profiles in Courage*. "Jack forgave so quickly," she said later, "but I never forgave Ted Sorensen." However, JFK himself obviously believed Sorensen's contribution was substantial. According to Jackie, Jack signed over all royalties to *Profiles in Courage* to Sorensen.

Profiles in Courage became an overnight bestseller and would go on to win a Pulitzer Prize for biography. Just as important, it served to elevate the young senator even further above his Senate brethren. Now Jack, meditating on the larger issues of morality and conscience in the public arena, was viewed as something more than your run-of-the-mill politician. Jack was a *statesman.*

"War hero, Harvard-educated, from one of the richest and most famous families in the nation, and now a Pulitzer Prize winner?" Smathers said. "Oh, did I mention good-looking, with a gorgeous, classy, and *smart* wife to boot? All the rest of us could do was just sit back and watch."

The Sorensen issue aside, Jack did not hesitate to publicly thank Jackie for her contribution to *Profiles.* The book would not have been possible, he wrote, "without the encouragement, assistance and criticisms offered from the very beginning by my wife, Jacqueline, whose help during all the days of my convalescence I cannot ever adequately acknowledge."

That summer, Jack bolstered his image even more with a seven-week tour of Europe. Yet again, Jackie proved a valuable asset, charming Pope Pius XII, French premier Georges Bidault, and, at a party thrown by Greek shipping tycoon Aristotle Onassis aboard his legendary yacht *Christina,* even Winston Churchill.

Jack was eager to meet his idol, even though there was no love lost between Churchill and Papa Joe. As FDR's ambassador to the Court of St. James's in the years leading up to World War II, isolationist Joe—already suspect because of his Irish roots—had argued against U.S. involvement in the looming fight against the Nazis.

On board the *Christina* fifteen years later, Churchill now appeared to be giving Joe's son the cold shoulder—although it was hard to tell if it was intentional. "The poor man was really quite ga-ga then," Jackie said. "It was hard going. I felt so sorry for Jack that evening because he was meeting his hero, only he met him too late."

That didn't explain, however, why Churchill seemed to lavish so much more attention on the other guests—particularly Jackie. "I don't know," Jackie said, glancing at her husband's white dinner jacket. "Maybe he thought you were the waiter, Jack."

If Jackie had hoped to have Jack all to herself during their European idyll, she was sadly mistaken. This time, it appeared that Jack even made a play for Jackie's sister Lee, right under the nose of Lee's first husband Michael Canfield, adopted son of the legendary publisher Cass Canfield. Gore Vidal insisted that Canfield claimed "there were times when I think she [Lee] went perhaps too far, you know? Like going to bed with Jack in the room next to mine in the South of France and then boasting about it."

Whatever constituted the last straw, Jackie was telling their traveling companions that she was no longer willing to put up with Jack's unfettered cheating. According to Peter Ward, a British friend who rendezvoused with them in Antibes, "they were split. She said, 'I'm never going back' in my presence several times."

Yet, less than a week later, Jackie and Jack were all smiles as they dined with Lee and Michael Canfield in Monaco. Jack had agreed to stop his philandering, but only because of what Jackie told him: she was expecting a child.

They told no one. "Jackie was a firm believer in waiting until it was obvious—at least three months—before making any sort of announcement," Janet Auchincloss said. "Just the immediate families knew." But in October, shortly after moving into Hickory Hill and starting to decorate the nursery, Jackie miscarried in her third month. Once again, Jackie and Jack made little of their loss and simply moved on. "They really," Yusha Auchincloss said, "didn't share their feelings with anyone."

Three months later, Jackie was expecting again. The child was due in September 1956, but it was clear that politics, not father-hood, was the first thing on Jack's mind. Adlai Stevenson, who had lost the presidency to Dwight Eisenhower four years earlier, once again had the nomination sewn up. As Democrats prepared to hold their convention in Chicago that August, however, the second spot on the ticket was up for grabs.

For months leading up to the convention, Jack and his minions lobbied hard to make it happen. At first, they left Jackie alone. "That was perfectly fine with her," said Arthur Schlesinger Jr., a Stevenson adviser who would become a key member of JFK's brain trust. "Jackie resented us all on some level, I'm sure. We were always underfoot, popping up out of nowhere, invading their privacy."

According to Hyannis Port friend and neighbor Larry New-man, Jackie simply "loathed politics and politicians." Gore Vidal agreed that the intensity of Jackie's feelings went far beyond mere resentment. "Jackie saw there was nothing glamorous about that world. It was just sleazy," Vidal said, "and boring." Whenever "the pols came into view," Chuck Spalding added, "you could see this desperate 'get me out of here' look in her eyes."

It was a look Jack's team of hard-core pols and tweedy Ivy League intellectuals knew all too well after the newlyweds rented their first home, a narrow nineteenth-century townhouse at 3321 Dent Place in Georgetown. These invaders strolled in and out of the house unannounced, left the toilet seats up, ground mud into the rugs, dropped cigarette butts everywhere—and smashed sev-eral of Jackie's favorite Sèvres ashtrays.

"I hate it, hate it, hate it!" Jackie complained to her friend Tish Baldrige after being trapped once again in the bathroom wearing nothing but a negligee, waiting for the coast to clear. "There are meetings in the living room, meetings in the kitchen, meetings in the hallways, and meetings on the stairs. Step outside for a breath of fresh air, and they are sitting on the front steps. Where am I supposed to go to get away from them?" At one point, Jackie told Baldrige that she was thinking of getting "a bullhorn and just blasting them every time I want to walk down the front stairs or use the bathroom."

Now that she was left to her own devices in the Virginia countryside, Jackie set out to transform the inside of Hickory Hill from an Eisenhower era, wall-to-wall eyesore into an antique-filled showplace. She paid special attention to the nursery, furnishing it in shades of yellow and white so that it would be appropriate for either gender. "She may have felt a little isolated out there, all alone while Jack was out in the world shaking things up," Jamie Auchincloss said. "She was very nervous about losing the baby, too."

It didn't help, Rose Kennedy pointed out, that Jackie responded to stress by chain-smoking two packs of Salems a day (Jackie later switched to L&Ms, and then to Newport menthols). "You really shouldn't smoke, my dear," Rose would admonish her daughter-in-law in that unforgettable cackle. "It's not healthy for the baby, you know." Jackie's response was to do a dead-on impression of Rose the minute she left the room—but not before lighting up. "She had a wicked sense of humor and was a superb mimic," George Plimpton said. "Her imitation of Rose even had Jack on the floor, absolutely convulsed with laughter."

Rose had a point, of course. Jackie's obstetrician, Dr. John Walsh, had repeatedly urged her to quit smoking, at least until after she had the baby. "My words fell on deaf ears," Walsh said of Jackie's smoking habit, which began back at Miss Porter's. "It was just a blind spot with her," added Dr. Janet Travell. "Yes, a lot of pregnant women did smoke in those days, but even then it was widely frowned upon. The medical community certainly knew you were risking complications if you smoked."

Still, Travell conceded that Jackie was "under a lot of stress, and apparently trying to kick a serious nicotine addiction wasn't something she could deal with at the time." For his part, Jack had no serious objection to Jackie's smoking habit, as long as it was done out of sight and away from cameras. She, conversely, went so far as to encourage Jack's cigar smoking (he had a particular fondness for Havana Upmanns) as a way of masking her cigarette smoke—a ruse she continued in the White House. "If anyone asks," Jackie shrugged, "I just blame his smelly stogies."

Jackie's hopes of being left alone for the rest of her pregnancy were dashed when Jack pleaded with her to join him at the convention in Chicago. When she balked, telling him that she was concerned she might miscarry again, Jack pointed out that Bobby's wife, Ethel, who was also eight months pregnant, would be there. (Jack's sister Patricia, married to the movie actor Peter Lawford, was even further along in her pregnancy and decided to remain home in Los Angeles.)

Not wanting to disappoint her husband or exclude herself from this important part of his life, Jackie accompanied Jack to Chicago. As it turned out, while Jack worked the convention floor Jackie was left to fend for herself at a breakfast for the Massachusetts delegation and a cocktail party for campaign wives.

Jack lost the vice presidential spot to Tennessee senator Estes Kefauver on the third ballot. Jackie, emotionally drained and physically exhausted, stood sobbing next to Jack as he thanked supporters gathered in their suite at Chicago's Conrad Hilton Hotel. "It's all too much to bear," she told Smathers. "I don't know how you all do it."

At that point, Smathers was surprised at how hard both Jack and Jackie were taking the defeat, but he wasn't particularly worried about the baby. "None of us knew about the first miscarriage," he explained. "Jack never said a thing. They kept that all private. Since Jackie was young and the Kennedys seemed to have a knack for producing children, there seemed to be no cause for concern."

Immediately after the convention, Jack told Jackie that he would not be returning with her to Hickory Hill. Instead, he was going to join his parents as they vacationed on the French Riviera, and then cruise the Mediterranean aboard a yacht with his brother Teddy and Smathers.

"What do you mean, Jack?" she asked incredulously. After all, she had done everything he had asked of her. "I'm due in a month," she pleaded. "Please don't leave me alone. I'm frightened."

Jack was frightened, too—of Joe. The senior Kennedy had angrily warned Jack that it was too soon to try for national office, that he must not squander his political capital making a futile vice presidential bid. Now JFK felt he had to make amends with his father.

IT WAS LESS EASY TO explain why Jack also felt free to take a Mediterranean cruise while his wife was back home about to have a baby. "For God's sake, Jackie," he said—Salinger, Spalding, Lowe, and others recalled that JFK routinely prefaced his remarks with "For God's sake, Jackie" or "Oh my God, kid" whenever he was irritated with her—"I'll only be gone for nine days. There are lots of people around to take care of you. You'll be fine until I get back." It wasn't as if he felt it was necessary even to be there when Jackie gave birth; Joe, for all his involvement in their adult lives, had not been present at the birth of any of his nine children.

But Jackie wasn't just worried about the baby. George Smathers conceded that Jack was going to have "his share of female company" on the trip, and that Jackie knew it. In the end, Smathers said, "there just wasn't anything she could do about it."

Instead, Jackie went home to Hammersmith Farm—and to her mother. While his wife tried to regain her strength back in Newport, Jack enjoyed the company of his friends and several female guests aboard a chartered forty-foot yacht. Jack had personally invited several of the women aboard but seemed most interested in one: "Pooh," an attractive Manhattan socialite who only spoke of herself in the third person: "Pooh is so glad you asked me to come along," "Pooh would like a daiquiri."

On the morning of August 23, 1956, Janet Auchincloss awoke to hear her daughter screaming for help. She pushed open the door to Jackie's room and found her on the floor, clutching her stomach. Jackie was rushed by ambulance to Newport Hospital, where doctors moved quickly to perform an emergency caesarean.

When she regained consciousness several hours later, Bobby Kennedy was at Jackie's bedside, holding her hand. It fell to Jack's brother to tell Jackie that doctors tried but failed to save the life of her stillborn daughter.

Jackie had also almost died in the process, hemorrhaging so badly that she required several blood transfusions. At one point her condition was so grave, Bobby told her, a priest had been called to her room. Not wanting to upset her, Bobby made no mention of the fact that he had already made arrangements for the unnamed baby to be buried in Newport. (Jackie and Jack had actually already picked out names, and if it was a girl, they agreed she would be named Arabella, after the ship John Winthrop took to New England in 1630.)

Out to sea and out of radio contact, Jack was blissfully unaware of the tragedy—and of the desperate attempts to reach him. While Bobby issued a statement citing "exhaustion and nervous tensions following the Democratic National Convention" as the cause, the *Washington Post* carried a dramatic front-page headline: SENATOR KENNEDY ON MEDITERRANEAN TRIP UNAWARE THAT HIS WIFE HAS LOST BABY.

Devastated and feeling abandoned by her husband, Jackie waited for three days before Jack put into port in Genoa and called home. Incredibly, he still hadn't been told of the baby's death; even that sad and emotionally draining task was left for Jackie to bear.

"Oh, Jack, Jack," she wept into the phone, "I'm so sorry. I know how much you wanted this baby." Janet Auchincloss was "horrified" at Jack's callousness in going in the first place and now tried to persuade her daughter to leave him. But rather than lashing out, Jackie seemed intent on blaming herself for both the miscarriage and the stillbirth.

Just two days after Jackie lost her baby, Pat Lawford gave birth to her daughter Sydney. Ethel would deliver her fifth child, Courtney, just two weeks later. To Jackie, these were not only painful reminders of her own loss, but proof that what the other Kennedy women had been whispering to one another was true: the haughty-seeming Miss Bouvier wasn't up to the physical demands of carrying a child full-term.

Jack would have none of it. According to Smathers, his friend looked "as if he'd been smacked in the face" when he learned the news. "It was a blow, a real blow. Jack didn't show his feelings if he could help it, and he didn't cry or anything, but it was clear he was in a state of shock. After that, he wasn't thinking clearly."

That became obvious when he informed Jackie he saw no reason to abandon his friends and fly home. "I'm not sure what that would accomplish," he told her over the phone. "I don't want to disappoint Teddy and the others. Why don't I finish up the last four days of the trip and fly back from Nice?"

Incredulous, Jackie lashed out over the phone. How could he be so callous and unfeeling? She lost the baby because he insisted she go to the convention. Now he wasn't going to interrupt his vacation over something as minor as the death of a child?

At first Jack remained silent, taken aback by his wife's sudden outburst but also trying to absorb all that had happened while he was literally out to sea. "Now Jackie . . ."

"This time I'm serious, Jack," she interrupted him before hanging up. The breathy little-girl-lost voice was gone, replaced with a steely resolve. "I cannot live like this. I need you here with me—right now."

Moments after hanging up the receiver, Jack relayed the details of the exchange to Smathers. "You better get your ass back there right away," Smathers told him bluntly, "if you plan on staying married—or on getting to the White House."

Jack wasted no time commandeering a car and taking the wheel himself. "We drove like a bat out of hell to the airport," Smathers said. By this time, apparently, it had dawned on Jack that the place for him to be was by Jackie's side. Conceding that it was "a shame" Jack didn't come to that realization immediately, Smathers also insisted that Jack "cared deeply" for Jackie and "felt terrible about hurting her feelings." In his own, guarded way, Jack "was concerned," Smathers said. "He was concerned."

It was too little, too late. "Jackie was miffed," Jamie Auchincloss said. "She gave him the silent treatment. She could be the warmest person in the world or so cold that it made your teeth chatter."

In contrast to Jackie's sulking, dark moods, and grudge-holding ("She could stay mad at you *forever*," George Plimpton said), Jack's temper would flare "but that was it. He'd blow sky-high over something, pound his fist on the desk, the whole deal," Pierre Salinger said, "and then five minutes later it was like it never happened." Smathers agreed that "even though Jack had a hell of a temper, he never held a grudge. It wasn't his style. Now, Jackie was something else entirely."

JACK ARRIVED IN NEWPORT THE day after their phone call, but it was too late. Jackie felt betrayed and abandoned, and held Jack accountable for her ill-fated pregnancies. Had it not been for the hectic pace of Jack's political career and the demands made on Jackie when she was at her most vulnerable, at this point in their married life they would already be the parents of two healthy children.

Within days Jack was back at work in Washington, making the most of his new post-convention status as a rising star of the Democratic Party. Jackie, meanwhile, divided her time between Newport and New York, giving rise to rumors of a split. But this wasn't just idle gossip; for at least the second time in their brief marriage Jackie was seriously considering divorce.

Joe, with whom Jackie had always shared a warm and joking relationship, would have none of it. When *Time* magazine claimed that the infamously ambitious Joseph P. Kennedy had offered Jackie $1 million not to divorce his son, Jackie phoned and cracked, "Only one million? Why not ten million?"

The offer was real and, according to Joe's longtime friend Clare Boothe Luce as well as Gore Vidal and others, she accepted it. "Yes, Joe did offer Jackie the money to stay with Jack," Vidal said, "and she took it. Happily."

Joe also agreed to rent a house for Jack and Jackie at 2808 P Street in Georgetown while they looked for a new home. There was no way, she told Jack, that she could return to Hickory Hill—not with its nursery so lovingly decorated for their baby. A few months later they sold Hickory Hill to Bobby and Ethel, who over seventeen years wound up having eleven children. "Wind her up," Jackie quipped, "and she becomes pregnant."

In March 1957, Jackie learned that she, too, was pregnant again. By now Jack had—with Joe's blessing, of course—decided to run for president in 1960. As much as she wanted to be part of her husband's life, Jackie made it clear that this time she would not subject herself to the strains of politics.

While her husband traveled the country making speeches (144 in the span of just ten months), Jackie busied herself decorating their new home—a redbrick Federal townhouse at 3307 N Street in Georgetown. Jackie instantly recognized the building as "an architectural gem" that she could turn into a warm yet stately home. Jack was drawn to the house for one very specific reason.

"He bought our house in Georgetown," Jackie said, "because the doorknob was old, which he liked."

Jackie flooded the rooms with expensive eighteenth-century French furniture (all on Joe's tab) and, to Jack's surprise, had no qualms about decorating the third-floor nursery in a style similar to the one at Hickory Hill.

Any hope of somehow avoiding a stressful pregnancy ended when Jackie learned that Black Jack Bouvier was upset with her for not calling with the news that she was expecting. "I'm the grandfather," he complained bitterly, "and I have to read about it in the *New York Times*?" A recluse living in a four-room apartment on New York's Upper East Side, the once-dashing Black Jack now spent weeks on end drinking alone.

Jackie, who was at the Kennedy compound in Hyannis Port, flew straight to New York to tell her father how sorry she was and beg his forgiveness. But instead of accepting his daughter's apologies, Black Jack lambasted her for turning her back on him in favor of the Auchinclosses and the Kennedys. "We may not have as much money," he told her. "But what we do have is considerably more valuable: breeding."

Throwing up her hands, Jackie flew back to Cape Cod. When Black Jack checked into New York's Lenox Hill Hospital complaining of stomach pains on July 27, the eve of Jackie's twenty-eighth birthday, she called to check on him. She was told her father was resting comfortably, he was likely to be released soon, and there was really no need for her to make a special trip to visit him.

Just five days later, Black Jack Bouvier lapsed into a coma. It was then that Jackie was informed for the first time that her father was suffering from terminal liver cancer.

Jackie and Jack rushed to the hospital, but it was too late. Black Jack died just forty-five minutes before they got there. He was sixty-six. As difficult as it was for Jack, he put a comforting arm around Jackie while the nurse on duty told them that Jackie's name was the last word on her father's lips.

"I know she cried a great deal when her father died," Yusha Auchincloss said. "It took her completely by surprise, and she was terribly, terribly hurt." Guilt-ridden over not being there for her father at the end, Jackie assumed the burden of making all the funeral arrangements—from writing the obituary to picking out the flowers and the coffin.

Matters only got worse when Jack was admitted to New York Hospital suffering from another virulent staph infection in his back. He quickly recovered but Jackie, now five months along, was beginning to buckle under the strain. "She was a basket case," Evelyn Lincoln said. "Everyone, including Jack, was worried about the baby."

On November 27, 1957—the day before Thanksgiving—Jackie gave birth by caesarean section to a seven-pound, two-ounce girl at the Lying-In Hospital of New York–Cornell Medical Center. Janet Auchincloss was especially struck by Jack's reaction, given the callousness he had shown over her daughter's stillbirth the year before. "I'll always remember Jack's face when the doctor came into the waiting room and told him that the baby was fine," she said, "the sweet expression on his face and the way he smiled." She was also impressed that Jack "seemed perfectly at home with babies," and marveled at the "sheer, unadulterated delight he took in Caroline from that first day on. The look on his face, which I had never seen before, really, was . . . radiant."

As Jackie came out of anesthesia, the first sight she saw was Jack walking toward her, their baby in his arms. A nurse propped Jackie up and then helped Jack hand the baby to her. This was a feeling that, until this very moment, she feared she might never experience. "Oh, Jack. Isn't she gorgeous?" she asked him. "Isn't she the prettiest baby girl you have ever seen?" They named her after Jackie's sister, Lee, whose full name was actually Caroline Lee.

Members of the Kennedy, Bouvier, and Auchincloss clans trooped in for a peek at little Caroline, and then friends began to arrive. Lem Billings was the first. Looking at the babies lined up in the hospital nursery, Jack clasped a hand on his friend's shoulder and asked, "Now, Lem, tell me—which of the babies in the window is the prettiest?" Lem, without hesitating, pointed to the wrong infant. "He didn't speak to me for two days," Billings recalled. "Jack was more emotional about Caroline's birth than he was about anything else."

Everyone was surprised at how effortlessly Jack had taken to fatherhood. The impact of Caroline's birth was so profound, in fact, that it enabled him to connect with others in a way he had not been able to before. "Caroline's birth was a magical thing for Jack," Lem observed. "It changed him. I'm not sure he ever would have had what it takes—that extra sparkle—to make it all the way to the White House. And her arrival really changed the whole situation with Jackie—made it stronger, at least for a while."

Other friends saw the changes, too. "Jack was able to release some of his emotions to her," Betty Spalding said, "and it freed him from the fear of it." That meant he could communicate with Jackie "better, and she with him. Until he had Caroline, he never really learned how to deal with people."

If Caroline's birth rekindled the romance in her marriage, it was in large part because it bolstered Jackie's flagging self-esteem. She no longer felt inferior to the prolific Kennedy in-laws, or in the shadow of either her own domineering mother or the equally domineering Rose.

In fact, no one took child-rearing more seriously than Mrs. JFK. "If you bungle raising your children," Jackie later said, "I don't think whatever else you do matters very much."

Once back at the house on N Street, Jackie took charge. Now that she was wife, mother, and mistress of the first home she considered entirely her own, Jackie called the shots—and hired a staff to implement them: a valet, two upstairs maids, a cook, a full-time chauffeur, a laundress, her own private secretary, and a personal maid who would remain with her for years to come, Providencia "Provi" Paredes.

Then, of course, there was the nanny, Maud Shaw. It was up to Nanny Shaw to change diapers, wake up for the midnight feedings, and make sure that the master and mistress of the house were not unduly disturbed by the presence of a newborn in the house. Still, Shaw gave credit to Jackie for paying attention to her children from the very beginning. In the coming years, Jackie would "do a lot of little things for Caroline," Shaw said, "dress her, and take her out, and play with her in the garden."

At the house on N Street, Jackie put an inflatable pool in the backyard and used a garden hose to fill it up herself. "We spent a number of hours playing in the swimming pool," she said, "and having these little afternoon teas and lunches together."

NO ONE WAS MORE SMITTEN with Caroline than Daddy. Yet Jack also saw something else in their daughter—a valuable political asset. "Jack's desire," Charlie Bartlett said, "was to get the bountiful positive publicity only a child might yield."

Jackie would have none of it. "No pictures of the baby, Jack," she insisted. "That's final. I'm not going to let our child be used like some campaign mascot. I don't care how many votes it costs you." But in April 1958, as Jack positioned himself to become his party's 1960 presidential nominee, Jackie finally caved in—with the understanding that Jack would take a break from campaigning that summer and take her to Paris. On April 21, *Life* hit the stands with a beguiling Kennedy family portrait on the cover. "It looks wonderful, Jack," Mommy said when he proudly showed the magazine to her. "And that's good because we won't be doing that again any time soon."

Jack, however, was not about to give up so easily. He would ultimately turn to photographer Jacques Lowe, a refugee from Nazi Germany who had befriended Bobby Kennedy, to create the Norman Rockwell image of a perfect American family, frame by frame. At times, Lowe found Jack the Front-runner to be "grumpy, awkward, and preoccupied. But he perked up whenever I asked him to sit with Caroline."

The charming, wholesome images seemed at odds with the fact that Jack soon returned to his extracurricular pursuits. In addition to a brief fling with Quincy, Massachusetts–bred actress Lee Remick, Jack began his sporadic, two-and-a-half-year affair with Marilyn Monroe. A year after divorcing Joe DiMaggio, Marilyn married the playwright Arthur Miller. The couple settled in bucolic Roxbury, Connecticut, but within months Marilyn was meeting Jack secretly at his suite in New York's Carlyle Hotel, a duplex that occupied the thirty-fourth and thirty-fifth floors and boasted two terraces and a glass-enclosed solarium—all with wraparound views of Central Park and the Manhattan skyline.

"As Jackie saw it," Betty Spalding said, "her main job was to keep Jack interested." That Christmas of 1957, she proudly handed Jack the keys to a white Jaguar sedan. Although she used only a small portion of the money her father had left her to purchase it, Jack insisted the British-made luxury car was "too showy." He promptly traded it in for Joe Kennedy's vehicle of choice—a sedate, dark green Buick.

This time Jackie was determined to keep a closer eye on her husband. She joined Jack on the campaign trail for the first time as he sought reelection to the Senate in 1958—a race he needed to win by a landslide as prelude to a White House run. She posed for pictures alongside the candidate, stared adoringly at him whenever he gave a speech, and helped man the phone bank with her Kennedy sisters-in-law as part of an "Ask Senator Kennedy" telecast paid for by Papa Joe.

Ironically, Jackie's very first campaign speech was not in English, but in French, delivered to members of Worcester's Cercle Français. Since Jackie also spoke Spanish and Italian, Jack took her to Boston's North End. When she addressed one crowd with a few phrases in flawless Italian, it erupted in cheers. Jack won his reelection with an unprecedented 73.6 percent of the vote.

By the time Jack formally declared his presidential candidacy on January 20, 1960, he had already logged tens of thousands of miles aboard his campaign plane—a ten-passenger DC-3 Jack named, with Jackie's blessing, the *Caroline*. Given her father's frequent absences, the real Caroline's first spoken word— "goodbye"—seemed particularly poignant.

The goodbyes weren't only for Daddy. Jackie gamely tagged along in her role as the candidate's adoring wife. Flying through blizzards, dense fog, and thunderstorms aboard the *Caroline* ("I'd be turning green, and they'd both just be sitting there reading,"

Lowe said), the Kennedys crisscrossed the country at a break-neck pace. Once airborne, Jack usually strategized or worked on speeches with Sorensen, O'Donnell, Salinger, and Powers between bowls of fish chowder—JFK's favorite dish. Jackie sat quietly doing needlepoint or reading Jack Kerouac—"an island of serenity in the chaos," Jacques Lowe said. "But you always knew she'd rather be someplace else."

Jackie, considered cold and aloof at first, gradually proved herself to be a valuable asset to the campaign. West Virginia campaign organizer Charles Peters worried that she was too "high-toned" for his state, but he admitted that he was "dead wrong. It turned out that the voters loved her. She was perceived as the princess, and they basked in her glamour rather than being offended by it." Pierre Salinger, who had signed on as Jack's press secretary, conceded that "Jackie did a credible job of concealing her natural distaste for politics from the voters. But God, she just hated it. She kept saying she knew her husband was involved in a 'great struggle'—meaning the race against Nixon—and that as his wife she knew she had to be a part of it."

Now that he was facing a tough battle for the White House against the well-financed, well-organized, and even better-known incumbent vice president, Jack wanted Jackie by his side in the general election. But that was not going to happen. When he returned from racking up primary victories in New Hampshire, Wisconsin, and West Virginia, Jackie told the candidate she was expecting another baby in December.

This time Jack did not even consider asking his wife to attend the Democratic National Convention in Los Angeles. He did not have to be reminded that the strain of campaigning in 1956 cost them the life of their infant daughter and almost killed Jackie in the process. "Now Jack understood what it was to be a parent," Larry Newman said. "He already saw his baby as a human being, and not a thing. . . . He was a changed man in 1960."

The day after Jack beat back a last-minute challenge by Texas senator Lyndon Johnson and secured the nomination on the first ballot, reporters descended on Hyannis Port wanting to talk to the candidate's wife. While Caroline careened about, Jackie apologized for her decision to stick close to home for the rest of her pregnancy. "I suppose I won't be able to play much part in the campaign," she allowed, "but I'll do what I can."

Privately, Jackie was less eager to oblige. Her spies at the convention—including her sister Lee, now married to Polish Prince Stanislas ("Stas") Radziwill—had kept her abreast of Jack's dates with Marilyn Monroe. (Marilyn told Jack's brother-in-law Peter Lawford that she found her time spent with JFK to be "very penetrating.")

"She was no dumbbell," Smathers said. "Jackie knew all about Marilyn and what they were up to at the convention." Much of the time, "what they were up to" occurred at Jack's secret Los Angeles hideaway in an apartment house owned by a close friend of Joe Kennedy, *Wizard of Oz* Tin Man Jack Haley.

Jackie assumed that Marilyn wasn't the only woman her husband had been involved with during this period, and she was right. On the eve of the pivotal New Hampshire primary back in March, Jack had begun an affair with a slender, blue-eyed, raven-haired twenty-six-year-old named Judy Campbell at New York's Plaza Hotel. Campbell, who had been introduced to JFK by Frank Sinatra, also happened to be the girlfriend of Chicago mob boss Sam Giancana. During the convention in Los Angeles, Campbell spent the night with Jack at Peter Lawford's Beverly Hilton Hotel suite.

Jackie wasn't worried about losing Jack to any of these women, but she did live in fear of one thing. "So long as she was not held to public ridicule," Gore Vidal said, "Jackie accepted Jack's womanizing as a fact of life. It's not that they didn't care about each other. I think she eventually grew quite fond of Jack, and he took a certain pride in her."

"Jackie was not threatened—not even by Marilyn Monroe," Clare Boothe Luce claimed. "But if somehow word had gotten out, it would have upset her terribly. She could not bear the thought of being publicly humiliated."

"Jackie was anxious, confused," said their Hyannis Port neighbor Larry Newman. "She thought a child would make all the difference, and it didn't, not really." As she faced the inevitable demands that would be made on her, said Newman, "there were plenty of moments when there was this look in her eyes—somewhere between sadness and panic." As for crowds: "They terrified her." Whenever she saw people approaching, or the car she was in was about to be swallowed up by the throng, "she always looked like a frightened deer."

Yet she was not about to let her true feelings show to the voters. "She hid it," Newman said, "from the press, the cameras, the public." But not, as it happened, from Jack's election team. "Get the hell out!" she shouted at Kennedy advance man Frank Morrissey when he came to drive her to meet Jack at Cape Cod's Barnstable Airport. "I'm staying right here!" It was to be Jack's triumphant homecoming, but at first Jackie did not want to give him the satisfaction of seeing her play the part of loyal wife.

She came around, of course, but not before telling Newman that she didn't want to go because the same thing always happened: She was going to run up the gangway and join Jack in the *Caroline,* and reemerge with him to the roar of the crowd. Then someone would shove a bunch of roses in her arms and Jack would then desert her to shake hands. "I hate it," she said. When everything happened exactly the way she predicted, Jackie, clutching her roses, turned to Newman and said, "What did I tell you?"

Even though Jack could always count on crowds being twice the size if Jackie was with him, he didn't seem particularly interested in her welfare on the hustings. Jacques Lowe said JFK was "never intentionally rude" to his wife, but instead was "very focused on what he was doing and not always paying that much attention to her. He could be walking out into a crowd and she'd be about a half-mile behind him, just trying to keep up."

According to Betty Spalding, this had less to do with campaigning than it did with Jack's "terrible manners" when it came to the opposite sex. "He didn't have any manners, in the sense of letting women go through the door first or opening doors for them or standing up when older women came into the room. He was nice to people, but heedless of people."

BEFORE THE CAMPAIGN AGAINST HIS old friend Richard Nixon started in earnest, Jack unwound with his family at Hyannis Port. Not that summers at the compound were ever particularly restful. Presided over by Caroline's fiercely competitive grandparents, "vacations" were invariably a frenetic blur of swimming, sailing, tennis, snorkeling, badminton, golf, and of course the compulsory games of rough-and-tumble "touch" football on the lawn. Always looking for ways to indulge his passion for speed, Jack would ignore his bad back and take the wheel of a golf cart, careering around the grounds as Caroline and her cousins held on tight and shrieked in terror.

Once she had settled back into the rhythm of life at Hyannis Port, Jackie was able to tamp down her own anxieties and offer words of comfort to her new sister-in-law, Ted's wife Joan. When Joan confided that Ted wasn't even bothering to hide his interest in other women, Jackie laughed it off. "Kennedy men are like that," she said. "They'll go after anything in skirts. It doesn't mean a thing."

UNLIKE JOAN, WHO CAME FROM a more traditional, suburban, upper-middle-class background, Jackie had had plenty of practice looking the other way. The same "boys will be boys" rationale had made it possible for Jackie to excuse her own father's womanizing. "People try to make them into John and Jane Smith of Dayton, Ohio," Vidal said. "But theirs is a world of money and power, and to the rich and powerful quaint things like fidelity and domestic bliss simply don't matter." To them, he continued, "sex is something you do like tennis. It can become quite competitive."

Jackie had time enough to sort out her feelings, and to contemplate what life might be like for her as first lady. In the meantime, she agreed to help Jack neutralize wife Pat Nixon's Republican cloth-coat image by gamely posing for photographs. For one shot, Jackie, who managed to stave off the inevitable baby bulge by smoking even more than usual, put on a one-piece bathing suit and a bathing cap to frolic with her husband on the beach. At one point she pretended to steady him in a dinghy before tipping the boat over, toppling Jack into the surf.

Despite her initial refusal to turn their daughter into a campaign "mascot," Jackie relented. After all, Nixon was trotting out daughters Tricia and Julie at the drop of a hat. Not to be outdone, Caroline was shown in one magazine layout after another hugging her teddy bear, napping, smiling at her parents, or simply staring wide-eyed into the camera. "She was," Lowe said, "a *phenomenally* photogenic child." Maud Shaw, of course, was nowhere to be seen in the photographs. As far as the voting public was concerned, Jack Kennedy's down-to-earth wife was raising their daughter without the help of a nanny. "It was perfectly fine," Shaw later said. "I understood they had an image to project, and she really was a wonderful mother to Caroline."

Being photographed was one thing, but Jackie still insisted that Caroline be kept out of the fray. She would not allow her daughter to be jostled and gawked at by the mob. "Jack wanted to cart Caroline out as often as he could," Lowe said, "but he wasn't about to defy Jackie when it came to their child."

Or at least not directly. Jack's personal photographer discovered early on that his boss had few qualms about letting staff members take the heat for something he wanted accomplished. "He'd tell us to do something Jackie expressly didn't want done," Lowe said, "and then play dumb."

"The campaign gave us a good idea of how things were going to work between them in the White House," Pierre Salinger said. "The president insisted on deniability when it came to Jackie."

"You know," added Lowe, "it was 'What? Who, me?' He didn't like any unpleasantness with Jackie. Jack would do anything to avoid an argument with her. He genuinely cared about her feelings, and tried his best, even with all the distractions and incredible pressures involved in running for the presidency, to keep her happy."

Notwithstanding the fact that the JFKs' little family was appearing on newsstands everywhere, Jackie and Caroline managed to lie low for the first twelve weeks as Daddy barnstormed the country nonstop. Perhaps too low. On the evening of September 12 Jackie was about to sit down for dinner at Hyannis Port with several Kennedys and Auchinclosses when the phone rang. "That's Jack!" she said excitedly. She had been waiting for his call from the campaign trail all day. Moments later, Jackie returned to the living room with, said one guest, "that blank, resigned look she always had when she didn't want anyone reading her emotions." Was something wrong? Rose Kennedy asked.

"Today's our anniversary," Jackie told everyone, "and Jack never mentioned it." In his defense, Jack, who had asked Evelyn Lincoln to send his wife flowers that day, later called to apologize.

Nothing had changed since that day a few years earlier when Gore Vidal asked Jackie if she didn't find her husband's political stardom exciting. "For Jack it is," she answered. "Not for me. I never see him."

Jackie would be the first to concede, however, that Jack had every reason to be distracted. The most critical moment in the campaign was fast approaching: September 26, when CBS was scheduled to air the first of four historic debates between Kennedy and Nixon.

Unbeknownst to all but two or three confidants, Jack was going into the first debate armed with a secret weapon. Just days earlier, he and Chuck Spalding decided to attend a party in New York after a strenuous day of campaigning. Bright and early the next morning, Spalding went out of town on a political errand for Jack, and came back to Jack's Carlyle Hotel suite "raring to go."

"I'm just pooped," JFK confessed, "completely wiped out. You went to the same party I did last night. . . . Where in the hell do you get all this energy?"

Spalding let JFK in on his little secret. In addition to helping Jack out in the campaign, Spalding had a high-pressure executive position on Madison Avenue and was going through a rough divorce that left him exhausted. At a friend's urging, Chuck went to see a mysterious Dr. Max Jacobson on East Seventy-second Street in New York. In the waiting room that afternoon were Broadway and film star Zero Mostel, singers Johnny Mathis and Eddie Fisher, and even Jack's old Choate classmate Alan Jay Lerner, the lyricist for such hit Broadway musicals as *Brigadoon, My Fair Lady*, and Jack's favorite, *Camelot*. ("And to think," JFK later joked when Lerner brought the New York cast of *Brigadoon* to perform at a state dinner for King Hassan II of Morocco, "neither of us thought the other would amount to anything.")

Spalding quickly discovered that Max Jacobson—"a loud, arrogant, kind of mad scientist type"—counted "half of Hollywood" among his patients. They were all apparently willing to overlook Dr. Max's scruffy appearance, his fingernails blackened with chemicals, and the bizarre knack he had for suddenly dozing off in strange places. (Once when the doctor fell asleep in a bathtub, longtime patient Eddie Fisher tried and failed to scrub Jacobson's fingers clean.) Nor was Dr. Max much of a stickler for hygiene. Fisher described the shiny black medical bag Jacobson carried as "a jumble of dirty, unmarked bottles and nameless chemical concoctions which he would just dump out on a table when he began to mix an injection." According to Jacobson's assistant, Harvey

Mann, "many of Max's patients ended up with hepatitis, because the office was filthy."

Spalding was indeed put off by Jacobson's brash behavior and unkempt appearance, but he rolled up his sleeve anyway. "I let him give me a shot," Spalding said. "Well, I went over the top of the building! I felt wonderful, full of energy—capable of doing just about anything. I didn't know exactly what he was giving me, but it was a magic potion as far as I was concerned."

Jacobson, later dubbed "Dr. Feelgood," was shooting up his high-profile clientele with amphetamine cocktails, mostly Dexedrine laced with steroids. The upside was immediately obvious: as a stimulant, these concoctions not only increased energy but infused the patient with a sense of power, confidence, and well-being. Conversely, amphetamines were highly addictive, often led to severe depression, and in some cases triggered symptoms of paranoid schizophrenia. For the moment, of course, Jacobson kept the downside of using amphetamines to himself.

"Well, if it's doing all that for you," Jack told Spalding, "then I want some. Can you put me in touch with this guy?"

Spalding hesitated. He told Jack that if anything went wrong, he didn't want to be responsible. Bobby Kennedy was fiercely protective of his brother, so Spalding figured that he'd run the idea by Bobby first.

Bobby not only urged his brother to see Max Jacobson; he soon counted himself among Dr. Feelgood's regular patients. Only days before the first debate, Jacobson cleared out his office and JFK entered through the garage. "The demands of his political campaign were so great he felt fatigued," Jacobson said. "His muscles felt weak. It interfered with his concentration and affected his speech."

The first shot was 85 percent speed and 15 percent vitamins—and within minutes Jack was a new man. His muscle weakness vanished and, according to Jacobson, JFK was instantly "cool, calm, and very alert."

The injections had another effect, as well. To alleviate Jack's back pain, Dr. Travell had increased the prescription for the time-release DOCA pellets in his thighs from 150 to 300 milligrams. Cortisone pills replaced the steroid injections he had also been getting twice a day. To offset any negative side effects, JFK requested—and was given—a daily dose of methyltestosterone. Normally, such elevated levels of testosterone increase muscular strength, raise energy levels, and sharpen mental focus. They also can lead to a quantum boost in libido. "It was pretty obvious," Smathers said, "that if Jack was a tiger before, he was even more of one now."

&

IT WAS NOT LONG BEFORE "we were *all* taking injections," Spalding said. "Jack, Jackie, Bobby, *everybody*." In most cases, Jacobson gave the shots twice a week, although Jack in particular sometimes demanded—and got—more. "I thought, this doesn't make any sense," Spalding recalled. "It's so simple. It wasn't until much later I found out it wasn't so simple after all."

Dr. Feelgood's influence would reach into the White House and have far-reaching consequences not only for the personal relationship of the president and his wife, but also for the nation. In the short run, Jacobson's amphetamine cocktails would simply help get JFK elected.

Those who listened to the first debate on the radio, including Lyndon Johnson, felt Nixon won decisively. But the millions who watched the two candidates square off on television were won over by Jack's tanned, relaxed appearance in contrast to Nixon's darting eyes, five o'clock shadow, and sweaty upper lip. In the words of debate producer Don Hewitt, who would become best known as the producer of CBS's *60 Minutes,* Jack "looked like a young Adonis."

Jackie had watched the first three debates from the comfort of home, but for the final face-off she showed up at the ABC studios in New York to lend moral support—and outshine a comparatively mousy Pat Nixon in the process. "Poor Pat Nixon," she said to Salinger. "She can look so New York chic, but they won't let her."

Chic was not always required, or even desired. It was inevitable that Jackie's own admittedly lavish spending habits, although willingly funded by an appreciative Joe Kennedy, would become a bone of contention. That fall, a newspaper reported that American women resented Jackie because in a single year she spent $30,000 (the rough equivalent of $240,000 in 2013 dollars) on Paris fashions alone. Jackie snapped back that she couldn't possibly spend that much unless she "wore sable underwear."

During the closing months of the campaign, Jackie saw her husband only a half-dozen times, and then fleetingly. When Jack decided he could spare two days to unwind in Palm Beach, she immediately joined him in Florida. "She was totally thrilled to see him," Maud Shaw recalled, "even if it was only for a short time."

Instead of spending time with his wife, however, Jack wanted to hit the links. Jackie was determined that he spend time with her, but Jack headed off for the golf course with Chuck Spalding as planned. When Jackie sent word pleading with him to return to the house, Jack grew remorseful—but not enough to want to call off his game. "Chuck," he told his friend, "go back to the house and see her."

Spalding wished he hadn't. "So I went up to her and she *flew* at me in a rage," he said. "I had never seen her so angry. She really went off the deep end, yelling and screaming at me."

"Hey, hey," Spalding said, hoping Jackie would regain the dignified aura for which she was already becoming famous. "We've been friends a long time. You and I are family. It's just a golf game. Why don't you come with us?"

Spalding's invitation fell on deaf ears. "She just looked at me, absolutely fuming, then turned on her heels and left."

As the race grew tighter, Jack begged Jackie to join him in New York for the jam-packed closing days of the campaign. Defying doctor's orders, she agreed. It was difficult for her to say no, since the campaign schedule drawn up for Jack had him shaking hands and delivering speeches a minimum of eighteen hours a day. "He just works so hard," she said, "and you know I think he hates it almost as much as I do, at least he says he does." Besides, she added, "It's the most important time of Jack's whole life. I should be with him."

As she had done so skillfully during earlier races, Jackie spoke Italian to crowds in Little Italy and Spanish in Spanish Harlem. The candidate and his eight-months-pregnant wife flirted with disaster, however, when they rode on the back of an open car during a ticker-tape parade through New York's "Canyon of Heroes." Three million screaming fans turned out, yanking at their sleeves, rocking the car—at several points along the route Jackie was convinced they were about to be hurled to the pavement.

A shaken Jackie returned to Hyannis Port to wait out the election and what remained of her pregnancy. Browsing through a copy of *Life,* she took little comfort in reading that someone had gone to the trouble of categorizing Jack's legion of hysterical female fans as "jumpers, shriekers, huggers, lopers, touchers, gaspers, gogglers, swooners, and collapsers."

Indeed, Jack was now inspiring the kind of frenzied reaction that had previously been reserved for Frank Sinatra or Elvis Presley. "It's hard to explain the hold he had on these young women," Nancy Dickerson said, chalking it up to what she called his "incredible sexual pull." Lowe said the atmosphere at every campaign stop was the same, and could best be described with one word: "orgasmic."

Even though she had already sent in her absentee ballot—casting a single vote for her husband and no one else, not even LBJ—Jackie was again recruited to accompany her husband to Boston on Election Day. "It doesn't matter that I'm tired and about to have a baby," she complained to Newman. "They need their picture of me smiling from ear to ear while Jack casts his vote."

Back in Hyannis Port, Caroline, who would soon turn three, raced into her father's arms as soon as he walked in the front door. They had not seen each other in two months. Jack ran his fingers through his daughter's blond curls, held in place by two powder blue ribbons.

Then Jackie ordered her husband to sit in his favorite wing chair while Caroline recited two poems by Edna St. Vincent Millay. "My candle burns at both ends," she began. "It will not last the night . . ."

"Wonderful, Buttons!" Jack said when she was done, clapping his approval. "Wonderful!" A half century later, Caroline would call this one of her most cherished childhood memories.

∽

THAT NIGHT OF NOVEMBER 8, 1960, it looked at first as if JFK might win a landslide victory. "Oh, Bunny," she said at 10:30 p.m., using her favorite nickname for Jack. "You're president now." But then Nixon surged ahead. While the entire Kennedy clan watched the seesawing results on television, precinct-by-precinct numbers were pouring in over the thirty phone lines installed on Papa Joe's veranda.

Realizing it was going to be "an all-night thing," Jackie went up to bed. "It was so sweet. Jack came up and sort of kissed me good night," she said, "then all the Kennedy girls came up, one by one, and we just hugged each other."

Jack stayed up until 4 a.m. and then, intent on not disturbing her, retired to the guest room next to theirs. At 8:30, Jackie woke with a start. "I went flying into his room to hear the good news," she said, admitting that she startled Jack to such an extent he "sprang" out of bed. "But no, there wasn't anything."

A little before 9 a.m. Ted Sorensen called Jack with the news that he'd won. Minutes later, the president-elect was soaking in the bathtub.

"Daddy, Daddy!" Caroline hollered as she ran into the bathroom. "You won! Miss Shaw told me to call you 'Mr. President' now."

As it happened, victory would not be certain for hours. When Nixon's camp finally did concede, it became clear that Jack had won the narrowest of election victories, squeaking by with a margin of less than one-fifth of 1 percent.

Ignoring his problematic back, Jack walked outside and gave Caroline a piggyback ride around the lawn. Then, still holding his little girl in his arms, he walked over to the gaggle of reporters waiting by a bank of microphones.

With all eyes on her husband, Jackie threw on a coat and raced down to the beach alone. Jacques Lowe was trying to assemble all the Kennedys together for a family portrait when he glanced out the window and saw Jackie "rushing down to the sea. That Wednesday morning when the rest of the family was jubilant and embracing each other and laughing it up, Jackie was deeply shaken," he said. "She was clearly in a state of shock."

Jackie, Lowe said, "definitely had ambivalent feelings about becoming first lady. She had always lived in a fairyland, in the role of the storybook princess. I'm not sure Jackie ever counted on being queen."

"Where's Jackie?" Jack asked. "Everyone's waiting to have their picture taken."

Lowe pointed to the solitary figure standing on the beach, holding her collar up against the cold, her hair whipping in the wind. "It's okay," Jack told Lowe. "I'll go get her."

Lowe watched as Jack walked briskly down to the water's edge and put his arm around her.

"What will happen now, Jack?" she asked. "What will happen to us?"

&

LOWE WATCHED AS THEY CHATTED for a minute or two more. "He obviously reassured her everything would be all right," Lowe said. "Then they hugged. It was a very moving scene." Once Jack brought Jackie back up to the house, she changed into a red dress and walked into the room where the rest of the family had gathered to have their picture taken. Everyone, including the hypercritical Rose and the Kennedy in-laws Jackie had once called a "pack of gorillas," leapt up and cheered. "You see," Jack whispered into Jackie's ear, "they know I couldn't have done it without you."

Come here any time and keep us company.
Because we are so lonely.

—JACKIE,

in a note to her friend Oleg Cassini

5

❧

"Our Strange Little Life"

*L*ess then a month away from her due date, Jackie was not about to take any more chances. She and Jack had planned on having the baby at New York Hospital, where Caroline was born, and that meant moving into Jack's Carlyle Hotel suite a week or so before the newest Kennedy was scheduled to arrive.

Until then Jackie was under strict orders from Dr. Walsh to stay home. While she rested, Jack shuttled between Washington and the Kennedy mansion in Palm Beach, where he and his father went over possible cabinet choices as they lounged by the pool.

Meanwhile, crowds gathered outside the N Street house, already cordoned off by the Secret Service, to catch a glimpse of the president-elect and his attractive family. Inside, the usual chaos prevailed as gruff, cigar-chomping pols mingled with JFK's band of bow-tied and bespectacled young advisers and distinguished future cabinet appointees like Dean Rusk and Robert McNamara. "I could be in the tub," Jackie said, and when she was finished return to find "Pierre Salinger holding a press conference in my bedroom." At one point Jackie complained that she'd nearly collided with Jack's national security adviser McGeorge Bundy on her way to the bathroom. "For God's sake, Jackie," JFK replied, "all you have to worry about right now is your inaugural ball gown."

On November 25, Jack returned to Georgetown for a quiet Thanksgiving dinner with his wife and daughter at their house on N Street—"my sweet little house," Jackie liked to say, "that leans slightly to one side." Midway through dinner, Jack informed Jackie that he intended to return to Palm Beach that night.

Jackie was crestfallen. Worried that this delivery might not be as easy as Caroline's turned out to be, she begged Jack to postpone his trip to Florida just a few weeks—until the baby was born. "Why can't you stay here until I have the baby?" she asked. "Then we can all go down together."

Jack refused. "Caroline had arrived on time," Jack's friend Bill Walton said, "and he saw no reason to think anything would be different this time around." Instead of remaining by his wife's side, JFK departed right after dessert.

Just one hour later, Maud Shaw heard a scream and rushed upstairs. Jackie was crumpled over on the edge of her bed, clutching her stomach. The bedspread, Shaw noted with horror, was stained with blood. Shaw grabbed the phone and called Dr. Walsh. Within minutes, Jackie was being rushed by ambulance to Georgetown Hospital. Sheet-white by the time it arrived, Jackie summoned enough strength to ask the emergency room doctors one question: "Will I lose my baby?"

Meanwhile the president-elect was in high spirits aboard the *Caroline,* puffing on a cigar and chatting about his plans for the transition. It was then that the news of Jackie's condition crackled over the radio. This time Jack was "stricken with remorse," Kenny O'Donnell said, "because he was not with his wife." Jack muttered to O'Donnell, "I'm never there when she needs me."

As soon as the *Caroline* touched down in Palm Beach, Jack called Georgetown Hospital and was told that Jackie was being prepped for an emergency caesarean. To get back to Jackie's side as quickly as possible, Jack commandeered the fastest plane available—the DC-6 press plane that trailed the *Caroline* to Florida.

As the press plane sped back to Washington, Jack clamped on the cockpit headphones and waited for news. It came a little after 1 a.m.: Jackie had given birth by caesarean section to a six-pound, three-ounce boy. Mother and child were healthy and resting comfortably. From the cockpit, Pierre Salinger announced the birth of John Fitzgerald Kennedy Jr., and the reporters cheered. It was only then that Jack, who just moments before had worried that this time he might lose both his wife and their child, lit another cigar, faced the press—and took a sweeping bow.

Salinger's glowing statement aside, Jackie and her son were not out of the woods—far from it. John Jr. would spend the first six days of his life in an incubator. It would be months before they would fully recover, both suffering near-fatal setbacks along the way.

John Jr. was less than a day old when Kennedy family nurse Luella Hennessey, flanked by Secret Service agents, wheeled Jackie in to see him in his incubator. Halfway there, a photographer lunged out of a storage closet and popped off a half-dozen flashbulbs before the agents confiscated his film.

Jackie was not prepared for this. "I feel," she said, "as though I've turned into a piece of public property."

Jack, meanwhile, made up for not being there for John's birth by visiting his wife and son three times a day. The mood at the hospital, *Life* magazine writer Gail Wescott said, was "almost carnival-like—innocent and exhilarating. It did not seem that anything could ever go wrong."

With Mommy in the hospital, JFK was less likely to rein in his high-spirited daughter—certainly not when there were cameras around. As for the baby, Caroline proudly claimed ownership; since she turned three just two days after John's arrival, she was told that he was her "birthday present." Caroline, according to Maud Shaw, "thought for a long time after that he *belonged* to her."

For the time being, Jack was perfectly happy to watch his little girl charm the press corps. While he conferred with political operatives and leaders from the top echelons of government, Caroline slid down bannisters, raced around the room, stuck her tongue out behind Daddy's back, pedaled her tricycle between reporters' legs, or—as she did during an important news conference—tottered around in her pajamas and Mommy's size-ten-and-a-half stiletto heels.

John Jr. was baptized on December 8 wearing JFK's forty-three-year-old christening gown. Because Jackie was still recuperating, the ceremony took place in the Georgetown University chapel. Asked who the baby looked like, all the Kennedys agreed John was the spitting image of his father. Janet Auchincloss insisted that the baby looked more like Jackie. When asked her opinion, Jackie replied, "I don't think he looks like anybody."

The day she was scheduled to leave the hospital, Jackie defied her doctor's orders and reluctantly accepted departing first lady Mamie Eisenhower's invitation to show her around the Executive Mansion. She didn't want to do it, but Jack insisted. "For God's sake, Jackie," he said, "you don't want to insult Mrs. Eisenhower. You've got to go." Family nurse Luella Hennessey was one of the few with the courage to speak up. "If you get on your feet now, you might die," she pleaded. "I don't care if he is the new president, he has no right to ask you to risk your life."

Jackie wished she had listened to the nurse. A promised wheelchair never materialized. Trailing Mamie, she schlepped through room after room, climbed up and down staircases—all the while grinning for photographers. Not once was she even offered a chance to sit down.

Once it was over and she was back home in Georgetown, Jackie collapsed. "I really had a weeping fit and I couldn't stop crying," recalled Jackie, who then flew down to the Kennedy estate in Palm Beach to recover. "It was something that takes away your last strength when you don't have any left. So that wasn't very nice of Mrs. Eisenhower."

Around this time, the baby suffered an even more distressing setback. Aboard the *Caroline* en route to Florida, Jackie was sufficiently alarmed about the baby's labored breathing to order Jack and his cronies to smoke their cigars at the opposite end of the cabin, away from John's bassinet.

At the Palm Beach mansion, things only got worse. It turned out that John Jr. suffered from an inflammation of the lungs' hyaline membrane—the same problem that would later prove fatal for another Kennedy child. "There was, thank God, this brilliant pediatrician in Palm Beach," Jackie said, "who really saved his life, as he was going downhill."

Just forty-eight hours after his son was pulled back from the brink of death a second time, Jack headed off as he did every Sunday in Palm Beach to Mass at nearby St. Edward's Church. No one had noticed that just outside, would-be suicide bomber Richard P. Pavlick waited on the street in his car packed with seven sticks of dynamite. Pavlick's plan: to crash into JFK's limousine as it pulled out of the driveway and onto North Ocean Boulevard.

Just as he was about to slam his foot on the accelerator, Jackie and Caroline stepped out to say goodbye. Then nurse Luella Hennessey emerged from the house with the baby in her arms. Unexpectedly overcome by the sight of the Kennedy children, Pavlick turned and drove away. His bizarre plot to kill President-elect Kennedy only came to light several days later, when Pavlick was pulled over for drunk driving. He was eventually convicted of attempted murder and sent to prison.

The ever-fatalistic Jack merely shrugged when told how close Pavlick came to murdering not only him but his family. Jackie, on the other hand, was petrified. "We're nothing," she told Tish Baldrige, "but sitting ducks in a shooting gallery."

Still weak, unable to hold food down, and suffering what she described simply as "complete physical and nervous exhaustion," Jackie returned to Georgetown on January 14 to start packing for the big move. The children stayed behind in Palm Beach with their father, Maud Shaw, and the new nanny hired to take care of John, Elsie Phillips.

Determined to leave her mark on the White House, Jackie had already hired old school chum Tish Baldrige, previously employed as publicity director for Tiffany & Company, to be her social secretary. "The world's greatest monument to bad taste" is how Jackie described the White House to Baldrige. "And the furniture—positively atrocious!"

To help fix the problem, Jackie hired New York interior designer Sister Parish, who promptly assembled a battalion of experts whose sole mission was to carry out the first lady's wishes. "Let's have lots of chintz," Jackie told Parish, "and gay up this old dump."

Surrounded by towering piles of packing boxes marked "Nursery," "Yellow Oval Room," "Queens' Bedroom," and "Children's Playroom/Solarium," Jackie and Parish spent hours going over the paint samples, wallpaper, drapery, and carpet swatches spread out on the dining room table. Jackie told Parish that she wanted to "restore" the White House, not simply "redecorate" it. "Everything must have a reason for being there, and that is a question of scholarship."

On January 18, Jack returned to Washington—but not home. Jackie became unraveled at the notion of Jack and his boisterous transition team invading her territory again; at her request, Jack instead moved in with his friend and neighbor Bill Walton.

The next day, waist-high snow blanketed the nation's capital, tying up traffic and throwing Frank Sinatra, producer of that evening's star-studded Inaugural Gala at the National Armory, into a panic. He needn't have worried. Crowds still huddled along the streets to catch a passing glimpse of their exciting new first couple, buoyed by what gala performer Leonard Bernstein called a "special blizzard festival mood."

The show itself came off without a hitch, although Jackie took offense at stand-up comic Alan King's skewering of marriage, and of wives in particular. "So awful, all these horrible jokes about marriage," she later told Arthur Schlesinger. "I mean, the wife is a shrew, and the—I just thought that's so sad when comedians do that . . ."

IF SHE WAS CONCERNED THAT Jack would take note, he was having too much fun toying with his Secret Service detail—vanishing down the service stairs, or darting off to greet someone he'd spotted in the crowd. Halfway through the program, Jackie realized she was simply too tired to go on. She slipped out during intermission and returned to Georgetown to collapse in her bed.

The irrepressible president-elect, however, was not about to call it a night. At a party thrown by his father at Paul Young's Restaurant, Jack took Red Fay aside to ask, "Have you ever seen so many attractive people in one room?" He then marveled at the fact that Papa Joe was flirting with every young woman there—"one of the smoothest operations," JFK sighed to his friend, "I've ever seen."

Back on N Street, Jackie quickly discovered that, as exhausted as she was, she remained wide awake. She was, she said, like a child "waiting for Christmas . . . I couldn't go to sleep." More to the point, she didn't want to fall asleep before Jack came home, not on their last night before moving into 1600 Pennsylvania Avenue. "It was such a night to share together," she said, "because that night, you know, we were in the same bed."

Actually, they were in bed together less than two hours; Jack didn't straggle in until shortly after 6 a.m., and he departed alone for early morning Mass at eight. Back by nine, he practiced his inaugural address in the ground-floor library while Jackie dressed upstairs. "Come on, Jackie," he yelled up the stairs after she'd kept him waiting past their scheduled departure for pre-inauguration coffee with the Eisenhowers. "For God's sake!"

America's next first lady appeared moments later looking like a character from Tolstoy in a beige coat with sable collar, matching muff, and the pillbox hat that would become her trademark. That, and the bouffant hairdo that was already being copied by millions of women around the world.

❧

PRECISELY AT NOON ON JANUARY 20, 1961, Jackie seemed un-fazed by the numbing 20-degree cold as she proudly watched Jack place his hand on the Fitzgerald family Bible and take the oath of office from Chief Justice Earl Warren. At that instant Jack became the first president born in the twentieth century, the first Roman Catholic president, and, at forty-three, the youngest person ever elected to the office.

Jack's inaugural address, with its bold "Ask not what your country can do for you" message, electrified the nation. But Jackie was prevented from following tradition and congratulating her husband on the dais with a kiss. "Everyone says," she recalled of that moment, " 'Why didn't you kiss Jack after?' " But knowing all too well his aversion to showing emotion of any kind in public, she held her own in check. Kissing, even after being sworn in as president, was something that "of course, he would never do."

Stuck far behind her husband with the other spouses, Jackie watched in frustration as Jack walked briskly up the red-carpeted steps and off the platform. "I so badly wanted to see him," she remembered, "just to see him alone." Finally, she caught up with him in the Capitol Rotunda as he was making his way to the traditional inaugural lunch with congressional leaders. As Jack turned toward her, she put her gloved hand on his cheek. "There was so much I wanted to say, but I could scarcely embrace him in front of all those people," she recalled. So she just looked into his eyes and said, "Jack, you were so wonderful!" She was startled by the way he looked at her with tears in his eyes. "He was smiling in the most touching and vulnerable way," she said. "He looked so happy."

It was then that a photographer emerged from behind a pillar and captured the moment on film. "In the papers it said, 'Wife chucks him under chin.' I mean that was so much more emotional than any kiss because his eyes really did fill with tears." She wanted to rewrite the newspaper caption to simply read "Oh, Jack. What a day."

Braving the frigid temperatures, the new president and his first lady rode in an open car from the Capitol Building to the White House. "I had absolutely no idea," she said, "about how to wave until Jack showed me."

The president seemed impervious to the cold as marching bands, military units, and floats—including one that carried members of his old PT-109 crew—paraded before him for three and a half hours. But after one hour on the reviewing stand, Jackie—shivering, fatigued, and looking ahead to the onerous prospect of having to dance at five scheduled inaugural balls—excused herself. "I'm exhausted, Jack," she said. "I'll see you at home."

Of course, "home" for Jack and Jackie was now the White House, where painters worked feverishly to complete the Kennedys' bedrooms, the newly configured family dining room (Jackie actually designed her own kitchen and dining room within steps of the West Sitting Hall, where the family congregated), and John's blue-and-white nursery. In the meantime, since Jackie was still recuperating from John's difficult delivery, it was agreed that Jackie would sleep alone at the opposite end of the hall in the Queens' Bedroom (so named because five queens had slept there). Jack would sleep separately from her their first night in the White House, across the East Hall in the Lincoln Bedroom.

That afternoon she did not budge from her quarters—not even to greet scores of Kennedy, Bouvier, and Auchincloss family members bused in for a private reception in the State Dining Room. When he returned from the parade shortly after nightfall only to be told that Jackie was still in bed, Jack was livid. That changed when he went upstairs and discovered his wife ashen-faced and motionless under the covers.

Realizing how tired and sick his wife really was, JFK went off for a dinner with new cabinet members, leaving staff with instructions to serve Jackie her dinner on a tray in bed. At 9 p.m., it was time to get dressed for the first ball. "I can't do it," she told Providencia "Provi" Paredes, her longtime personal maid. "I can't get out of bed. I just can't move."

"I was *frantic*," remembered Jackie, who immediately called Dr. Travell. Within minutes the president's personal physician was at Jackie's bedside. "She had two pills," Jackie said, "a green one and an orange one. She told me to take the orange one." The orange one, Travell told her as she swallowed the pill, just happened to be Max Jacobson's favorite drug: Dexedrine. "Thank God," said Jackie, who jumped out of bed and was dressed in half the time she usually took. "It really did the trick." She never found out what the green pill was, although Jackie conceded that she would always wonder.

It was the president's turn to gaze adoringly when Jackie appeared wearing a white silk crepe gown with a bodice embroidered in silver thread, all beneath a floor-length cape with a high mandarin collar. Diamond pendant earrings on loan from Tiffany and white opera gloves completed the look. Jack escorted her down to the Red Room, where a small group of friends were waiting. "Darling," Jack said as he lifted his champagne glass, "you've never looked lovelier."

That evening, Jackie was radiant. At each of the first three inaugural balls they were scheduled to attend, a gasp went up from the crowd as the dazzling Jackie and Jack, in white tie and tails, made their entrance accompanied by "Hail to the Chief."

But as they headed to the fourth ball, said Jackie, "it was like Cinderella and the clock striking midnight, because that pill wore off and I just couldn't get out of the car. I just crumpled. All of my strength was finally gone."

She urged him to go on without her, but that was hardly necessary. Daily doses of cortisone were giving Jack the stamina of a twenty-year-old athlete. He quickly met up with Red Fay and Fay's date for the evening, Angie Dickinson. It was not JFK's first encounter with the striking, blond, twenty-eight-year-old actress; they had reportedly gone skinny-dipping in Peter Lawford's pool the night Jack secured his party's nomination. "He was the killer type," Dickinson said of their relationship, "the kind your mother hoped you wouldn't marry." As for the sex: "It was," Angie allegedly said, "the most exciting seven minutes of my life."

This time things were different. When Fay asked if the equally stunning Kim Novak could tag along, Jack suddenly grew circumspect. "I can just see the papers tomorrow," he said. "The new President concludes his first day speeding into the night with Kim Novak and Angie Dickinson while his wife recuperates from the birth of their first son."

Instead, the president went on to the next balls alone before winding up at 2 a.m. dropping in on a small party at the Georgetown home of an old friend, columnist Joe Alsop. Two hours later, when he finally arrived back at the White House, Jack was still so excited that he went straight to the Queens' Bedroom and woke Jackie up. After they shared a few details of the evening's festivities, she went back to sleep while he went across the hall and crawled into Abraham Lincoln's huge, elaborately carved rosewood bed.

Far from being angry with her husband for partying without

her until dawn, Jackie felt guilty "for not participating in those first shining hours with Jack. But at least I thought I had given him our John, the son he had longed for so much."

It was only a few hours before Jackie joined her husband in the Lincoln Bedroom. "It's the sunniest room," she remembered of that first morning. "I mean, you feel like two children again. Think of yourself in Lincoln's bed!"

After Jack headed off for the Oval Office ("with that wonderful spring in his step," Jackie recalled), she found herself back in the Queens' Bedroom with leg cramps so debilitating she couldn't walk. Dr. Travell was in the process of treating Jackie's problem ("She had my leg up in the air trying to get some kink out of it") when "who burst in the door but Jack and President Truman. Poor President Truman just turned scarlet. I don't think he'd ever seen a woman but his wife in bed in a nightgown before." That night and for several nights after, Jackie and Jack ate supper on trays in the small Lincoln Sitting Room. "You know," she later said wistfully, "I loved those days."

Lincoln's rooms were, in fact, Jackie's refuge, her "secret place." Those times when she felt overwhelmed—and there were many— Jackie would "go and sit in the Lincoln Bedroom. It gave me great comfort. When you see that great bed, it's like a cathedral. To touch something I knew he had touched was a real link with him. I used to sit in the Lincoln Bedroom and I could really feel his strength. I'd sort of be talking with him. Jefferson is the president with whom I have the most affinity. But Lincoln is the one I love."

Once the inauguration hoopla was over, Jackie really only needed a few days to regain her strength. While Jack worked in the West Wing, the first lady perched on the edge of her antique slant-front desk and had candidates for household jobs brought to see her, three at a time. They were astonished to see that at home the glamorous Jackie Kennedy wore riding boots, a plain white shirt, jodhpurs, and no makeup—and that she smoked.

As it turned out, Jackie always wore pants if she wasn't expecting visitors and went barefoot whenever she could. "Jackie laughed at the way people expected her to be dressed up like a cover for *Vogue* every minute of the day," Tish Baldrige said. "She'd walk in a room with that wild dark mane of hers, toss off her shoes, and sit cross-legged on the floor. And everyone standing there would look at each other thinking 'Now what do we do?' "

"I love it when they get that panicky look in their eyes," Jackie confided to Baldrige. "Sometimes I feel like telling them, 'No, I don't wear a pillbox hat to bed—but I do wear one when I bathe!' "

Even judged against her fellow first ladies, Jackie was a mind-spinning tangle of contradictions. No more qualified an authority than White House Chief Usher J. B. West believed hers was "the most complex personality" of all the modern first ladies. "In public she was elegant, aloof, dignified, and regal," said West, who served every president from FDR to Richard Nixon. "In private, she was casual, impish, and irreverent." Jackie also had "a will of iron," West said, "and more determination than anyone I have ever met. Yet she was so soft-spoken, so deft and subtle, that she could impose that will upon people without their ever knowing it."

Mommy and Daddy were waiting at the airport to meet them when Caroline and her brother finally arrived from Palm Beach. Caroline sat between her parents for the ride back to her new home; in this pre-car-seat era, Jackie held John fast in her arms.

As the limousine pulled up to the White House gates, Jackie told Caroline that this was to be her new home. "Wow," she said, gazing out over the snow-covered grounds. "It's very big." At the edge of the driveway stood "Frosty," a regulation snowman with buttons for eyes and a carrot nose—all topped off with a big white panama hat. As soon as the rear doors of the president's car swung open, Caroline clambered out and raced toward the snowman. Jack and Jackie watched approvingly as their little girl, fresh from several weeks in the Florida sunshine, playfully poked Frosty in the stomach.

No one was happier than the president to have his children back. Since the inauguration, he had been pestering Jackie to have them both flown up from Palm Beach. Jackie kept reminding him that intense paint fumes made the children's end of the family residence uninhabitable, but Jack insisted. "You've got to bring them back soon," he told her. "I really miss them."

Jackie had other reasons for postponing the children's arrival. "As odd as it sounds, those first few days were the first time since Jack started running for president that they could be alone," Lowe said. "Jackie wanted to savor those moments, because I don't think she believed they would last very long."

There was also no way of telling how long the Kennedys' honeymoon with the press would last. "We were all flying pretty high," Salinger admitted. "There was this euphoric feeling about what we were going to do for the country—I mean, we were all very young. Older hands knew the higher the expectations the greater the fall."

JACK'S PRESIDENCY WAS NOT YET one hundred days old when the honeymoon came to an abrupt halt. On April 17, JFK suffered not only his first major foreign policy defeat but the first significant failure of his political career when twelve hundred Cuban exiles launched an abortive invasion of Cuba. Jack authorized CIA support for the military action but at the last minute canceled promised U.S. air strikes in support of the attack. The chairman of the U.S. Joint Chiefs of Staff condemned JFK's decision to call off air support, which doomed the Bay of Pigs invasion from the start, as "absolutely reprehensible, almost criminal."

Publicly, the American president remained the very picture of strength and confidence. But privately, the Bay of Pigs fiasco left him deeply shaken. For only the second time, Jackie saw her husband weep. At 8 a.m. the morning after the attack, Jack walked into Jackie's bedroom and, she recalled, "he started to cry. Just sobbed and put his arms around me. It was so sad. He cared so much . . . all those poor men who you'd sent off with all their hopes high and promises that we'd back them and there they were, shot down like dogs."

JFK was so despondent that the attorney general, his younger brother Bobby, paid a special visit to Jackie in the East Wing. "Please stay very close to Jack," he asked her. "I mean, just be around all afternoon." Jackie said Bobby wanted her "not to go anywhere, just be there to comfort him because he was so sad."

Even as her husband grappled with crises that would bring the world to the brink of nuclear war, Jackie set out to transform the White House from a "soulless office building" into a majestic showplace for the nation, to celebrate the arts, and to create an aura of high style and sophistication so extraordinary it would make the French "ashamed of Versailles."

Yet nothing she could do, Jackie later said, would ever be as important as the contribution she made as Jack's wife and partner. Inside the White House, she later observed, "you were hermetically sealed. . . . And I decided the best thing I could do was to always make it a climate of affection and comfort for him when he was done for the day." At least that way, she added, "we could sort of live our strange little life in there."

Jack could have had a worthwhile life without me. But mine would have been a wasteland, and I would have known it every step of the way.

—JACKIE

&

My wife is a shy, quiet girl. But when things get rough, she can handle herself pretty well.

—JACK

*If Jack turned out to be the greatest president of the century
and his children turned out badly, that would be a tragedy.*

—JACKIE

&

*If Mrs. Kennedy had her way, the White House would be
surrounded by high brick walls. And a moat with crocodiles.*

—J. B. WEST, CHIEF WHITE HOUSE USHER

6

⚬ℓ⚬

"Keep Her Riding"

"Admit it," the president of the United States said as he leaned back and lit his second cigar of the day. The senator from Florida, sitting just to the right of the president's desk in one of the nineteenth-century cane-backed chairs Jackie had handpicked for the Oval Office, was already beginning to squirm. He took a long drag on his cigarette before answering.

"Admit what?" George Smathers asked.

"You told me not to marry Jackie," JFK said with a wry smile. "You said that she was too young and not sophisticated enough. I want you to admit right here in the Oval Office and right now that you were wrong. Dead wrong."

Until now, it was always Jackie who delighted in needling Smathers. "I remember what you told Jack," she would whisper into his ear as they danced together in the East Room during a state dinner. "You told him I wasn't *good enough* for him." For the rest of her life, in fact, she would bring this up to Smathers every time they met, without exception.

"Oh Jackie, for God's sake," Smathers would reply, "I was just *testing* him. I wanted to see if he really loved you!" Smathers knew Jackie "didn't buy it, but she was nice enough to make a running joke out of it. I'm not so sure she thought it was so funny at the time."

Smathers' definition of "sophistication" may have differed somewhat from the norm. What he meant at the time was that Jackie might not be able to tolerate her husband's womanizing. It was Smathers, after all, who accompanied Jack on many skirt-chasing expeditions. Years earlier the two men had even tried to convince their fellow congressman Richard Nixon to cheat on his wife, Pat, during a fact-finding mission to Europe; they provided him with the names and numbers of women to contact in Paris—a note Nixon promptly crumpled up and threw away.

Right now, however, the president wanted an answer. "Look, George," he said, waving his hands over his desk. "Look at this magnificent desk we're sitting at. The detail, the craftsmanship, the history. It's only here because of Jackie, and that goes for the rest of this place."

The mammoth *Resolute* desk, carved from the timbers of the British warship HMS *Resolute* and given to President Rutherford B. Hayes by Queen Victoria in 1878, was indeed as good a symbol as any of all that Jackie had been able to accomplish during their first year in office. This was the same desk FDR sat behind as he delivered his famous "Fireside Chats" on the radio, and Jackie discovered it languishing under a canvas sheet in the basement.

Jack was so enamored of the desk that he asked her to have

a copy made to use after he left office. Jackie also worked with Dr. Travell and the New York's Gunlocke Company to design a special, high-backed, leather-upholstered swivel chair to alleviate Jack's back problems while he worked in the Oval Office. JFK intended to take that chair with him when he left office as well.

The desk would become famous for reasons that had nothing to do with history or weighty matters of state. Visiting world leaders, cabinet members, or presidential advisers could be thrashing out some important issue when a curious sound might emanate from inside the desk.

"Is there a rabbit in there?" the president would ask just as the hinged door beneath the desk popped open and John made his entrance. The toddler then ran around the room, whooping and making faces while Jack clapped his approval.

The *Resolute* desk was not, as it happened, Jackie's biggest find. That distinction went to James Monroe's historic 1817 Bellangé pier table, which for decades had been disguised under a thick layer of gold radiator paint. There were other treasures that had been abandoned in storerooms and closets: the Lincolns' china service, busts of Columbus and Martin Van Buren, a superb portrait of Andrew Jackson, the Monroe gold and silver flatware service.

Yet treasure-hunting of this sort—"spelunking," she called it— was only a small part of the task. With the help of Sister Parish and the Kennedys' old friend Bill Walton, a *Time* correspondent who gave up journalism for a career as an artist, Jackie set up the White House Fine Arts Committee with Winterthur Museum founder Henry Francis DuPont as its chairman. The name DuPont set the bar in terms of wealth and taste for the rest of the committee's membership, which included Mrs. Paul Mellon,

Mrs. Henry Ford II, Mrs. Charles Engelhard, Mrs. Albert Lasker, and Mrs. C. Douglas Dillon.

Committee members, as it turned out, contributed far more than just their time, expertise, and the cachet of their names. Mary Lasker donated a nineteenth-century Savonnerie rug for the Blue Room, Bunny Mellon provided Rembrandt Peale's portrait of Thomas Jefferson, and the C. Douglas Dillons shipped an entire roomful of Empire furniture to the White House along with one piece Jackie personally helped move into a place of honor in the Red Room—Dolley Madison's sofa.

Instead of choosing an American to head up the restoration, she gave the job to France's most revered decorator, Stéphane Boudin. The flamboyant seventy-two-year-old president of the Paris decorating house of Jansen had a knack for re-creating the ceremonial grandeur of the Louis XVI and Empire periods—precisely the look Jackie was going for.

Rather than risk a backlash for not choosing a homegrown designer, Jackie simply concealed Boudin's involvement from the public. In the process, she also had to referee the inevitable battles between the high-strung Boudin and DuPont, an unyielding stickler for historical verisimilitude. Jackie allowed Boudin to prevail everywhere except the Green Room, which DuPont filled with spindly eighteenth-century American tables and chairs. Jackie braced herself and escorted Boudin to the Green Room for his first glimpse of DuPont's vision. Boudin gasped. "But," he said, "it's full of *legs.*"

Notwithstanding the magnanimous gifts and hundreds of thousands of dollars donated by the first couple's wealthy friends, Jackie still had to figure out a way to finance the massive restoration effort. Jackie came up with the idea of publishing the first

White House guidebook—*The White House: An Historic Guide*— which not only financed the restoration but went on to sell more than 4.5 million copies, earning tens of millions of dollars for future White House projects.

Jackie then had to convince a skeptical public that it had all been worth it. Jack, like the rest of the nation, sat glued to the set when Jackie gave the first televised tour of the White House on Valentine's Day, 1962. Unlike Jack, a seasoned pro when it came to TV, Jackie was petrified at the thought of appearing for a full hour on prime time. "My husband," she whispered to veteran CBS correspondent Charles Collingwood before going on the air, "is making me do this, you know."

The president did fulfill his promise to Jackie to make a brief appearance at the end of the show, but he really needn't have. Drawing an astounding 46 million viewers (the taped program was broadcast on CBS and NBC on February 14, and on ABC the following day), Jackie's White House tour ranked at the time as the most-watched prime-time broadcast in the history of the medium.

JFK "took such pride in what she accomplished," Ted Sorensen said, "because it really was a minor miracle. When you tinker with something as cherished as the White House it really takes guts and vision and skill. All these things Jackie had in abundance." Given Jackie's highbrow tastes and the fact that she was a known Francophile, Jack feared a backlash. He was "surprised at what a superb diplomat she was," Tish Baldrige said. "It astounded him that she was able to do it, but even more so that she was able to sell the idea of changing the White House so brilliantly." Now whenever Jack spoke of his wife, Arthur Schlesinger said, "his eyes brightened."

George Smathers saw that look right now. "Of course I'll admit it, Mr. President," he said. "I wish I'd never said it, and I sure wish you'd never *told* her I said it!"

In a matter of months the new first lady had also made giant strides toward her goal of creating what she called "an American Versailles," in the process setting a new standard for entertaining at the White House. Ultimately, she and Jack would play host to seventy-four world leaders and preside over fifteen state dinners—each more dazzling than the last.

For the first of these—a dinner for Tunisia's diminutive President Habib Burguiba—Jackie dazzled in an off-the-shoulder Cassini gown of pale yellow silk organza. Overturning 150 years of tradition, she unilaterally replaced the long banquet tables that had always been used in the East Room with round tables, decreeing that the president and first lady sit at separate tables, and that each of the other tables be hosted by a dignitary. Jackie also hired a French chef, René Verdon, and employed the talents of noted horticulturist Bunny Mellon to advise her on floral arrangements. (Mellon also redesigned the Rose Garden and the East Garden as part of Jackie's restoration project.)

The most audacious effort—and the first state dinner ever to be held outside the White House—was for Pakistan's president Muhammad Ayub Khan. When JFK said he wanted to repay Khan for sending five thousand troops to fight a communist insurgency in Laos, Jackie suggested holding a candlelit dinner on the lawn of Mount Vernon, with its sweeping views of the Potomac.

"It was a logistical horror show," recalled Baldrige. Among other things, there was no electricity at Mount Vernon at the time, so giant generators had to be brought in. A tent pavilion had to be set up, as well as a stage for the National Symphony Orchestra. Everything—White House tables, china, silver, glassware—had to be trucked in by the Army, while the Navy was enlisted to transport the 150 guests fifteen miles downriver to George Washington's stately home by boat. Each of the four vessels had its own trio of musicians, who serenaded guests during the hour-long cruise.

Although the guest list for the historic dinner was dominated by the names of cabinet members and other high-ranking government officials, there were also contributors to Jackie's restoration efforts, including the DuPonts, the Mellons, and a little-known diamond merchant named Maurice Tempelsman. Some thirty years later, Tempelsman would become, with the exception of John Jr., the most important man in Jackie's life—her lover and devoted companion in her final years.

"I thought she was crazy for even suggesting it," Baldrige said of the ambitious state dinner on the grounds of Mount Vernon. "But everything went off without a hitch. It was a magical night. Unforgettable." Baldrige gave full credit to the first lady. "Sometimes I thought they should have made Jackie the head of the joint chiefs. She knew how to marshal forces and make things happen."

With the exception of the president and his brother Bobby, who wore black tie, all the men wore white dinner jackets. Jackie wore a sleeveless white organza dress with an emerald green sash and stole designed by Cassini. Everyone watched the Continental Fife and Drum Corps in their eighteenth-century uniforms perform drills and then, at the end of the show, take aim with their muskets and fire blanks directly at the press corps. A cameraman waved a white flag, and Jack wept with laughter.

THERE WOULD BE OTHER MAGICAL nights that year. In November 1961, the legendary Spanish cellist Pablo Casals performed at a state dinner for Puerto Rico's governor, Luis Muñoz Marín. It was the first time Casals had been to the White House since 1904, when he performed for Teddy Roosevelt. Among the guests was Teddy's acid-tongued daughter, Alice Roosevelt Longworth, who had been present for Casals's 1904 White House performance.

Among the 153 guests that night was Leonard Bernstein. "Fires are roaring in all the fireplaces," he said. "The food is marvelous, the wines are delicious, people are laughing, *laughing out loud*, telling stories, jokes, enjoying themselves, glad to be there . . ." It was, he continued, "like a different world, utterly like a different planet."

Although Jack willingly deferred to Jackie on cultural matters ("Pablo Casals? I didn't know what the hell he played—someone had to tell me"), he always rose to the occasion with toasts, speeches, and banter that sparkled as brightly as Jackie's haute couture. At the historic April 1962 dinner honoring forty-nine Nobel laureates, Jack lauded the group as "the most extraordinary collection of talent, of human knowledge, that has ever been gathered together at the White House, with the possible exception of when Thomas Jefferson dined alone."

Jefferson aside, Jackie personally made sure that the guest lists for these affairs glistened with the most celebrated names in arts and letters. Attending a May 11, 1962, dinner for French minister of culture André Malraux were playwrights Tennessee Williams and Arthur Miller, actress Geraldine Page, director Elia Kazan, choreographer George Balanchine (who coaxed Margot Fonteyn and Rudolf Nureyev into performing at the White House), Charles and Anne Morrow Lindbergh, and artist Andrew Wyeth.

There was one group that Jackie tried but failed to get barred from all state dinners—the press. "Their notebooks bother me," she sniffed in a memo to Tish Baldrige. "I think they should be made to wear big badges and be whisked out of there once we all sit down to dinner."

The new, gilt-edged atmosphere in Washington was no less apparent to the rest of the world. "They certainly have acquired something we have lost," British prime minister Harold Macmillan admitted, "a casual sort of grandeur about their evenings, pretty women, music, beautiful clothes, champagne." Schlesinger went further, gushing that the Kennedys had ushered in a "new Augustan age of poetry and power."

To be sure, not all visiting dignitaries were as refined in their tastes as Jackie Kennedy or André Malraux. In anticipation of Indonesian strongman Sukarno's arrival, Jackie asked the State Department to dig up a copy of a book published about his art collection so she could place it on the coffee table in the West Hall.

"Mr. President," she told Sukarno proudly as she reached over to pick up the book, "we have your art collection here." Then, with Jack sitting on one side of him and Jackie on the other, Sukarno sat on the sofa and began leafing through the glossy, full-color volume. Each painting was of a young woman naked to the waist, with a hibiscus in her hair. "And this is my second wife," Sukarno said as he leafed through the book. "And this is my . . ."

"They were like Vargas girls!" Jackie said, comparing Sukarno's paintings to the Alberto Vargas nude pinups that appeared in American men's magazines. "I caught Jack's eye and I was *trying* not to laugh . . ."

The Kennedys took their show on the road that first spring of

1961, starting with a two-day visit to Canada in May that doubled as a warm-up for a major European tour the following month. That trip would take them to Paris, London, and, most important, a summit meeting with Soviet premier Nikita Khrushchev in Vienna.

"Jack already knew that Jackie would be a huge asset on the trip," Salinger said, pointing out that in 1960, when French president Charles de Gaulle first met her at the French embassy in Washington, he remarked that "the only thing I want to bring back from America is Mrs. Kennedy." The feeling was mutual; as a child, Jackie had named her pet poodle "Gaullie" because "he was straight and proud and had a prominent nose."

Trouble was, the first lady was suffering from intense migraines and simply didn't want to go. "Everyone forgets that she wasn't feeling well that first year," Baldrige said. Jackie was "making this tremendous effort to restore the White House, and she just didn't have the energy to do much of anything else."

Before the trip, Jack and Jackie spent a restful four days at the palatial Palm Beach estate that belonged to their friends Charles and Jayne Wrightsman. While the president played golf, his first lady slid deeper into depression. "The state visits were daunting for her," Baldrige said. "She wasn't trying to be difficult. She was simply tuckered out—and frightened, because at just thirty-one she knew so much was expected of her."

Just as Jackie had intervened after his back operations years earlier, Jack took matters into his own hands. He summoned Max Jacobson to Palm Beach, where Secret Service agents picked him up at his hotel and took him to meet "Mr. and Mrs. Dunn"—the aliases chosen for Jack and Jackie.

Jack didn't beat around the bush. He told Jacobson that he

was worried about his wife—that she had almost died twice after the birth of their son and now suffered periodic bouts of depression and headaches. Would she, JFK wanted to know, be healthy enough to accompany him on his trips to Canada and Europe?

The only way he could find out was by examining Jackie. Escorted into her room by Provi, Jackie's maid, Jacobson found the first lady propped up on the bed. "I feel terrible, Dr. Jacobson," she said, "so tired—and this awful headache . . ."

"The least I can do for you," Jacobson told her in this thick German accent, "is to stop your migraine." After Dr. Feelgood injected her with his usual potent "cocktail" of speed mixed with vitamins, Jackie pepped up considerably. "Why, Dr. Jacobson, my headache is completely gone," she said in amazement. "I feel so much better already." The first lady did not bother to ask what was in the syringe Jacobson had just used to inject her. Thrilled at the immediate results, Jack rolled up his sleeve and asked Jacobson to do the same for him.

In Ottawa, Jackie, wearing a red wool suit designed by Oleg Cassini to mimic the uniforms of the Royal Canadian Mounted Police, wowed the public and parliament leaders alike. For JFK, the trip proved disastrous for reasons that had nothing to do with international diplomacy. At a tree planting ceremony on the grounds of Government House, Jackie turned a few dainty spadefuls of earth while her Dexedrine-fueled husband proved his prowess by plunging his shovel into the ground like a ditch digger. Instantly, he felt a searing pain in his back—a pain that, sadly, wasn't going to be going away anytime soon.

Once again, a frustrated and angry Jack was hobbling around the White House on crutches. Jacobson was called back to the White House and, after giving both the president and first lady their shots—a stronger dose than usual in JFK's case—was informed that he and his black bag would be accompanying them to Europe at the end of May.

Now both riding high—literally—on Jacobson's potent amphetamine "treatments," the Kennedys were greeted by more than a million Parisians who lined the streets screaming "Jacqui! Jacqui!" as their motorcade sped by. The climax of the visit was a glittering state dinner at Versailles's Hall of Mirrors, where Jackie, wearing a Givenchy gown of white silk embroidered with flowers and four diamond "flame" clips in her hair, continued to charm de Gaulle with her knowledge of French history and culture. When Jackie explained to her host that her grandparents were French, he replied, "So were mine!"

At one point during the visit, de Gaulle told Jack, "Mrs. Kennedy knows more French history than most Frenchwomen." Jack was delighted. "My God," he told Jackie, "that would be like me sitting next to Madame de Gaulle and her asking me all about Henry Clay!"

Jack was more than happy not to be the center of attention. "I do not think it entirely inappropriate for me to introduce myself," he told his hosts. "I am the man who accompanied Jacqueline Kennedy to Paris."

Although Jack got an extra boost from Jacobson in Vienna ("The meeting may last for a long time. See to it that my back won't give me any trouble when I have to get up or move around"), Khrushchev ridiculed Jack's handling of the Bay of Pigs fiasco and made no attempt to conceal his lack of respect for the inexperienced American president. The summit with the pugnacious Soviet leader was the "worst thing in my life," Jack privately told journalist James Reston. "He savaged me." For the first time in his life, British prime minister Macmillan observed, JFK had "met a man wholly impervious to his charm."

Jackie, on the other hand, bowled Khrushchev over. At the state banquet held in Vienna's Schönbrunn Palace, Khrushchev insisted on sitting next to the U.S. first lady all evening. Wearing a seductive, skintight pink mermaid dress by Cassini, she tried to impress him with her knowledge of Tolstoy, Chekhov, Dostoevsky, and Pushkin. Instead, he began preaching to her about how many more schoolteachers there were in the Ukraine than there had been under the czar. In response, Jackie proclaimed, "Oh, Mr. Chairman, don't bore me with statistics."

A ballet performance followed dinner at the Schönbrunn, and when the dancers came swooping toward the guests of honor, Jackie again whispered in the Russian leader's ear. "They're all paying most attention to *you*, Mr. Chairman," she told him. "They're all throwing their flowers at you."

Khrushchev merely laughed. "No, no, it is your husband they are paying attention to," he said. "You must never let him go on a state visit alone, he is such a wonderful-looking young man."

Tish Baldrige, who stood on the sidelines clutching a large black binder bulging with schedules and other tour information, watched with no small degree of awe as Jackie worked her charms on one notoriously prickly head of state after another. "When Jackie could get Khrushchev's ear, and he would lean close to her," Tish said, "the President was proud and pleased. After all, he couldn't get Khrushchev to lean close to *him*."

Soon they were trading lines "like Abbott and Costello," Jackie later said. At one point she bantered with Khrushchev about the three dogs the Soviets sent into orbit. "I knew all the names of those dogs—Strelka and Belka and Laika. So I said, 'I see where one of your space dogs just had puppies. Why don't you send me one?' " Khrushchev merely laughed, but "by God, two months later, two absolutely ashen-faced Russians come staggering into the Oval Room with the ambassador carrying this poor terrified puppy." Its name, Ambassador Anatoly Dobrynin told Jackie, was Pushinka.

"That trip completely changed the way he saw her," Baldrige said of the president. "One minute she was a wife complaining about his cigar ashes being ground into the carpet. The next she was charming heads of state and entire nations, arising like the queen of the world."

THE KENNEDYS STOPPED OVER IN London on their way home, attending both the christening of Jackie's niece Anna Christina Radziwill at Westminster Cathedral and a dinner hosted by Queen Elizabeth and Prince Philip at Buckingham Palace. Immediately after the palace dinner, Jack flew back to Washington without Jackie; the first lady had decided to remain behind and tour Greece with her sister and her husband as a guest of Greek prime minister Konstantinos Karamanlis.

This jaunt was fine with JFK, with one stipulation: under no circumstances, he warned Clint Hill, should Mrs. Kennedy be allowed to cross paths with Aristotle Onassis. The Greek ship owner, well on his way to becoming one of the world's richest men, had been arrested by the FBI in 1953 and charged with the illegal operation of U.S. war surplus ships. Onassis posed for a mug shot, was fingerprinted and then thrown into a holding cell with male prostitutes, muggers, and a group of Puerto Rican nationalists who had just been accused of shooting up Congress.

He eventually paid a fine (he preferred to call it a "ransom") of $7 million. The FBI investigation into a broad range of Onassis's shady business dealings was ongoing, and, simply put, JFK did not want the first lady anywhere near him.

Not that the president had anything against Greek tycoons in general. Since Prime Minister Karamanlis was far from wealthy, he turned over some of his official hosting duties to yet another Greek shipping magnate, Markos Nomikos. In addition to a lavish villa in the village of Kavouri, Nomikos offered Jackie and her party the use of his 130-foot yacht, the *Northwind.*

First port of call: the thyme-scented village of Epidaurus, where Jackie watched a special performance of Sophocles's *Electra* in Greece's perfectly preserved fifth-century B.C. amphitheater. After some expert water-skiing off the back of a small boat, it was on to the island of Delos—reputedly the birthplace of Apollo—before proceeding to the picturesque island of Hydra.

AT EVERY STOP, CHURCH BELLS rang, boats blew their horns, and locals turned out in force to cheer the American first lady. Rather than depart for Mykonos on schedule, Jackie and the Radziwills popped into a local hangout for a quick drink. When the other patrons began dancing the spirited *kalamatianos* popularized in the United States by the films *Never on Sunday* and *Zorba the Greek,* Jackie leapt up and joined right in.

Once back in Athens, Jackie, trailed by a pack of tourists and photographers, toured the Acropolis and the Parthenon before having a private luncheon with King Paul and Queen Frederika. As she left, the dashing Crown Prince Constantine, twenty-one-year-old heir to the throne, took her on an impromptu joyride in his new dark blue Mercedes convertible. Caught by surprise, Clint Hill and the other Secret Service agents gave chase in a follow-up car, careening along the tortuous roads toward the port of Piraeus and on to the villa in Kavouri where she was staying. Jackie was beaming when the Secret Service caught up with her. "She knew she had put us to the test," Hill wrote in his memoir, *Mrs. Kennedy and Me,* "and she loved it."

In stark contrast to Jackie's sun-splashed escapade, Jack was having anything but fun. The trouble began on the flight home from London. Unable to fall asleep aboard Air Force One, he ambled into the main cabin wearing his nightshirt and asked Jacobson if he could do anything to help. Dr. Max dove into his battered black medical bag, filled another syringe—this time with Librium—and administered the shot to the president "to help him sleep. He wanted," Jacobson said, "to be in his best form for the return to the USA."

Once he was back in the Oval Office, however, Jack was coping with more than just affairs of state; he was dealing with ever-more-crippling back pain triggered by the tree planting in Ottawa. Ordered by his physicians to go to Palm Beach to recuperate, Jack brought along Dr. Travell, Chuck Spalding—and two attractive staffers in their twenties known to everyone as "Fiddle" and "Faddle."

Priscilla Weir, who acquired the nickname "Fiddle" because as a young child she couldn't pronounce Priscilla, was yet another Miss Porter's alumna. Jill Cowan, a member of the wealthy Bloomingdale's department store family, inevitably became "Faddle" after the two women shared an apartment in Georgetown. Hired during the 1960 presidential campaign—they thought it would be amusing to introduce themselves as Fiddle and Faddle and wear the same dress—Weir now worked for Evelyn Lincoln, while Cowan clipped wire copy and answered telephones for Pierre Salinger.

Fiddle and Faddle often swam with the president in the White House pool, and their easygoing, flirtatious manner raised eyebrows. Rumors flew, but Jackie seemed very matter-of-fact about the giggly pair. Once, while giving a foreign journalist a White House tour, she stuck her head in Salinger's office and blurted out in French, "And this is one of the young ladies who is supposed to be sleeping with my husband."

IRONICALLY, ANOTHER OF HER HUSBAND'S reputed White House lovers—Jackie's press secretary Pam Turnure—was on the road with her boss in Greece while JFK "relaxed" in Palm Beach with Fiddle and Faddle. "The only indication I ever had that Jackie knew about all of Jack's women," Betty Spalding said, "was when they were in the White House and she asked me if I knew if he was having an affair with Pamela Turnure. I said I didn't know, but even if I did I wouldn't tell her."

More than once when she felt her back was against the wall, Jackie took action. "Jackie put up with the situation because she loved him, in her way," Gore Vidal said. "However, she would not accept being humiliated—and he was very careful that she *not* be humiliated." However, "when things started to leak out, when she became threatened, she sent him a message."

One of those times occurred, George Smathers remembered, after Jackie found a pair of panties peeking out from under a pillow in JFK's bedroom. "Would you please shop around and see who these belong to?" she asked him. "They're not my size."

In Palm Beach, Jackie was overheard firing off another zinger when she returned from the beach. "You'd better get down there fast," she told Jack. "I saw two of them you'd really go for."

JFK confided in Smathers that, more than once, Jackie—"the only person during the whole time in the White House who ever told Jack off"—asked him flat out if the stories were true. "Jackie," the president replied in one instance, "I would never do anything to embarrass myself."

"Well," she shot back angrily, "you're embarrassing *me!*"

JFK's Air Force aide, General Godfrey McHugh, had dated Jackie before she met Kennedy and was well aware of the president's extramarital activities. Early on, McHugh said, "Jackie knew about his women." Her friend Ralph Martin agreed. "You know, in the end Jackie knew everything. Every girl. She knew her rating, her accomplishments . . ."

That didn't mean she took Jack's cheating lightly. "She didn't like Jack's fooling around. She was damn mad about it," Smathers conceded. "But she was willing to look the other way as long as he was careful."

As it happened, Jackie was never really satisfied with this "arrangement," and had taken steps to do something about it. Unbeknownst to even their closest friends, the first lady was regularly sharing the most intimate details of her marriage—including the devastating emotional toll of her husband's rampant infidelity—with someone far outside the Kennedys' social orbit. In May 1961, after spraining her ankle playing touch football with Bobby's brood at Hickory Hill, Jackie was treated by RFK's neighbor, a young, square-jawed cardiologist and professor of medicine at Georgetown University named Frank Finnerty. Jackie was so captivated by Dr. Finnerty's bedside manner that she asked if she could call him every now and then just to talk about things that had been troubling her.

Flattered, Finnerty agreed. For the rest of JFK's presidency, Jackie essentially treated the physician as her therapist, calling twice a week to unburden herself about problems in her relationships with friends and family, the stresses of living life in the public eye, and—most alarmingly—her complicated marriage.

"She wanted me to know she was not naive or dumb, as people in the White House thought," Finnerty recalled. "She did know what was going on." She did not, he added, want people to think she was "strange and aloof, living in a world of her own."

Jackie conceded that her husband was so promiscuous and his extramarital conquests so numerous there was no way either she or he could possibly identify them all. She had no compunction about listing the names she did know, confident that they would mean nothing to Finnerty. The mention of one name, however, took the thirty-seven-year-old doctor's breath away. More than any of JFK's other lovers, Marilyn Monroe "seemed to bother her the most"—in large part because Marilyn was a loose cannon who could go public at any time, causing a scandal that would obliterate her husband's reputation, destroy her marriage, and hold her up to public ridicule. (Even after JFK's assassination, Jackie confessed to the Reverend Richard T. McSorley, a Catholic priest, that she was still deeply troubled and confused by her husband's affair with Marilyn.)

Over a period of weeks and months, Finnerty listened as Jackie calmly outlined her theory about Jack's philandering—that he had inherited this "vicious trait" from Joe Kennedy, that he was simply driven by hormones, and that he had no real feelings for any of these women. Motivated less by jealousy than by frustration and despair, Jackie had no illusions about getting Jack to stop. But she did wonder if her own sexual inadequacies had pushed Jack away.

To a gob-smacked Finnerty, Jackie described her husband's usual modus operandi in bed: "He just goes too fast and falls asleep." Was there something she could do to change that? There was, and after some understandable hesitation Finnerty spelled out in clinical detail how foreplay could be used to improve their sex life.

It was essential that, in trying to persuade Jack to change his approach in bed, no mention be made of Jackie's unconventional therapist-patient relationship with Dr. Finnerty. So Jackie concocted a tall tale that she told her husband over dinner at the White House. It began with Jackie confessing to her priest that something was lacking in her sexual relationship with her husband. The priest, she went on, then referred her to her obstetrician, who recommended several illustrated books on the subject. As a result, Jackie was now full of new information about how they might spice things up in bed. Surprised and obviously pleased at his wife's newfound expertise—and, said Finnerty, that she would "go to that much trouble to enjoy sex"—Jack happily obliged.

The ploy worked, and Jackie informed her co-conspirator that relations between the president and first lady had improved significantly—although not enough to stop Jack's skirt-chasing. If nothing else, from this point on Jackie had no reason to blame herself for her husband's sexual compulsions.

As Jackie's Grecian idyll drew to a close in June 1961, she was on the phone with Jack every night consoling him about his badly injured back. Apparently his Palm Beach interlude, punctuated by long swims in the Wrightsmans' heated saltwater pool with

Fiddle and Faddle, did nothing to alleviate the agonizing pain. On his return to Washington, Jack was not even capable of climbing down the stairs of the presidential aircraft on crutches. In a dramatic and humbling turn of events, JFK had to be lifted off Air Force One on a cherry picker.

To be sure, the papers were full of stories about JFK's back troubles. But the public remained largely unaware of just how crippling those problems really were. "People don't understand just how bad off Jack was during his presidency," Smathers said. "He could barely stand up much of the time, much less walk. He leaned on Secret Service agents all the time."

"Look closely at the photographs," Jacques Lowe said. "He tried to avoid it when someone was taking a picture, but occasionally he is caught off guard, leaning. He was always leaning—on tables, on desks, on windowsills, the backs of chairs." According to Tish Baldrige, JFK "had this uncanny knack of leaning up against a wall and going to sleep. He could sleep *standing up*, which always astounded me." Moreover, Jack "had this little trick," she continued. "He would put on his sunglasses, and people thought he was watching a parade or whatever, and the whole time he'd be sleeping behind those glasses! I'd catch him doing it all the time."

Although no one ever heard him complain, there were times when, according to Salinger, JFK would "wince, or go absolutely white." It was at moments like those, he said, that "you knew he was feeling pain that would make anyone else scream. Not a word of complaint about his health or how he was feeling, ever."

There were many times when the pain was so severe the president "could hardly dress himself," Smathers recalled. Just prior to attending a political banquet in Miami, the Florida senator had to put JFK's shoes and socks on for him. Like Franklin Roosevelt, who hid the fact that he was wheelchair-bound from the general public, Jack successfully concealed the extent of his crippling back trouble. What made this achievement even more remarkable is that, unlike FDR, he accomplished this subterfuge without the cooperation of the press. "Jack even managed to hide it from them," Smathers said.

That first summer of his presidency, JFK spent long weekends in familiar surroundings at Hyannis Port, seeking what respite he could from mounting crises both foreign (Khrushchev's shocking decision to build a wall dividing East and West Berlin, mounting tensions in Cuba and Southeast Asia) and domestic (civil rights protesters attacked and beaten in Alabama). "The Cape was his escape hatch," said Ted Sorensen, who admitted that during this period JFK was "agitated and deeply disturbed" by the belligerence of the Soviet leader. "Hyannis Port was where he felt most at home, and where he could regroup mentally and physically."

For Jackie, life at their four-bedroom "cottage" in the Kennedy compound offered such a welcome escape from the pressures of being first lady that she planted herself there for the entire summer and early fall. With the exception of a few forays back to Washington, usually to check on the restoration or host an official dinner, Jackie, Caroline, and John would not return full-time to the White House until late October.

Until then Jackie enjoyed unnerving her Secret Service agent, Clint Hill, by showing off on water skis behind Ambassador Kennedy's fifty-two-foot cabin cruiser, the *Marlin*. (She pushed the envelope even further by having four-year-old Caroline ski with her.) There was also swimming in the surf and in Joe Kennedy's pool, tennis matches, golf at the nearby Hyannis Port Club, nude sunbathing, and the inescapable rough-and-tumble of Kennedy-style touch football.

During the week, after the president's sprawling entourage departed and she was finally alone with the children, Jackie liked to paint on a small easel set up on the porch while listening to chamber music. Other times, she grabbed one of the books recommended by the erudite Arthur Schlesinger and lolled poolside wearing a skimpy bikini and oversized dark glasses, her hair tied back with a brightly colored kerchief. "She was gorgeous," their neighbor Larry Newman said. "It made you sad seeing her there all alone, knowing what he was up to back in Washington. Why Jack bothered to look at any other woman, I'll never know."

AT THE END OF SEPTEMBER 1961, Jack joined Jackie in retreating from the pressures of Washington. This time, they spent ten days together at Hammersmith Farm, taking leisurely cruises on Narragansett Bay aboard the ninety-two-foot presidential yacht, the *Honey Fitz* (renamed by Jack in honor of his colorful maternal grandfather, legendary Boston mayor John Francis "Honey Fitz" Fitzgerald). "We sit for hours on the terrace just looking at the bay and drinking in the beauty and all one's strength is renewed," Jackie wrote to her mother, who was traveling with Uncle Hughdie in Europe. "You would never guess what this vacation has done for Jack. He said it was the best he ever had."

JFK returned to the Oval Office looking tanned and rested, but it would not take long for the aura of well-being to fade. Early in September 1961, United Nations secretary-general Dag Hammarskjöld was killed in a plane crash. In a blatant move to increase their influence over the international body, the Soviets moved quickly to replace the secretary general with a troika made up of the Soviet Union, the United States, and the theoretically non-aligned nations.

JFK flew to New York to make America's case for scrapping the Soviet plan before the UN General Assembly, but on the eve of his speech he was stricken with laryngitis—the apparent result of a steady diet of stress and cigars. When Max Jacobson arrived at Jack's Carlyle Hotel suite, he found the president still dressed in his pajamas—and virtually mute. "So, Max," Jack whispered as he pointed to his throat, "what are you going to do about this?"

"I can cure your laryngitis in time for the speech, Mr. President. But only if I inject the drug in your neck, directly below the larynx. I'm afraid," he added, "it may be very painful."

"Do what's necessary," Jack shrugged. "I don't give a hoot."

There would be other, similar emergencies where Dr. Feelgood would be called upon to work his magic: for example, just before an important reception in the East Room during the Steel Crisis ("Now I can go downstairs to shake hands with several hundred intimate friends") and the day National Guard troops were called in to help desegregate the University of Mississippi ("Wasn't that a ball breaker?"). Later, Dr. Max (who referred to JFK as "the Prez" when talking to his wife and staff members) would do multiple duty injecting the president, first lady, and members of their inner circle at the height of the Cuban Missile Crisis.

Apparently even Jacobson, aware that Dr. Travell and other physicians treating the president vehemently objected to his methods, entertained doubts about whether his was the right approach. Although JFK assured him that the regular four-times-weekly injections weren't interfering with his work, Jacobson handed Jack his letter of resignation. JFK tore it up.

"The President was very fond of Max Jacobson, and it wasn't just because of the boost he was getting from those shots," conceded Pierre Salinger, who claimed JFK often urged him to avail himself of Dr. Feelgood's services. "He came to rely on Max to bolster Jackie's spirits. The quicksilver changes in her mood were getting pretty hard for him to take."

"Jackie could be absolutely giddy and enchanting," her half brother Jamie Auchincloss said, "and then you'd turn around, and for no apparent reason, she'd just turn off as if someone had flipped a switch." These shifts could spell the abrupt end of even a long friendship. "She was one of the most emotionally self-sufficient people ever," Jamie marveled. "You'd be in her life one moment, and out the next. Gone. And it really didn't seem to bother her one bit."

Oleg Cassini could understand Jack's frustration in dealing with his wife's shifting moods. "She might be very warm one day and freeze you out the next," he said. "She did this to everyone, even her closest friends. You never really knew where you stood with Jackie. I never quite knew on which foot to dance."

Dr. Max's magic bullets may have helped Jack and Jackie cope in the short run, but Dr. Travell and her colleagues grew increasingly concerned about how they might interact with the dozen or so other drugs Jack was taking for his Addison's-related problems (cortisone, testosterone, Florinef), chronic colitis (paregoric, Metamucil, Lomotil), recurring urinary tract infections (penicillin), allergies (antihistamines), and of course his back (Novocain, procaine).

Travell and Salinger both pleaded with the president to get rid of Jacobson, but to no avail. Even Gore Vidal, who had been a patient of Jacobson's, was "horrified" to learn he was treating Jack.

"Watch out," he warned Jackie. "Stay away from him. I know him well. Max drove several people mad."

The man who introduced Max to the Kennedys, Chuck Spalding, was also having second thoughts. At one point, Jacobson's bizarre behavior and his own dependence on the injections made Spalding "very frightened. . . . The whole thing had gotten so completely out of hand."

With nowhere else to go, Salinger turned to Jack's brother Bobby. Even though he had also sampled Dr. Feelgood's wares, RFK intervened in his capacity as attorney general, demanding that Jacobson hand over samples to the Food and Drug Administration for testing. Since neither amphetamines nor steroids were officially determined at the time to be either addictive or harmful, the FDA gave Dr. Max's pick-me-up cocktails its seal of approval.

Not that it mattered to the president. "I don't care if there's panther piss in there," JFK said, "as long as it makes me feel good."

The last time Max Jacobson treated Jack was on the eve of his fateful trip to Dallas. Until then, the doctor and his shiny black medical bag would make dozens of trips to Washington, New York, Hyannis Port, the Kennedys' weekend retreat in Virginia, and Palm Beach on behalf of his friend "the Prez." Chuck Spalding, who himself was trying to get off the drugs, watched warily from the sidelines, "praying that Jack wouldn't get so hyped up he'd accidentally start World War III. If you're President, I suppose you should be more careful. But at the time we all needed a boost."

For all the energy she poured into her official duties, Jackie unhesitatingly described herself as "a wife and mother, first and foremost." J. B. West agreed that the most glamorous first lady in American history was "never more animated or happy" than when she was spending time with Caroline and John.

In addition to the elaborate playground Jackie had built for the children—including the trampoline concealed by evergreens ("All they'll be able to see is my head, sailing above the tree-tops")—there were also doghouses for Pushinka and Charlie, the Kennedys' feisty Welsh terrier; Clipper (a German shepherd given to Jackie by her adored father-in-law); and an Irish wolf-hound with the unimaginative name Wolf, a gift to JFK from a priest in Dublin.

Eventually, Jackie provided pens for lambs, guinea pigs, ducks, and a beer-guzzling rabbit Caroline named Zsa Zsa. Bluebell and Marybell, the children's hamsters, lived in Caroline's room with her favorite pet, a canary named Robin. Far and away the most famous first family pet was Caroline's pony Macaroni, who shared temporary stalls on the White House grounds with Leprechaun, the pony Jackie purchased for John. Unfortunately, it turned out that John, like his father, was intensely allergic to horses. As far as Daddy was concerned, the growing menagerie was fine—as long as the animals kept a respectful distance.

Jackie felt much the same way about the Secret Service. In a confidential memo, the head of the Kiddie Detail relayed the first lady's wishes to Secret Service chief James J. Rowley. "Mrs. Kennedy feels strongly, though there are two children to protect, it is 'bad' to see two agents 'hovering around.' If Mrs. Kennedy is driving the children, she still insists the follow-up car not be seen by the children."

Jackie, the memo continued, was "adamant" that the agents

"not perform special favors for John Jr. and Caroline or wait upon them as servants." That meant agents were "not to carry clothes, beach articles, sand buckets, baby carriages, strollers, handbags, suitcases, etc., for Caroline and John Jr., and the children must carry their own clothing items, toys, etc." She asked that agents "drift into the background quickly when arriving at a specific location, and remain aloof and invisible until moment of departure." The bottom line was that she felt it was "bad for the children to see grown men waiting upon them."

The first lady's insistence that the children not be "either spoiled or smothered" extended to matters of safety. Whenever they were at Hyannis Port, for example, Jackie wanted the agents to back off. "Drowning is my responsibility," she said, adding that the Secret Service was "not responsible for any accident sustained by the children in the usual and normal play sessions." In the end, she reiterated, if anything happened to the children in the course of their simply behaving like children, it was "the sole responsibility of Mrs. Kennedy."

A Lindbergh-style kidnapping aside, few things bothered agents more than the possibility of Caroline being injured or worse while horseback riding. Their first instinct was to jump on mounts of their own and tail Caroline as she rode Macaroni. But as the agent assigned to protect the first lady, Clint Hill, learned early on, it was pure folly to try to keep up with Jackie as she tore across the Virginia countryside on horseback. "After seeing Mrs. Kennedy ride," he recalled, "I sure as hell knew I couldn't keep up with her."

The same was true of her daughter. Jackie bluntly informed the Secret Service that even as a child Caroline was "a better rider than the Secret Service agents. In fact, Caroline would probably be safer riding with other children than she would be with a Secret Service agent who has a very limited knowledge of horses."

Besides, Jackie had broken her collarbone tumbling off a horse when she was a little girl, and as a newlywed suffered such a serious fall while riding with the Piedmont Hunt that she was knocked cold, swallowed her tongue, and turned blue before being revived by another rider. She expected Caroline "to have her share of riding spills and accidents. How else will she learn?"

In this, Jack, whom Ben Bradlee described as "looking like Ichabod Crane with his legs flying" when he tried to ride, was in full agreement. At Hyannis Port, Kiddie Detail agent Joseph Paolella sprang into action when Caroline took a nasty fall off Macaroni. "Caroline, get up!" yelled JFK, who continued rocking on the porch. "Get back on the horse." Jackie, when told of the incident, nodded in agreement. "You don't even have to ride," she said, "to know that old saying about conquering fear."

That November of 1961, Jackie took a notable tumble of her own, not far from Glen Ora, the leased country house (at $600 a month, or around $4,800 today) that would become her sanctuary. Located just forty miles from Washington, in historic Middleburg, Virginia, Glen Ora sat on four hundred manicured acres at the epicenter of the state's horse country. With its pale yellow stucco walls, gunmetal gray slate roof, white shutters, and peaked dormers, the 180-year-old main house more closely resembled an overgrown cottage in the Cotswolds than a baronial hunt-country estate.

&

WHILE THE WHITE HOUSE ARMY Signal Agency installed an elaborate command center near the stables, built guardhouses, and scoped out landing zones for Marine One, the presidential helicopter, Jackie wasted no time setting up a simple metal-framed swing set (swings, slide, glider) between the six-bedroom main house and the Olympic-sized pool.

Even before Jack was sworn in to office, the first lady had arranged to spend most of her time here, a spot just remote enough and protected enough for her to preserve something of her privacy. And since this was to be the first family's home away from home, Jackie hired Sister Parish to redo the interior at a cost of $10,000—the equivalent of at least $80,000 today. (Unfortunately, when they moved out eighteen months later, the owner insisted on having the place put back just as it was, triggering another heated quarrel between Jackie and the president over her spending.)

At Glen Ora, Jackie relied heavily on her longtime friends Paul and Eve Fout, who owned the nearby farm where Jackie briefly boarded her frisky bay gelding, Bit of Irish, and Rufus, a considerably better-behaved pinto. "Jackie wanted her kids to have what she grew up with," Eve Fout said, "and to make their lives normal and fun."

That meant taking Caroline and John on picnics, pushing them on the swings, watching them swim, giving them baths, and putting them to bed—"all the normal things a mother should be able to do with her children without feeling you're constantly watched."

Soon Jackie and the children were leaving the White House for Glen Ora every Thursday afternoon, returning late the following Monday. Jack, who would arrive Saturday afternoon and depart the next day, was not nearly so enamored of the place. "He hated it, actually," Jackie conceded. "There was nothing for him to do there. He'd sleep all Saturday afternoon, and then he'd watch television from his bed. It was just a letdown for him." At one point, Jack told her, "I don't really care about Glen Ora because all I use it for is sleep."

Jackie did what she could, conspiring with Paul Fout to surprise Jack on his forty-fourth birthday with a very difficult four-hole golf course at Glen Ora—"9,000 square yards of pasture," Ben Bradlee recalled, "filled with small hills, big rocks, and even a swamp." The first day out, Bradlee added wryly, JFK "shot the course record—a 37 for four holes."

As it happened, the president was a fairly decent golfer—"competitive as hell with a natural swing," Bradlee determined, "but erratic through lack of play." JFK was far too impatient to ever go looking for a lost ball, "but he was great fun to play golf with because he didn't take the game seriously and kept up a running conversation." The chitchat, as Spalding and other golfing buddies attested, was liberally laced with profanity, "Bahsted!" ("Bastard!") being the preferred expletive whenever Kennedy sliced a drive or landed in the rough. Jack also enjoyed giving a running commentary while he played—"With barely a glance at the packed gallery, he whips out a four iron and slaps it dead to the pin"—and liked to unnerve his competitors by pointing out that the golf bags lugged around by his Secret Service agents contained guns, not clubs.

JFK appreciated his wife's efforts to get him to warm up to the place, but Glen Ora would never be to his liking. "So dark, so small, so boring, I can hardly wait to get the hell out," he told Red Fay. "The whole reason for Glen Ora," Paul Fout said, "was to be nice to Jackie." That, and remembering Black Jack Bouvier's advice: "Keep her riding and she'll always be in a good mood."

The Fouts belonged to the highly selective Orange County Hunt Club (the Duchess of Windsor was refused membership), and on the basis of Jackie's horsemanship invited her to join. Sailing over hedges and fences, skimming over ponds and ditches, Jackie became a local fixture in her knee-high leather boots, black leather gloves, tight-fitting tan jodhpurs, black jacket, and helmet. "She knew how to ride," said fellow foxhunting enthusiast Oleg Cassini. "It was a religion with her." It was also the reason Jackie claimed to dislike being called *first lady.* "It always," she said, "reminds me of a saddle horse."

Careful to tread lightly on the sensibilities of her press-shy neighbors, Jackie insisted that she was not worthy of being considered a part of the hunt country life. She loved Glen Ora for the privacy it afforded her ("People there let me alone") and the chance to accompany Caroline when she took Macaroni out for a ride.

Glen Ora was, Jackie said, "the most private place I can think of to balance our life in the White House." But she quickly discovered that there was really no escape—not even in the Virginia countryside. Out riding with the Piedmont Hunt one Friday morning that November, Jackie and her horse Bit of Irish were about to jump a rail fence on the estate of Paul Mellon when a local photographer named Marshall Hawkins leapt out of the bushes and startled them. Bit of Irish jolted to a halt, hurling the first lady over the fence headfirst.

Miraculously, Jackie managed to beak her fall with her hands and was unhurt. But she quickly called Jack and insisted he intervene to stop the embarrassing photo from being published in *Life* magazine. "It was on private property," she argued. "It's clearly an invasion of my privacy."

Jack was not about to tangle with the press over this. "I'm sorry, Jackie," he said, "but when the First Lady falls on her ass, it's news."

Jackie was a woman full of love and full of hurt. They were two private people, two cocoons married to each other. She felt it was up to him to reach more than he did. But he couldn't.

—LINDY BOGGS, JACKIE'S FRIEND

&

We are like two icebergs — the public life above the water, the private life is submerged.

—JACKIE

7

∞

"It Was a Real Look of Love"

"*A*nd what does your new puppy eat, Mrs. Kennedy?"

"Reporters," Jackie replied with a straight face. There was silence, followed by nervous laughter. The first lady had done little to disguise her antipathy toward the press—particularly the "news hens" who were traditionally assigned to cover the wife of the president. There were a few obligatory press luncheons and receptions that Jackie dutifully attended. For the most part, however, she seemed to take particular pleasure in snubbing women reporters, branding even seasoned veterans like UPI's Helen Thomas, *Washington Post* columnist Maxine Cheshire, and Associated Press writer Frances Lewine as "harpies."

Jackie simply felt that overnight she had been reduced to an object, a commodity. At Jack's urging, she had cooperated for back-to-back articles in *Ladies' Home Journal, McCall's, Life, Red-*

book, and *Look.* It gradually dawned on her that, no matter what she agreed to, the public's appetite for stories about the first family would never be satisfied. Jackie was beginning to feel, she told Lowe, as if she was being viewed as something other than human. "There ought to be a nicer word than *freak,*" she said of the way she was being treated, "but I can't think of one."

Jackie was, understandably, even more concerned about how all the unwanted attention might psychologically damage Caroline and John. "She was a lioness protecting her cubs," Salinger said. "You didn't want to cross her. From the moment she set foot in the White House, she wanted to keep them out of the spotlight. She made this abundantly clear to me on many occasions. Whenever a photo was taken of Caroline or John that she hadn't signed off on, I could be certain to catch hell for it."

"They have all the pictures of Macaroni they need," Jackie wrote to the beleaguered press secretary when a harmless shot of Caroline on her horse was picked up by the wire services. "I want no more—*I mean this*—and if you are firm and will take the time you can stop it. So please do."

The photographers themselves were not immune to Jackie's wrath. She "could strike terror in your heart," *Look* photographer Stanley Tretick said at the time. "She was a tough babe." Tretick found out the hard way when he ignored Jackie's express orders not to take photos of Caroline playing with her cousins at Hyannis Port and did anyway. When the pictures appeared in *Look,* Jackie bawled out JFK for letting it happen.

"Get that fucker Tretick on the phone!" Jack yelled to his secretary. Ted Sorensen later told Tretick he was "so angry" it was a good thing he wasn't there at the time. "Thank God," the photographer said, "I was out shopping at the local Safeway."

Jacques Lowe watched as Jackie became increasingly "paranoid about the press. But Jack knew they were a great asset for his administration. He was proud of them. He wanted to show them off." The president, Baldrige agreed, "saw a photo op behind every tree."

The result, Lowe observed, was that the push-pull over pictures of the children "got to be a game between the two of them, with me stuck in the middle." Lowe was not alone. At one point, Salinger simply told Jackie that the president was behind a new batch of Caroline and John pictures that had popped up in the press. "I don't give a damn," she blasted back. "He has no right to countermand my order regarding the children."

Yet Jackie was not completely clueless when it came to the children and publicity. As long as Jackie was handed complete control of the final product, she was perfectly happy to have publications like *Life,* the *Saturday Evening Post,* and *Look* run heartwarming stories on John and Caroline.

These tightly managed glimpses of the first family captivated the American public: JFK clapping while his children dance and twirl around the Oval Office; Caroline and John showing off their Halloween costumes while Daddy cracks up; Caroline sitting in a horse cart with her mother at Glen Ora or riding Macaroni on the White House lawn.

Yet the president wanted more. Reluctant to provoke a confrontation with his wife, he often waited until she went out of town—usually to Glen Ora—before inviting photographers in to work their magic. "As soon as she snuck out," Tretick said, "I snuck in." Publicity wasn't the only area of disagreement between the Kennedys when it came to their children. It wasn't long before JFK, elected at a time when crew cuts and close-cropped hair were the norm, tired of John's long, European-style cut. He wasn't alone; soon the White House was inundated with letters demanding the president's son get a haircut. Some outraged citizens even sent in money to pay for it.

Jackie wouldn't budge on the issue; she found the Little Lord Fauntleroy look to be "perfectly appropriate for a young American boy his age." Eventually, JFK took Nanny Shaw aside and told her to at the very least trim John Jr.'s bangs. Anticipating Jackie's reaction, Jack promised he would take the blame. "If anyone asks you," he told the apprehensive nanny, "tell them it was an order from the President."

The open affection between Jackie and the children had been expected, but photographers were particularly impressed with the tenderness JFK showed toward Caroline and John. Tretick was struck by Jack's "almost sensual" interest in the boy whom people around the world knew as "John-John." John F. Kennedy Jr. had acquired the nickname John-John because whenever the president called the boy's name over and over again ("John! John!") he came running. To family members, however, JFK's son was always just "John."

One night, Tretick recalled, John was sitting on the floor of the Oval Office while the president talked to him. "And then he just kind of reached for the boy and pulled his pajama up—you know, bathrobe and pajama—and he kind of rubbed his bare skin right above his rear end. He wanted to touch him."

Another time, Jack threw John over his knee as if to spank him, but tickled him instead. "He was having fun with him," Tretick said. "It was a genuine thing between the two of them."

John usually had to wait for Daddy to be going either to or from the office before they could play "Going Through the Tunnel," his favorite game. While JFK stood tall with his legs apart, John would go through them over and over again. "John never tired of this game," Maud Shaw said. "I'm sure the President did."

Not that he ever let it show. Ignoring his bad back, Jack would grab his children and toss them in the air, tickle them, and roll around on the floor with them. The president also took the time to perfect his skills playing peekaboo, leapfrog, hide-and-go-seek, and tag. "The children could be playing all over him," Baldrige said, "and he could still be conducting a conference or writing a speech."

JFK also never tired of making up stories for the children on the fly—about John in his PT boat sinking a Japanese destroyer and Caroline foxhunting with the Orange County Hunt and winning the Grand National; about Maybelle, a little girl who hid in the woods; about a giant named Bobo the Lobo, and about the Black Shark and the White Shark, both of which subsisted on a diet of socks.

For the young parents, holidays took on a new meaning. On Valentine's Day, Jackie helped Caroline cut out and color heart-shaped cards to give to her classmates. They dyed Easter eggs together in the White House kitchen, lit sparklers on the Fourth of July, and watched the Macy's Thanksgiving Day Parade on television. Caroline and John had a ringside seat for the lighting of the national Christmas tree, decorated the family tree at the house in Palm Beach, and used the White House switchboard to place a direct call to the North Pole.

Some holidays were more problematic than others. The idea of taking them trick-or-treating posed what, on the surface, appeared to be a security nightmare. Nevertheless, one Halloween night Arthur Schlesinger was standing on the doorstep of his

Georgetown home handing out candy to trick-or-treaters when a mask-wearing mother spoke up.

"Come on, now, children," she said, "it's time to go to the next house."

"The voice," Schlesinger recalled, "was unmistakably Jackie's."

John was unquestionably adorable and would go on to overshadow his sister as an adult. At Camelot's zenith, however, Caroline was the bigger attraction. No less than the glittering state dinners and headline-grabbing trips abroad, the little girl's Norman Rockwell life of ponies, toys, and tea parties contributed greatly to the Kennedy mystique. As the *New York Times* put it, no one had seen the public make such a fuss over a child "since Shirley Temple shot to international fame."

As much as she abhorred incessant incursions on her family's cherished privacy, Jackie became truly incensed whenever someone tried to make money off the Kennedy name. "They are now selling Caroline Christmas dolls—*with wardrobe*," Jackie complained to Pierre in yet another angry memo. "Can't you do something about this?"

Joe Kennedy had no trouble understanding America's love affair with the president's children. He doted on Caroline, in particular—just as he doted on Jackie. J. B. West recalled that whenever the ambassador came to visit, Jackie "danced down the halls arm in arm with him, laughing uproariously at his teasing." The first lady and Joe "were buddies," said Hamilton P. "Ham" Brown, the Secret Service agent assigned to protect the president's father. "She loved him, and he admired her, respected her. He was grateful that Jackie had stuck by the President through everything, sure. But it was more than that. There was a very tight bond of affection between them that was unlike anything else in that whole family. They always lit up when they saw each other."

In mid-December 1961, the president and his wife headed off for another whirlwind goodwill tour, this time of Puerto Rico, Venezuela, and Colombia. Once again—and very much to Jack's delight—the first lady was a huge hit, embracing children in orphanages, visiting elderly patients in hospitals, and conversing in fluent Spanish with dignitaries and common folk alike. Crowds chanted "JFK" and "Viva, Miss America!" wherever the couple went.

On December 18 they stopped over in Palm Beach on the way home to see Joe, and so Jackie could also start moving things into the house that would serve as their new base during the Christmas holidays. So as not to crowd the rest of the Kennedy family, this time Jack and Jackie rented a luxurious eight-bedroom estate just a mile away from Papa Joe's La Guerida. The new winter White House, boasting a heated pool and four hundred feet of ocean frontage, belonged to the elder Kennedys' wealthy friends C. Michael Paul and his wife, Josephine Bay Paul, head of the Wall Street brokerage firm Kidder & Company.

The next day, Grandpa Joe took Caroline to the airport to wave goodbye to Air Force One as her daddy departed for Washington. Once he handed Caroline off to Maud Shaw, Joe headed for the links to play a round with his favorite niece, Ann Gargan. The president's seventy-three-year-old father was about to tee off on the eighth hole when he suddenly became faint. Gargan took her uncle home, and he went upstairs for a nap. Four hours later, after Gargan checked in on him and discovered he could neither speak nor move, an ambulance was finally summoned.

The seventy-three-year-old family patriarch had suffered a massive stroke that left him paralyzed on his right side and only able to utter the word "no," which he did repeatedly. "It was frustrating for him, obviously," Agent Brown said. "But it was also hard on the President and the First Lady. He always came to his dad for advice, and she just loved him."

From this point on, the man who put JFK in the White House was confined to a wheelchair, capable of understanding everything being said around him but incapable of communicating his thoughts. Although his face was often contorted and he sometimes drooled, Jackie made sure he was still included in White House functions. She always sat next to Joe at lunches and dinners, talking to him, helping him with his food, and kidding with him as she had always done.

Jack also was careful to include his father in conversations and deliberations, turning to him for reassurance even when he had no hope of deciphering what Joe was trying to say. Lifting off the Hyannis Port lawn aboard the presidential helicopter, JFK looked down at his father slumped in his wheelchair. "It's all because of him, everything," he told Chuck Spalding. "None of this would have happened if it weren't for him. We owe it all to him."

After her White House tour television special drew 77 percent of the viewing public in February 1962, Jackie could easily claim to be the most admired woman in America—perhaps the world. During an earlier screening in the White House movie theater, she nursed a drink while the president puffed on one of his favorite Upmann Havanas. As the lights went up, CBS producer Perry Wolff recalled, Jack "looked at her with adoration and admiration. There was an emotional connection in that couple, I have no doubt. It was a real look of love."

No one appreciated that look from her husband—or the change in the public's perception of her—more than Jackie. "Everyone thought I was a snob," Jackie later recalled. "Jack never made me feel like a liability to him during the election, but I *was*. Now everything that I'd always done suddenly became wonderful, and I was so happy for Jack, because even though it was for only three years together in the White House, he could be proud of me then. You know, because it made him happy, it made *me* so happy."

Not long after, the first couple threw one of their famous dinner parties for twelve—this time in honor of Russian composer Igor Stravinsky. As he approached the head of the receiving line, Leonard Bernstein was greeted by Stravinsky with a bear hug and kisses on both cheeks. "There was all this Russian kissing and embracing going on," Bernstein recalled, when from the far corner of the room came a familiar voice. "Hey," JFK said, "how about me?" Bernstein called the moment "so endearing and so insanely unpresidential, and at the same time never losing dignity."

Unfortunately, the moments at these White House soirees were not always so dignified. Jackie might have a drink and a glass of wine or champagne, and the president seldom had more than one drink—often a daiquiri, a glass of wine, or a Dubonnet, sometimes a martini or a Scotch—but their overexcited guests frequently got caught up in the moment. That evening, the great Stravinsky got so drunk he had to be literally carried out of the party.

This paled in comparison to a raucous dinner for eighty held the previous Veterans Day for Fiat tycoon Gianni Agnelli. At that affair, a well-lubricated Lyndon Johnson crashed to the dance floor while attempting the Twist, and Gore Vidal got into a tiff with Bobby Kennedy after daring to place his hand on Jackie's shoulder—a quarrel that turned so nasty Jackie banned Vidal from the White House forever.

WITH THE FIRST LADY'S STOCK seemingly at an all-time high, Jack, said Tish Baldrige, "felt it was time for Jackie to take her act back on the road." In the fall of 1961 JFK accepted invitations extended by India's Jawaharlal Nehru and President Muhammad Ayub Khan of Pakistan to visit their countries. While Kennedy was fond of the Pakistani leader, he could not bear Nehru's sermonizing. "That sanctimonious fucker," Jack said. "He's the worst phony you've ever seen." But the cracks in the relationship between India and the United States were beginning to show, and something had to be done.

Over the next four months, Jackie caused something of a diplomatic kerfuffle by postponing the trip three times; the excuse was always sinus trouble, even though during this same period she taped her TV special, hosted a number of White House parties, rode to the hounds with the Orange County Hunt, and waterskied off the back of the *Marlin* in Palm Beach.

Jackie was actually working up the courage to head out on her own. "Jack is always so proud of me when I do something like this," she said, "but I can't stand being out in front." In March 1962, she set out on her first solo trip abroad—cautiously billed, at the first lady's request, as a "14-day semiofficial cultural goodwill tour" of the Indian subcontinent. "Solo" was something of a misnomer as well. For company on the road, Jackie had her sister, Lee; her maid, Provi; her favorite Secret Service man, Clint Hill; her hairdresser, sixty-four pieces of luggage—and sixty journalists.

But first, Jackie stopped over in Rome for a private audience with Pope John XXIII. Cassini had created a full-length black dress for the occasion, worn with a lace mantilla borrowed from her sister-in-law Ethel Kennedy. Jackie and the pope chatted in French for more than thirty minutes—the longest private audience with a foreign dignitary John XXIII had ever granted during his papacy. (Jack would never get the chance to meet the charismatic John XXIII, who died on June 3, 1963.)

In his capacity as U.S. ambassador, noted Harvard economist John Kenneth Galbraith—at six feet, eight inches a towering figure in every sense of the word—greeted Jackie when her plane landed in New Delhi on March 12, 1962. In the coming days, Jackie saw the Taj Mahal by moonlight, fed pandas, jumped horses, took a boat ride down the Ganges, teamed up with her sister to ride a thirty-five-year-old elephant named Bibi, recoiled at the sight of a mongoose fighting a cobra, left a bouquet of white roses at Mahatma Gandhi's shrine, partied with the Maharaja and Maharani of Jaipur at their famous nine-hundred-room "Pink Palace," and chatted for hours with India's first prime minister as they strolled the private gardens of his official residence. Nehru became so enamored of his American guests, in fact, that he asked Jackie and Lee to stay with him.

The Bouvier sisters were not disappointed; over the course of their stay in the prime minister's residence they were guests of honor at several elaborate banquets where they were entertained by dancers in brilliantly colored saris twirling to the music of a sitar orchestra. "Nehru was a lonesome man," said Galbraith, "who loved the company of beautiful and intelligent women."

Just as they had in Europe and South America, thousands of people turned out to cheer the woman whom one overwrought

Indian journalist described as the new "Durga, Goddess of Power." "Jackie Ki Jai! Ameriki Rani!" ("Hail Jackie! Queen of America!") the crowds shouted as she rode in the back of an open car, responding with a gesture of *namastes*, the palms-together Indian greeting.

The reception in Pakistan was no different: tens of thousands lined the streets to catch of a glimpse of Jackie riding in an open car from Lahore Airport with President Ayub Khan. As a token of his gratitude for the state dinner previously given in his honor at Mount Vernon, Ayub Khan presented Jackie with a spectacular emerald, ruby, and diamond necklace and the gift she would come to regard as the best she had ever been given by a foreign leader: a magnificent ten-year-old Thoroughbred bay gelding named Sardar.

Karachi, Rawalpindi, and the Khyber Pass were all on Jackie's itinerary in Pakistan, but none matched the beauty and wonder of the Shalimar Gardens in Lahore. "I only wish," she told her hosts, "my husband could be with me."

Not surprisingly, by the time she left Pakistan for a three-day stopover in London, Jackie—who was "adamant" about taking a nap every day rather than be "run into the ground"—was nonetheless on the verge of collapse. She seemed none the worse for wear, however, when the Radziwills threw a party for her that included Cassini, British actress Moira Shearer, and legendary photographer and costume designer Cecil Beaton on the guest list. This time Oleg, who at several White House parties had taken it upon himself to demonstrate the Twist to guests more familiar with the foxtrot, taught Jackie an even more au courant dance: the Hully Gully.

On her return to the States, there was the inevitable criticism from Republicans in Congress that military aircraft had been used to transport Sardar to the United States from Pakistan. But not even that could dim what was another diplomatic triumph for America's thirty-two-year-old first lady. The trip not only smoothed over relations with India, in particular, but on the home front Americans were captivated by photographs of Jackie and Lee riding elephants and camels and touring the grounds of the Taj Mahal.

"The President expected Jackie to seduce Nehru the way she seduced de Gaulle and at the very least charmed Khrushchev," Galbraith said. "She did not disappoint." In the end, the ambassador said, Jackie did nothing less than remove all the "bitterness" that had existed between India and the United States. "Jackie had to walk a tightrope, never appearing to take herself too seriously, and at the same time maintaining a certain aura of . . . *majesty* is the only word I can think of to describe it."

In terms of Jackie's role in enhancing American prestige abroad, journalist Theodore White noted, JFK "knew just how valuable she was." The political payoff back home was just as significant. "The President used to call me into the Oval Office to look at the headlines and the pictures, grinning from ear to ear and saying 'That's our girl!' " Salinger remembered. "Jackie made you proud to be an American, and that feeling translates into votes."

NONE OF THIS WAS ABOUT to stop Jack from seeing other women while his wife was half a world away. Less than twenty-four hours after Jackie departed for India, Jack headed off to Florida for a few days of "girling" with fellow Lothario George Smathers.

Jackie was under no illusions about what was going on on the home front, although the identities of some of her husband's lovers would have shocked her had she known. One was a gorgeous, dark-haired, multilingual, twenty-seven-year-old mother of two named Helen Husted Chavchavadze. Helen was the ex-wife of Romanov descendant David Chavchavadze and, incredibly, the first cousin of the man Jackie once intended to marry, John Husted.

Jack began his affair with Helen Chavchavadze when Jackie, then five months pregnant with John, was resting at Hammersmith Farm. To compound the irony, Helen and Jack hit it off at yet another intimate dinner party thrown by Charles and Martha Bartlett, the same couple who played matchmaker to Jack and Jackie. On the way home after dinner, Chavchavadze glanced in her rearview mirror and saw Jack's white convertible. He followed Helen to her Georgetown house, and they tumbled into bed.

Their affair continued sporadically during the campaign, but after Jack was elected, Helen assumed that JFK would no longer engage in such risky behavior. She was wrong. Days after taking office, Jack and Smathers sauntered into Chavchavadze's Georgetown house. She felt that by "paying a call" in "broad daylight," Jack was sending an unmistakable message: " 'I am a free man. The Secret Service are not going to stop me . . . I will be free to see the women I want to see in the White House.' "

Chavchavadze never knew if Jackie found out about her clandestine affair. If Jackie did, she never let on. Over the next two years, Jackie invited Helen to several parties at the White House. JFK, in turn, invited Helen over when Jackie was out of town. Chavchavadze came to view JFK's "incorrigible promiscuity" as a "guilt-free compulsion"—behavior he viewed as completely natural and certainly not immoral or "wrong."

By this time, JFK had already raised the bushy eyebrows of British prime minister Harold Macmillan with offhand comments about his sex drive. "I wonder how it is with you, Harold?" Jack asked when the two leaders conferred in Bermuda. "If I don't have a woman for three days I get a terrible headache." (At least Macmillan was spared Jack's surprisingly candid admission to Smathers that he was "never finished with a girl" until he had "had her three ways.")

Diana de Vegh was only twenty-two and had just graduated from Radcliffe when JFK found a place for her on the staff of National Security Adviser McGeorge Bundy. Like most of the other young women Jack surrounded himself with, De Vegh was smart, beautiful, well-bred, spirited—and drawn to power. She was looking, De Vegh later confessed, for a man "who would think I was charming and make me feel safe—like Daddy's best girl." Their trysts, which occurred only when the first lady was out of town, took place almost exclusively in the Lincoln Bedroom.

None of the women with whom Jack was involved seemed to be aware of the others. That was certainly true of aspiring painter Mary Pinchot Meyer, an heir to the Pinchot dry goods fortune who had known Jack since his days at Choate. Brought up in Manhattan and on a 3,600-acre estate in Pennsylvania, Mary was also the sister of Ben Bradlee's wife, Tony, a former roommate of Pam Turnure, and a distant relative of Diana de Vegh. In fact, in the late 1950s and early '60s, the rich, blond, Vassar-educated Pinchot sisters had achieved a certain fame as two of Washington's most intriguing women.

Jack happened to share that view, making frequent passes at Tony even while her husband, his good friend Ben Bradlee, was standing only a few feet away. Tony rebuffed JFK's advances. Her more adventurous sister did not.

Mary had been married to dashing journalist-turned-CIA agent

Cord Meyer, but they split after the second of their three sons was struck by a car and killed. From that point on, she indulged in several brief affairs, careful to avoid any long-term emotional entanglements.

On January 22, 1962, Meyer began an intimate relationship with JFK—a fact she shared with only one person, her friend and confidante Anne Truitt. According to Truitt, the affair would last more than a year.

Like Helen Chavchavadze, Meyer was a frequent dinner guest at the White House. The guest lists for these soirees were prepared by the first lady but run by JFK for his approval (ironically, Jack and Jackie went over the lists with another of his lovers, Turnure). Although Jackie was aware of her husband's peccadilloes and knew the identities of several of his lovers, she may well have been totally in the dark about Jack's affair with Mary Meyer.

She was not alone. "Mary was a free spirit—a sensualist and maybe a little wilder than the rest," Cassini said. "I think she was one of those wealthy young women who were not quite sure of themselves and therefore look for approval in the eyes of powerful men. But she never let on that she was sleeping with Jack." NBC anchor Nancy Dickerson was dating Meyer's ex-husband, Cord, at the time, "so I was paying attention to those things. I knew Jack was fond of Mary Meyer," Dickerson said, "but nobody remotely suspected they were having an affair. None of us knew."

Not Smathers or Spalding or—even more astonishingly—Ben and Tony Bradlee. Much later, in October 1964, Mary was taking her customary walk along the towpath of the Chesapeake & Ohio Canal along the Potomac River when someone grabbed her from behind and shot her twice under the cheekbone, execution-style. She was forty-three. A young black man named Raymond Crump Jr. was subsequently arrested, tried, and acquitted of the murder. It was only after Mary's death that the Bradlees stumbled upon her diary—and a detailed account of her affair with JFK.

"To say we were stunned doesn't begin to describe our reactions," Bradlee wrote in his memoirs. "Like everyone else we had heard reports of presidential infidelity, but we were always able to say we knew of no evidence, none." Given the frequent passes JFK made toward Tony Bradlee—including one party aboard the presidential yacht, *Sequoia*, when he literally chased her around the cabin—the Bradlees' sweeping denial about Jack's womanizing rang hollow. Nevertheless, Mary Meyer was undoubtedly successful at keeping her relationship with the president a secret from even those closest to her.

The Bradlees turned the potentially explosive diary over to the CIA with the understanding that it would be destroyed. When the diary mysteriously reappeared a dozen years later, the original was returned to Tony. She promptly burned it.

In March 1962, however, Jack's clandestine affair with Mary Meyer was still fresh. According to CIA counterintelligence chief James Angleton, who read the explosive contents of Mary's diary, she and the president shared three joints of marijuana in the Yellow Oval Room of the White House. The diary also allegedly described a "mild acid trip together, during which they made love."

At the same time, Jack was forced to call it quits with another lover. Over lunch at the White House, FBI director J. Edgar Hoover confronted Jack with evidence that for two years he had been seeing Judith Campbell. Campbell's relationships with mobsters Sam Giancana and Johnny Roselli—two men who had been enlisted by the CIA in botched attempts to assassinate Fidel

Castro—were of "grave concern" to Hoover. (Years later, both Giancana and Roselli would be rubbed out in classic mob hits.)

After breaking up with Judy Campbell over the phone, Jack flew to California to find solace in the arms of the paramour Jackie worried most about: Marilyn Monroe. On Bobby's advice, Jack was no longer staying at the Palm Springs home of Frank Sinatra, the mob-connected singer who had slept with both Campbell and Marilyn before introducing them to JFK. Risking Sinatra's enmity, Peter Lawford was now arranging for the president and Marilyn to meet secretly at the Palm Springs estate of Bing Crosby.

One of Crosby's other guests, California Democrat Philip Watson, inadvertently wandered into a bungalow on the property and came across JFK "wearing a turtleneck sweater" and a soused Marilyn "dressed in kind of a robe thing. It was obvious they were intimate," Watson said, "that they were staying together for the night."

Marilyn's condition that night was typical. She had always grappled with severe psychiatric and emotional problems, made worse in recent years by alcohol and prescription drug abuse. At thirty-six, she realized her sex-symbol days were numbered and began to see a new role for herself: as the second wife of the president. Confiding the most intimate details of the affair to her friend Jeanne Carmen, Marilyn was convinced JFK was about to leave Jackie for her. "Can't you just see me," she asked Carmen, "as first lady?"

It was a dream she also shared with a former boyfriend, Robert Slatzer. "Marilyn told me that the President planned to divorce Jackie and marry her," Slatzer said. "She believed it because she needed to believe it."

Tellingly, during this period Marilyn would get up at parties and sing "I Believe in You," the hit song from the 1961 Broadway smash *How to Succeed in Business Without Really Trying*, to herself in a mirror—just as protagonist J. Pierpont Finch does in the musical. "It became her personal anthem," journalist and friend James Bacon said. "Marilyn was so riddled with self-doubt—with self-loathing, really. . . . The idea that the President of the United States was in love with her, would leave his wife for her—to Marilyn, that would have been the ultimate revenge."

After Marilyn introduced "I Believe in You" to Jack, he also became obsessed with the tune. He played Robert Morse's version from the original cast album of *How to Succeed in Business Without Really Trying* at the White House so frequently that another lover who soon came on the scene, Mimi Beardsley, felt compelled to learn the lyrics so she could sing along. The song, Beardsley later said, "seemed to light up some pleasure center deep inside his brain."

There was never any possibility of Jack divorcing Jackie, or of Marilyn becoming first lady. Yet Jack led Monroe on. According to Peter Lawford, Marilyn, wearing a black wig and dark glasses, masqueraded as his secretary aboard Air Force One. She wore the same disguise at 1600 Pennsylvania Avenue, where she stayed more than once when Jackie was out of town.

Despite understandable skepticism that Monroe could have gone unnoticed as a guest of JFK at the White House, Smathers, Lawford, and Spalding were just a few of the eyewitnesses to her presence there. "I know because I saw Marilyn at the White House," Smathers insisted. "She was there." How often? "A lot."

That didn't mean, Chuck Spalding observed, that Jack was more serious about Marilyn than he was about any of the other women he managed to juggle simultaneously. "Marilyn fell into the girlfriend category," Spalding said. "Jack never considered her on a par with Jackie."

Apparently no one told Marilyn. Peter Lawford claimed that Monroe called the White House and told Jackie of the affair, and of Jack's alleged promises to her. "Marilyn, you'll marry Jack, that's great," Jackie reportedly responded in that breathy voice that sounded not unlike Monroe's. "And you'll move into the White House and you'll assume the responsibilities of first lady, and I'll move out and you'll have all the problems."

Jackie's half brother Jamie Auchincloss had "no trouble" believing the confrontation between Marilyn and Jackie took place. "It sounds," he concluded, "like the kind of gutsy thing my sister would say." Either way, Jackie chose not to dwell on her husband's problematic love life. Exhausted from her travels in India and Pakistan, Jackie scooped up the children and took them to Palm Beach, where she spent most of April recuperating.

As was so often the case when Jackie simply decided to disappear, the president stood in for her at ceremonial events—in this case, hosting a White House luncheon for the Duchess of Devonshire. But one White House event Jackie wasn't about to miss that month was a state dinner for the Shah of Iran and his much younger wife, the breathtaking Shabanou Farah Diba. "Their sex life," Vidal said, "had been the object of intense speculation in Washington. Sex and power fascinated Jack and Jackie the way it does everybody else. They thrived on gossip."

There was the matter of what to wear. Jackie was not accustomed to being outdone by any woman in terms of fashion, but the Farah Diba presented a real challenge. JFK couldn't resist needling his wife about the beautiful young Iranian empress with an unlimited budget. "You'd better watch out, Jackie," he warned her. "You'd better put on all your jewels."

At first, Jackie scrambled to borrow tiaras, necklaces—anything she could from wealthy friends. Finally, Tish Baldrige recalled, "Mrs. Kennedy did a very crafty thing. She took off all her jewels except for one in her hair"—a diamond sunburst pin.

At the dinner, the empress arrived wearing a shimmering gown of embroidered gold silk and "every jewel in the whole Iranian kingdom on her back, front, and head," Baldrige said. These included Iran's famous peacock crown, and a necklace that glistened with twenty-carat diamonds and gumball-sized emeralds. Cassini, who had designed Jackie's pink-and-white dupioni silk gown for the occasion, admitted that it was "difficult to take your eyes off the Shabanou. She literally glowed in the dark."

JFK spent much of the evening teasing his wife. "Are you *sure* you did the right thing?" he asked, glancing over at the young empress. "You know, she's pretty good-looking, Jackie . . . I bet her clothes bill is even more than yours."

If there was a competition brewing between Farah Diba and Jackie, at least eighteen-month-old John left no doubts as to where he stood. When the Shabanou bent down to hand the little boy a daffodil, John shouted "No!" and pulled away. Nanny Shaw was mortified. Mom, apparently not so much.

Jackie had come to dread the first half of May, and with reason. These two weeks, more than any other, were packed with back-to-back breakfasts, lunches, teas, receptions, and ceremonies—a schedule that would, in Theodore White's words, "have floored lesser mortals."

After hosting a diplomatic reception and then sitting through lunches held in her honor by the Congressional Club and the

Senate Ladies Red Cross, Jackie headed to the U.S. Navy subma-
rine base in Groton, Connecticut, to christen the nuclear sub
Lafayette before hosting a luncheon for the Norwegian prime minister the following day.

BY MID-MAY, JACKIE FELT SHE had earned the right to flee to
Virginia—ostensibly to indulge her true passion by competing
in the Loudoun Hunt horse show. In truth, she was escaping the
possibility of being humiliated on national television.

To celebrate the president's upcoming forty-fifth birthday, a
gala Democratic Party fund-raiser was held at New York's Madison
Square Garden on May 19, 1962. More than fifteen thousand
party faithful showed up at the televised event to be entertained
by the varied likes of Peggy Lee, Jack Benny, Ella Fitzgerald, Maria
Callas, Jimmy Durante, and Harry Belafonte.

The president's wife had planned to be there for the star-studded celebration as well. But when she learned that the evening's
entertainment also included an appearance by Marilyn Monroe,
Jackie opted for the Virginia countryside. Taking her mind off the
spectacle unfolding in New York by focusing on the competition,
Jackie won a third-place ribbon riding Minbreno, a horse she
co-owned with her hunt country neighbor Eve Fout.

Jackie had not retreated to Virginia before taking some precau-
tions. Before departing, she made sure Rose, Ethel, and Jack's
sisters Eunice and Pat were going to encircle JFK on the dais. "I
suppose that way," Gore Vidal observed, "it looked a little less like
the presidential stag party it was."

After Marilyn missed several cues to make her entrance—
the star kept people waiting as a way to build tension and

anticipation—master of ceremonies Peter Lawford intoned, "Mr. President, the *late* Marilyn Monroe."

The throng exploded with cheers when Marilyn, bundled in white ermine, suddenly materialized beneath a spotlight. Foggy from pills (talking to her later that evening was "as if talking to someone under water," Schlesinger observed), Marilyn shed her furs to reveal a shimmering, flesh-toned gown that she had literally been sewn into moments before. Monroe later said she was dressed in "skin and beads," but Adlai Stevenson, for one, claimed he "didn't see the beads!" None of this was a surprise to Jack; the hair-obsessed president had even lent Marilyn his stylist, who blew up her platinum bouffant into an exaggerated flip.

Standing at the microphone, perhaps the greatest screen sex goddess of all time was suddenly seized by stage fright. "By God," she later confessed thinking to herself, "I'll sing this song if it's the last thing I ever do." Jack smiled broadly as Marilyn finally launched into her seductive, breathy version of the birthday song—"Happy Birthday, Mr. *Pres-i-dent*"—and a giant cake was wheeled out. "I can now retire from politics," JFK announced with Marilyn standing beside him, "after having 'Happy Birthday' sung to me in such a sweet, wholesome way."

Even by JFK's own standards, this moment, played out before a national audience, appeared incomprehensibly reckless. Yet Kennedy knew that, at least in the case of Marilyn, it was best to simply hide in plain sight. "At the time," Salinger said, "it was just inconceivable. Remember, this is way before Ronald Reagan. Americans put the President of the United States in one box and a big movie star like Marilyn Monroe in another. I know I did."

Salinger, who had virtually unrestricted access to JFK in the West Wing, conceded that he heard gossip but insisted that he "could honestly say I never caught him with another woman." He also admitted that he assumed the president was unfaithful because he kept pressing his press secretary to cheat on his wife. "So," Salinger concluded, "I took that to mean he was having affairs, too." Those "dalliances," said Tish Baldrige, were "kept hidden . . . I hadn't the slightest inkling that anything was going on. None of us did. We were all just doing our jobs and, in retrospect, I guess we were ridiculously naive."

It wasn't just White House staff members who were kept in the dark. "I never saw any evidence of Jack's cheating," Charlie Bartlett said. "He hid his infidelity completely." Similarly, Ben Bradlee wrote years later that he and Tony "were always able to say we knew of no evidence, none."

Incredibly, the Washington press corps, for decades assumed to have actively shielded JFK from scandal, was also apparently unaware of Jack's extramarital shenanigans. "I was right there every day," UPI White House correspondent Helen Thomas said, "and I didn't know a thing. Period." CBS correspondent Charles Collingwood, a particular favorite of the Kennedys, claimed he "never heard a word spoken about JFK cheating on his wife—not a word," while *Washington Star* columnist Betty Beale said the press was "totally in the dark. I mean *totally*." Legendary CBS producer Fred Friendly conceded that "John F. Kennedy had pretty much the whole world under his spell and the press was no exception. The bottom line is that they didn't *want* to find out anything unflattering about the President so they didn't go looking for it. But you really didn't dig into people's private lives in those days. It was such a different time then . . ."

It helped that Jack, perhaps more than any other president, had a genius for compartmentalizing his life—putting Jackie and the children in one cubicle, White House staffers in another, his Kennedy relatives in another, Administration officials in another, the press in another, close personal friends in yet another, and his lovers each in a compartment of their own. "I do not remember everything about him," Ted Sorensen said, "because I never *knew* everything about him. No one did."

That evening after the Madison Square Garden birthday gala, the president was among one hundred guests at a party thrown in his honor at the East Sixty-ninth Street home of United Artists chief Arthur Krim. Early on, Jack and his friend Bill Walton watched from their perch on a staircase as Marilyn, who had never been introduced to Bobby before, pressed the attorney general up against the wall. Bobby "didn't know what to do or where to look," said Walton, who along with Jack was "rocking with laughter" the whole time.

Marilyn's precarious mental state became more apparent when Walton stumbled upon her standing in front of a bedroom window, entertaining guards positioned on the rooftop of an adjoining building with a "naked erotic dance. I couldn't believe it!"

Marilyn ducked into Jack's limousine and accompanied him back to the Carlyle just seven blocks uptown, entering the hotel through the garage. This was one of only several ways Jack learned to get in and out of his New York base of operations undetected.

Early in the 1960 campaign, when he gave his Secret Service detail the slip, agents had realized JFK was using a secret underground passageway beneath the Carlyle to call on some of Manhattan's most desirable socialites in townhouses just a few blocks away. Chuck Spalding tagged along on several of Jack's subterranean adventures, which he called "bizarre." Flashlights in hand,

Spalding and the president trudged through the passageway while agents consulted their underground maps. The president and his detail, Spalding theorized, "got a kick out of the cloak-and-dagger aspect of it."

The night Jack spent with Marilyn following his famous Madison Square Garden birthday party would be their last together. That spring into summer, Marilyn was becoming increasingly unhinged. After word got back to Washington that Marilyn was openly boasting of her affair with the president of the United States, Jack asked George Smathers to intervene.

"Marilyn was surprised that Jack was upset," Smathers recalled. "She was in a haze much of the time and, frankly, I don't think she knew she was spilling the beans." In the meantime, however, Jack was informed that the mob had taped his romps with Marilyn at Lawford's house in Santa Monica—"and that was the final straw," Smathers said. "He had to break it off and get as far away from Marilyn as possible."

Monroe was not about to go quietly. When she could no longer get through to Jack, she began calling his brother. It was not long before Marilyn was telling friends that Bobby planned to leave Ethel and marry her.

The fling with RFK came as no surprise to singer Phyllis McGuire of the top-selling 1950s pop group the McGuire Sisters. Phyllis had replaced Judy Campbell as mob boss Sam Giancana's girlfriend and was told by Giancana and others that Jack had, in "true Kennedy fashion," passed Marilyn on to his younger brother. Apparently there was proof: audio tapes of Marilyn's trysts with both Kennedy brothers, which found their way into the hands of J. Edgar Hoover. Bobby did not have to be told; realizing that he risked bringing down his brother's administration, RFK cut off all contact with Marilyn.

BY THIS TIME, JACK WAS involved with someone new—another Miss Porter's alum named Marion "Mimi" Beardsley (later Beardsley Fahnestock Alford) who, at nineteen, was twenty-six years JFK's junior. A tall, slender, preppy WASP, Mimi was only a high school senior when she came to the White House to interview Tish Baldrige for the school paper. Introduced to the president during that visit, she was offered a chance to work as a summer intern in the White House press office after her first year at Massachusetts's Wheaton College. "He just couldn't," Mimi admitted, "resist a girl with a little bit of Social Register in her background."

Her fourth day on the job, Mimi was invited by Dave Powers to join the president for a swim in the White House pool. While Fiddle and Faddle paddled around, sipping wine and giggling, Mimi put on one of the dozen or so women's swimsuits always kept hanging on the dressing room wall and dove in. Within minutes, JFK appeared wearing a dark swimsuit, looking "remarkably fit for a 45-year-old man." According to Mimi, he "slid into the water and floated up to me. 'It's Mimi, isn't it? . . .' "

Nothing happened in the pool that day but small talk. Afterward, Mimi joined a small group—Dave Powers, Kenny O'Donnell, Fiddle, Faddle, and the president—for daiquiris in the West Sitting Room. Jackie and the children, Mimi was told matter-of-factly, had already left for Glen Ora. At some point during the proceedings, the slightly tipsy teenager was led upstairs by Jack for a personal tour of the family quarters, ending at the first lady's bedroom. It was there, on the edge of Jackie's bed, that Mimi lost her virginity to the president.

Only days later, 1.5 million people lined the streets of Mexico City just to catch a glimpse of Jack and Jackie as they arrived in an open car. "Mexican emotions literally exploded," Baldrige said, "at the sight of a young, bareheaded John F. Kennedy." But once again it was Jackie who stole the spotlight with her beauty, grace, and spectacular wardrobe (for this south of the border trip she had asked Cassini to design dresses in eye-popping "sun colors" of lime green, sky blue, and hot pink). Whether visiting children's hospitals or lunching with Mexican president Adolfo López Mateos, she impressed her hosts with unscripted remarks delivered in impeccable Spanish.

Once the four-day visit was over, Jackie headed off for what wound up being a three-month vacation. No longer willing to spend her holiday cheek by jowl with the rest of the clan, she convinced her husband to rent a seven-bedroom house outside the Kennedy compound from popular tenor Morton Downey, who also happened to be an old friend of the Kennedy family. The Downey house was located on Squaw Island, less than a mile from the rest of the Kennedys, and Jackie made it clear that she intended to divide her time between there and Glen Ora.

In the meantime, Jack was left to his own devices back in Washington. "Frankly," Baldrige said, "we all felt rather sorry for the President because there were these long stretches when Jackie was never there." Smathers saw things a little differently. "There were times when he wanted Jackie around, when he missed her and the kids," he said, "but then he knew that being at the White House could put her in one of those black moods of hers. So naturally, after a while he started looking forward to her being out of town so he'd be free to do what he wanted."

Helen Chavchavadze, Diana de Vegh, and especially Mary Meyer took up the slack that summer. None were as bold as the guileless intern Mimi, who made no attempt to conceal her sleepovers with the president; each morning when she awoke in JFK's bed, she was politely greeted by JFK's trusted valet, George Thomas ("Too discreet and loyal," she recalled, "to ever hint that he disapproved of my presence").

As with the other women in what one Secret Service agent called JFK's "private stock," there was nothing remotely romantic about the way Jack treated Mimi. "I don't remember him *ever* kissing me—not hello, not goodbye, not even during sex," Mimi later wrote. Nor would she ever call him anything but "Mr. President." But Mimi also insisted what they had was "sexual, intimate, passionate."

With the exception of Marilyn, it appears none of Jack's other lovers considered themselves to be in serious competition with Jackie. "I never knew if Jackie knew," Helen Chavchavadze conceded, "but I felt uncomfortable about her." Mimi did not share Chavchavadze's sense of apprehension concerning Jackie, but she was impressed with "the great care the President took to shield his wife from his infidelities. I believe he placed her on a pedestal as the perfect partner. . . . And he planted that pedestal in a private space where all his 'other women,' including me, would never be permitted to enter."

"I JUST HATE TO BE a *thing*," Marilyn told writer Richard Meryman for a *Life* magazine cover story that hit newsstands on August 3, 1962. The next evening, after quarreling with Bobby, she called Peter Lawford from her home in the Brentwood section of Los Angeles. Marilyn's psychiatrist had just left after giving her a sedative, she was drinking, and she had also taken sleeping pills. "Say goodbye to Pat," she slurred to Lawford, "say goodbye to the President, and say goodbye to yourself, because you've been a good guy." On Sunday morning, August 5, Marilyn's lifeless, nude body was found sprawled on her bed. The official cause of death was acute barbiturate poisoning—a "probable suicide," ruled Los Angeles County coroner Thomas Noguchi.

The American public reacted to Marilyn's sudden death with shock and disbelief. Yet no one made a connection between the doomed sex goddess and the handsome president. "The President and Marilyn Monroe? Lovers? Are you kidding me?" Tish Baldrige asked incredulously. "You might just as well have said little green men from Mars had just landed on the White House lawn. That would have been far more plausible to most Americans."

Jack, who was spending that weekend with Jackie and the kids on Cape Cod, made no public comment about Marilyn's death. Behind the scenes, however, JFK's reaction to the news confirmed Jackie's worst suspicions. Peter Lawford and Bobby were burning up the lines to Hyannis Port. Among other things, there was genuine concern that evidence at Marilyn's house—not to mention those tapes the FBI now allegedly had in their possession—might tie her to the Kennedys.

Damage control was something about which Jackie had become all too familiar. "The possibility that she might be humiliated or embarrassed really got to her," Smathers said. "She didn't like it, not one damn bit." While Jack returned to the White House to carry on business as usual, an irate and frustrated Jackie

1

"They were both such private people,"
Pierre Salinger said, "but they could be very
affectionate when they thought nobody was
looking." Here are two such private moments—at the Kennedy Compound in Hyannis Port, Massachusetts, and when Jackie
waited until they were in the family car to
welcome her husband home from a campaign trip in 1960.

2

3

4

She had not yet recovered from
John Jr.'s birth and he was suffering excruciating back pain, but
even seasoned photographers
gasped when the new president
and his first lady left the White
House for the first of five inaugural balls.

Just weeks after the inauguration, Jackie was indulging her one true passion: riding to the hounds with the Piedmont Hunt and jumping horses at Glen Ora, the Kennedys' rented estate in Middleburg, Virginia.

7

8

Another rare display of tenderness (top), this time after welcoming their first state visitor, Tunisian president Habib Bourguiba, at Blair House. The next day, Jack was standing in Evelyn Lincoln's office when he spotted Jackie passing in the hallway and called to her, "Come in and watch this." Minutes later she, JFK, and Vice President Lyndon Johnson were glued to TV coverage of Alan Shepard's historic blastoff into space.

9

11

10

12

Princess Grace of Monaco's gaze (top) spoke volumes when she and Prince Rainier visited the White House in May 1961. The following week, the first couple embarked on their first official trip to Europe, where they charmed Soviet premier Nikita Khrushchev, Charles de Gaulle (above), and Queen Elizabeth and Prince Philip. JFK was "bowled over" by the way his wife handled herself.

13

With the president's brother Bobby clutching Justice Department files, Jackie and Jack prepare to helicopter from Otis Air Force Base to Hyannis Port in late June 1961. Once at Hyannis Port, Jack and Jackie go for a sail aboard *Victura*.

14

15

16

"With the possible exception of when Thomas Jefferson dined alone." At the famous White House dinner for Nobel laureates in April 1962 (top), JFK chatted with novelist Pearl Buck while Jackie got an earful from poet Robert Frost. At a later dinner for French culture minister André Malraux, the hosts conferred in the hallway while an orchestra played on.

18

After her breathless rendition of "Happy Birthday, Mr. Pres-i-dent" at Madison Square Garden on May 19, 1962, Marilyn Monroe met up with JFK and RFK at a private party. Jackie, who made sure she was in Virginia at the time, later confessed she was deeply hurt by JFK's relationship with Monroe. On JFK's actual forty-fifth birthday ten days later, he tore into gifts at a surprise party thrown by White House staffers. That night, another party—this one while cruising aboard the *Sequoia* (below).

19

At the 1962 America's Cup banquet in Newport, Rhode Island, the first lady enter-
tains her husband with the latest gossip from New York.

Jackie sat at her husband's feet aboard the destroyer *Joseph P. Kennedy Jr.* as they watched the America's Cup races in Narragansett Bay.

Irving Berlin's Kennedy-inspired musical *Mr. President* turned out to be a dud when it previewed at Washington's National Theatre on September 25, 1962. But the crowds waiting outside for a glimpse of the president and his glamorous wife as they exited the theater didn't care. The opening night party for six hundred at the British Embassy turned out to be one of the year's social highlights.

24

"Buttons! John! *John!*" The Kennedy children came running to the Oval Office as soon as they heard Daddy clap his hands. With publicity-wary Jackie riding horses in Virginia, JFK felt free to invite photographers in to snap away.

Along with the Radziwills and their growing menagerie, the president's family celebrates Christmas 1962 in Palm Beach, Florida (top left). Four days later, JFK proudly looks on as his wife speaks Spanish to some of the forty thousand Cuban exiles gathered at Miami's Orange Bowl to welcome returning Bay of Pigs prisoners. In 1963, the first family stuck with tradition and attended Easter Mass at Palm Beach's vine-covered St. Edward's Church.

29 "Anyone for ice cream?!" With that, a dozen Kennedy cousins summering at Hyannis Port would come running to jump on Uncle Jack's golf cart for a wild ride into town. Just days before going into premature labor with Patrick, Jackie, who hid her heavy smoking habit from the nation, relaxes with a book and a cigarette aboard the *Honey Fitz*.

33

Drawn closer than they had ever been by Patrick's death, Jack and Jackie hold hands as they leave the hospital at Cape Cod's Otis Air Force Base. JFK explained the loss of their little brother to Caroline and John, then brought home a new cocker spaniel puppy to lift everyone's spirits.

JFK at the wheel. With the president as their chauffeur, the first family drew crowds when they decided to take an impromptu weekend tour of the Civil War battlefield in Gettysburg, Pennsylvania. On September 15, 1963, Jackie and Jack—still reeling from Patrick's death—leave Hammersmith Farm in Newport (below) for a cruise aboard the *Honey Fitz*.

36

In her first official act as first lady since Patrick's death shattered the Kennedys' world, Jackie joined her husband in greeting Emperor Haile Selassie of Ethiopia at Washington's Union Station on October 1, 1963. By the end of the month, Jack could laugh at the witch (Caroline, holding the requisite black cat) and her skeleton sidekick (John) when they surprised Daddy in the Oval Office. Just nine days before the fatal shots rang out in Dallas, the family was photographed one last time on the Truman Balcony of the White House (below), listening to the bagpipes of Scotland's Black Watch Regiment.

39

fled with Caroline and twelve Secret Service agents to Ravello, the picturesque village on Italy's Amalfi Coast where the Radziwills rented a clifftop villa with a breathtaking view of the Bay of Salerno. Abruptly leaving the country was Jackie's "way of telling him," Smathers said, "that he'd gone too far this time."

The paparazzi shadowed her every move, clicking away as Jackie shopped, water-skied, dined, swam, sunbathed, visited local nightclubs, and simply strolled Ravello's narrow streets. Unfazed, she took Caroline to an ice cream party with local children at the home of an American friend. Later that day, Jackie scrawled a ten-page letter to "Dearest, Dearest Jack" in which she lamented being apart: "I miss you very much . . . I know I exaggerate everything but I feel sorry for everyone else . . ." In the end, she told her husband that thinking of him was "the only thing I have to give & I hope it matters to you."

But in Washington, Jack was fuming over gossip that his wife had decided to extend her Italian escapade from two weeks to four because of another Radziwill house guest, the suave and very rich Gianni Agnelli. The president was able to keep his temper in check until wire services ran photos of Gianni and Jackie swimming together off Agnelli's eighty-two-foot sloop the *Agneta.* In a cable fired off to his wife, Jack demanded A LITTLE MORE CARO-LINE AND LESS AGNELLI. The next morning, papers around the world were filled with photos of the first lady and the Italian auto magnate scuba-diving together.

La Bella Jackie, as she was now being called in the local press, won even more Italian hearts after a devastating quake struck Naples some twenty miles away. "The past two weeks have reaffirmed my admiration and affection for the people of this part of the world," she said in a statement. "That they, who give so much in heart and spirit, should suffer loss of life and home is truly a calamity."

The first lady's heartfelt remarks proved her worth as a goodwill ambassador once again, but that didn't prevent Jack from placing several transatlantic calls pleading with Jackie to stay away from Agnelli and return home. "He could be very jealous when it came to Jackie," Salinger said, "and it wasn't just because he was worried it might look bad. He was always imagining she might be up to something, and you'd have to reassure him."

Oleg Cassini confirmed that JFK was very possessive when it came to his wife, even more so after they entered the White House. "But if she had slept with somebody other than him," said Cassini, whose own reputation as a Don Juan made him suspect to JFK at the beginning, "it would have been disaster for her." The designer felt that, beyond being perpetually "irritated" over her husband's infidelities, Jackie had no interest in getting even.

Once again, Jack was able to separate the other women in his life from the unique relationship he had with his wife. "Believe it or not," Betty Spalding said, "Jack was jealous of Jackie seeing *any* other man, even a pal like Bill Walton, because he was convinced she was doing the same thing he was doing."

It wasn't all work and no play for Jack that summer, either. He did manage a long weekend sailing off the coast of Maine and a trip to Los Angeles, where he was mobbed by squealing, swimsuit-clad women as he tried to take an impromptu dip in the Pacific.

At the end of August, the first lady and Caroline finally joined JFK and John in Newport. For the next six weeks, Jackie and the children stayed at Hammersmith Farm while Jack spent much of his time conferring with advisers about Soviet intentions in Berlin and Cuba.

☙

EVEN BEFORE SHE LEFT RAVELLO, Jackie was drawing up guest lists for the small weekend dinner parties she hoped would entertain Jack in Newport. For the president, nothing could top what they had planned for September 15: watching the eighteenth America's Cup final between the American sloop *Weatherly* and Australia's first-ever contender, the *Gretel,* in Narragansett Bay.

On the eve of the race, the Kennedys—he in black tie and nursing his customary Cuban panatela, she bare-shouldered in another provocative sheath by Cassini—seemed right at home presiding over the official America's Cup reception at the Breakers, once the palatial summer "cottage" of the Vanderbilts. For much of the evening the president and first lady were locked in intimate conversation; sitting at a long banquet table, she leaned close in and whispered bits of gossip, and he reacted with amazed looks and the occasional burst of laughter. "Of course everybody was staring at them," Salinger recalled, "wondering what they were saying to each other. They looked like a happy young married couple out on a date, having the time of their lives."

Yet when he stood to speak that night, Jack waxed poetic about his connection to the sea—words that decades later would be quoted at the funeral of his own son. "We have salt in our blood, in our sweat, in our tears," he told the well-heeled crowd. "We are tied to the ocean. And when we go back to the sea, whether it is to sail or to watch it, we are going back from whence we came."

☙

THE NEXT DAY JACK AND Jackie sidled up to each other again, this time watching the *Weatherly* defeat the *Gretel* from the deck of the destroyer *Joseph P. Kennedy Jr.* At times, Jackie sat at her husband's feet while he watched the race through binoculars. "It was just like the dinner at the Breakers," Salinger said. "They were exchanging intimacies, and everyone else was trying to read their lips."

On September 23, Jackie made a quick solo stop in New York to attend the nationally televised opening of Philharmonic Hall, the first of several travertine-and-glass buildings that were to make up the new arts complex called Lincoln Center. After conducting the world premiere of a new work by Aaron Copland, the Kennedys' old friend Leonard Bernstein committed a social gaffe for which he was excoriated in the press: he kissed Jackie on the cheek. What bothered Jack, apparently, wasn't that Bernstein kissed his wife. It was the fact that Bernstein was "dripping wet" while doing it. "That sweaty, awful conductor kissing this gorgeous creature, coast to coast on television, was just not permissible," Bernstein recalled of the ensuing public outcry. "Horrible."

Jackie merely laughed it off. "Oh, Lenny, really," she later told him. "People treat me like some porcelain doll, and I'm around horses all day that sweat *buckets*. And that's hardly the most disgusting thing I see them do."

The Kennedys began to wind down their ten-day September vacation by hosting a lunch for Ayub Khan. Eager to show the Pakistani president how thrilled she was with Sardar, the horse he had given her, Jackie insisted they ride together at Glen Ora. The following evening, the Kennedys attended a special performance of Irving Berlin's new Kennedy-inspired musical, *Mr. President,* at Washington's National Theatre. While Berlin's show bombed, the extravagant midnight dinner dance for six hundred thrown at the British Embassy afterward was—thanks to the presence of Jack and Jackie—one of the year's social highlights.

As expected, necks craned as the president and first lady, this time wearing a shimmering pink silk gown that had been given to her by King Saud of Saudi Arabia, made their entrance. Surprisingly upbeat given the theatrical fiasco they had just endured ("An old-fashioned dud" was the verdict of the New York *Journal-American*), Jackie and Jack mingled, laughed, and danced until 2:30 a.m.—only leaving when JFK literally took Jackie's arm and pulled her toward the exit. Everyone marveled at the first couple's stamina—unaware that they were both being bolstered by regular amphetamine and steroid shots, courtesy of Max Jacobson.

"They weren't faking it," said Jacques Lowe, who never failed to be amazed by the way the Kennedys "brought the world to a complete standstill" whenever they walked into a room. "They enjoyed being in each other's company. Jackie wanted her privacy and she wasn't always around, but she more than made up for that when she was. Alone, they were incredible, but together—and I know it sounds corny to say it—they were magic."

The next day, JFK summoned Dr. Max for another series of shots, this time to give him the energy to deal with the looming prospect of race riots in the South. Just days after the centennial of the Emancipation Proclamation, twenty-eight-year-old James Meredith had been barred from registering as the first black student at the all-white University of Mississippi by that state's governor, Ross Barnett.

Forced to confront the volatile issue of race relations head-on, Kennedy canceled plans to join Jackie and the children at Hammersmith Farm and hunkered down with his top domestic advisers. After a series of conflicting reports from the field and bizarre phone conversations between Jack and a vacillating Barnett ("You knew the man was an inferior person to begin with," Jackie sniped), the president addressed the nation. He pledged that Meredith would register safely the next day. He then sat down at a table that had been owned by Ulysses S. Grant and signed an executive order sending federal troops to desegregate Ole Miss. They did—but not before rioters armed with rocks, bottles, and guns killed two people and injured two hundred.

Twice during the crisis—at midnight and then at 5 a.m.—Jack woke Jackie in Newport to vent his frustrations. "Oh, my God!" he told her over the phone. "You wouldn't believe this." Jackie was impressed by her husband's self-control as he worked through the night to get Army troops to the Ole Miss campus. "There was never rage there," she recalled. "It was just so hopeless. I guess that was one of the worst nights of his whole life."

Yet Jackie was moved that the president took time out from conferring with his team of domestic advisers to reach out to his wife. "You know, I was so touched that he called me," she said, "and just wanted to talk."

JFK may have been motivated, to some degree, by guilt. Around this time, Mimi Beardsley informed Dave Powers that she might be pregnant—no surprise, really, since JFK never used condoms and Mimi knew nothing about birth control. Abortions were illegal at the time, but Powers told the coed to stay calm. Within an hour, he put her in touch with a woman in Newark, New Jersey, who, in turn, gave her the number of a doctor willing to do the job. The need for Powers to distance himself and the president from the whole procedure was obvious. "Even the docile White House press corps," she later wrote, "couldn't have averted their eyes from that story." As it turned out, Mimi wasn't pregnant, and no mention was made of the episode again. But, she would admit decades later, "I shudder to think what other cleanup jobs Dave Powers was asked to do for his boss."

On October 9, Jackie packed up the kids and returned to Washington. The next night, she and Jack hosted an intimate dinner party that included Federal Aviation Administration chief Najeeb Halaby, noted San Francisco architect John Warnecke, Bill Walton, and Walton's supposed date for the evening—Mary Meyer. Although JFK and Meyer had been alone at the White House several times, this was the first time she and Jackie actually sat across from each other at the dinner table. To make matters even more awkward, JFK had to be helicoptered to Baltimore to give a speech; he could only stay with his guests for drinks in the Yellow Oval Room and then return after dinner for coffee.

That evening, according to the other guests, there were no stolen moments or knowing looks from Mary or Jack. Jackie, who spent part of the evening deep in conversation with Warnecke about efforts to save Washington's historic Lafayette Square, held down the fort until the presidential helicopter returned shortly after nine. "Lovely and gracious but totally inscrutable—that's how they handled things," said Baldrige. "If Jackie knew someone was sleeping with her husband, she'd never let on—and certainly not to the person in question. That just wasn't her style."

Cassini, one of the relative chosen few frequently invited to the first couple's intimate White House dinners, chalked it all up to Jackie's "natural dignity. She was a woman of great pride. If she and Jack had had a fight ten minutes before, she would *never* have shown it."

"They both considered 1600 Pennsylvania Avenue sacrosanct," Baldrige agreed. "She wore a mask."

I want to be with you, and I want to die with you—and the children do too—rather than live without you.

൙

They did have a sex life. She talked about that intimately with me. She loved him dearly, and I felt they were getting much closer together.

8

∂⌀

"But What About All the Children?"

*J*ackie stretched out languidly in the warm sun of an Indian summer, glad to be back at her beloved Glen Ora. In keeping with her usual routine, she had arrived with the children the previous day, hoping for another much-needed break from the pressures of Washington. She was surprised when Provi said the president, who had been speaking in Chicago, was on the phone.

"I'm coming back to Washington this afternoon," he said. "Why don't you and the children join me there?"

When she asked him why, Jack paused for a moment. "Well, never mind," he said. "Why don't you just come back to Washington?"

"There was something funny in his voice," she recalled. "I could tell something was wrong. . . . That's the whole point of being married—you just must sense trouble in their voice and mustn't ask why."

But she knew why. Four days earlier, National Security Adviser McGeorge Bundy had rushed to the residence at 8 a.m. to show the president aerial photos taken by a U-2 spy plane the night before. The images showed the clear presence of offensive nuclear weapons in Cuba—intermediate-range Soviet missiles capable of striking the United States capital.

For the next week, the president maintained what appeared to be a normal schedule while top-secret meetings went on at the White House. JFK went ahead with planned trips to Connecticut and the Midwest, then returned to meet with members of the Executive Committee of the National Security Council—ExComm— to devise a strategy for coping with this newest threat to world peace.

This business-as-usual ruse worked so well that even White House staffers were unaware that key ExComm members were secretly camping out at the Executive Mansion, some sleeping on cots and couches. Jack let his wife know that the situation was serious, and that for the moment the best thing to do was keep everyone—including the Soviets—in the dark. "We can't let them know that we know what they're up to—not yet," he said. "We don't want to tip our hand."

It quickly became apparent that JFK's options were few. The United States could take out the missiles with an air strike, invade Cuba, negotiate a settlement through the United Nations, or enforce a naval blockade of the island. Jack's first impulse was for decisive military action, preferably an air strike to take the missiles out before they were fully operational.

From the outset, Secretary of Defense Robert McNamara strongly disagreed, arguing for a blockade. Positions seesawed back and forth until Bundy, backed by the Joint Chiefs, surprised everyone by calling for an air strike. It was then that Deputy Secretary of Defense Roswell Gilpatric, who happened to be one of Jackie's closest friends, made a case for caution that was elegant in its simplicity. "Essentially, Mr. President," he said, "this is a choice between limited action and unlimited action, and most of us think that it's better to start with limited action."

Early on, Secret Service agent Clint Hill had tried to gently broach the subject of what might happen in the event things spiraled out of control. J. B. West had already given the first lady a tour of the bomb shelter beneath the White House, and that, said Hill, was where she and the children would be taken if there weren't time to evacuate.

"Mr. Hill," Jackie stated flatly, "if the situation develops, I will take Caroline and John, and we will walk hand in hand out onto the south grounds. We will stand there like brave soldiers, and face the fate of every other American."

Jack knew Jackie too well to solemnly confront her with the worst-case scenario. He was far too cool even in such times of crisis, Jackie explained, "to say, 'Sit down, I have something to tell you.' " But when she heard of contingency plans to evacuate her and the children to the underground facility at Camp David, the presidential retreat high atop Maryland's Catoctin Mountains, Jackie protested. "Please don't send me away to Camp David," she pleaded with Jack, who presumably would have stayed behind with his top advisers in the crowded White House bomb shelter in the event of a nuclear attack. "Please don't send me anywhere if anything happens, we're all going to stay right here with you."

"But Jackie . . ."

"Even if there's no room in the bomb shelter in the White House . . . ," she went on. "Please, then I just want to be on the lawn when it happens. I want to be with you, I want to die with you, and the children do too—rather than live without you."

Jack looked deep into her eyes. "All right," he said, "then I promise, I won't send you and the children away." Jackie detected a sense of relief in her husband's voice. "He didn't really want to send me away, either," she said of that moment. Later, Jackie was shocked to learn how many wives of top government officials did depart Washington, leaving their husbands behind. "My God," she said. "I don't think that shows you love your husband very much!"

Now that she was being summoned back to the White House from Glen Ora, Jackie knew things had taken a turn for the worse. New photos of the missile sites in Cuba showed that the Soviets were now assembling SS-5 missiles capable of striking any target in the United States. The president would soon have to take action that would inevitably bring the world closer to nuclear war than it had ever been. He wanted his wife and children close at hand.

At Glen Ora on October 20, Jackie woke Caroline and John from their naps and asked Clint Hill to call for a helicopter to take them all back to Washington. Early the next morning, J. B. West was awakened at home by an urgent call from the first lady. Minutes later, he was entering the family quarters of the White House through a side door, so as not to arouse suspicion.

"Thank you so much for coming, Mr. West," she said matter-of-factly. "There's something brewing that might turn out to be a big catastrophe—which means we might have to cancel the dinner and dance for the Maharaja and Maharani of Jaipur Tuesday night." As it happened, the Kennedys would still entertain the visiting Indian dignitaries that Tuesday with a small dinner party. In fact, they would entertain virtually every night during the crisis, partly to keep up their own morale and particularly to maintain the illusion of business as usual.

Jackie would describe the rest of the thirteen-day crisis as "a time when there was no day or night"—just round-the-clock meetings, cables, briefings, and phone calls interspersed with catnaps and the rare two hours of uninterrupted sleep. At one point, Bobby donned riding clothes and drove to the White House in a convertible—all part of ongoing attempts to fool the press.

One night, Jackie drifted over to Jack's bedroom wearing a diaphanous nightgown and saw her husband lying on the bed and talking—or so she thought—on the phone. "I'd been in and out of there all evening," recalled Jackie, who ran toward her husband's bed only to have him wave her away. "Get out! Get out!" JFK shouted. When she turned, Jackie realized that owlish, stiff-collared McGeorge Bundy was standing there. "Poor puritan Bundy," she laughed, "to see a woman running in her nightgown. He threw both hands over his eyes." Another night, the president and first lady awoke to see a sheepish Bundy standing at the foot of the bed with an urgent cable.

"That's the time I've been closest to him," said Jackie, who never ventured far and made a point of sleeping with Jack "even if it was only for a nap." At times, she waited outside the Oval Office or eavesdropped at the door of the Treaty Room, where ExComm members thrashed out opposing views.

Jackie was surprised when, on the spur of the moment, Jack asked her to join him for a walk around the grounds. "It's funny," she said. "You know, he didn't very often do that. We just sort of walked quietly, then we'd go back in. It was just this . . . vigil."

Even Jackie, a master at concealing her emotions, was impressed by Jack's ability not to surrender to despair. But as he pondered the very real possibility of a global thermonuclear war, JFK's mask of confidence slipped during one of their strolls on the South Lawn. "We've already had a chance," he told Jackie, "but what about all the children?"

On Monday evening, October 22, JFK sat at his desk in the Oval Office and spoke to the nation. In his seventeen-minute address, he outlined the dimensions of the Soviet military buildup just ninety miles off the coast of Florida, and demanded that the Soviet Union "halt and eliminate this clandestine, reckless, and provocative threat to world peace."

He then warned both Cuba and the Soviets that he had "directed the armed forces to prepare for any eventualities," and spelled out the immediate steps the United States was taking— most notably, a naval blockade of Cuba aimed at halting Soviet ships with cargo that included offensive weapons.

"My fellow citizens," JFK concluded, "let no one doubt that this is a difficult and dangerous effort on which we have set out. . . . The cost of freedom is always high—and Americans have always paid it. And one path we shall never choose, and that is the path of surrender and submission."

Now they played a waiting game. Would the unrepentantly bellicose Khrushchev up the ante, pushing the world ever closer to nuclear Armageddon? Or would the Soviets, fearing the consequences of a direct military confrontation, simply back down?

In the meantime, Jack explained to his wife that, contrary to her dramatic statement, no one was going to go standing on the White House lawn if war was imminent. He did, however, have the unenviable task of deciding who would be joining his immediate family in the emergency national headquarters carved out of Virginia's Blue Ridge Mountains, thirty miles outside Washington. "I'm afraid," JFK later told Ben and Tony Bradlee over dinner, "neither of you made it."

Understandably, Jackie was smoking up a storm, and both she and Jack were leaning more heavily than ever on the good services of Dr. Feelgood. Now Max Jacobson, who had been greatly influenced by Swiss rejuvenation pioneer Dr. Paul Niehans, was adding animal cells to his injections—including placenta, bone, and liver cells. He did not volunteer the information to either the president or the first lady and, he later said, "they never asked."

Indeed, by mid-1962 the Kennedys had become so dependent on Jacobson's pick-me-ups that Jack, concerned that the press would eventually find out what the shady Dr. Feelgood was up to, repeatedly invited him to move into the White House. That way, the president reasoned, Jacobson could merely be described as a member of JFK's medical team and be more easily shielded from the press by the Secret Service.

Dr. Max declined to leave New York, where he numbered among his patients some four hundred multiple sclerosis sufferers. "I could never abandon them," explained Jacobson, who nevertheless continued to make himself available to JFK and Jackie virtually around the clock. Jacobson also refused the president's periodic attempts to pay him, claiming this was merely his way to pay back the adopted country he loved. After Max discovered several hundred-dollar bills a Secret Service agent had surreptitiously planted in his coat pocket, the doctor mailed the money back to JFK.

"They both had remarkable stores of energy," Chuck Spalding said, "but I doubt if they could have functioned at the level they did without Max's help. He was a crazy guy, and even then I worried about what he was doing. Max was also indispensable. They needed him."

Jack also needed close friends to confide in during this tense period, and Spalding was called more frequently than most. "He'd find me, wherever I was," Chuck said, "and call me up in the middle of the night. Just to relieve his tension, I guess. He would talk about anything from Voltaire to girls, always warm and funny."

While millions of frightened Americans emptied out supermarkets, practiced air raid drills, and flocked to churches to pray, Jackie tried to bolster her husband's spirits. Toward that end, she quickly threw together a small dinner party to take place immediately after Jack's ominous-sounding address to the nation.

"Jackie tried to be upbeat," said Oleg Cassini, one of the half-dozen guests. "But it was a tense evening." McGeorge Bundy drifted in several times, and when Jack got up to take a call, Cassini followed him. The president's mood was "detached, fatalistic." Yet Cassini was impressed with how his friend "refused to seem depressed or overwhelmed by the immensity of the moment."

Cassini was also among the guests at a dinner party the next evening, this one thrown together to substitute for a dinner dance that had originally been planned for the Maharaja and Maharani of Jaipur. This time, Jackie shuttled between her guests in the State Dining Room and the West Hall on the second floor, where JFK and David Ormsby-Gore, British ambassador to the United States, squatted on the floor, going over the latest missile photographs.

Once again, Cassini was impressed with Jack's air of "elegant fatalism. He believed, 'I'll do my best, in my style, and leave the rest to God.' Jack could be serious, even solemn, yet never defeated or deflated. He always had that spark, for want of a better word. This was equally true of Jackie."

The next morning—Wednesday, October 24—JFK was meeting with ExComm members when word came that Soviet cargo ships carrying missiles were turning back. "We're eyeball to eyeball," Secretary of State Dean Rusk said, "and I think the other fellow just blinked."

Jack remained cautious. The United States still had to find a way to remove the Soviet missiles already on the ground in Cuba. "Well," he said after one long puff on his cigar, "we still have twenty chances out of a hundred to still be at war with Russia."

Later, Oleg Cassini managed to get JFK alone for a few moments. "Mr. President," he asked, "are you saying war is still possible?"

"Oh yes," JFK replied without hesitation. "It's possible, all right."

Nevertheless, the world breathed a giant sigh of relief. Spalding was driving from Connecticut to his office in Manhattan when he heard the news on his car radio. He pulled over and called the White House from the first phone booth he could find. "You did it! You did it!" Spalding told Jack.

"So I trust," JFK said nonchalantly, "the boys on Wall Street are pleased as well." Spalding, like most of his countrymen, had been "sweating bullets" about the outcome. Yet "here the world had been pulled back from the brink of nuclear destruction, and he was calm enough to make that kind of casual, witty remark."

With events apparently still moving in the right direction, Jackie headed off for Glen Ora that Saturday to ride in the opening meet of the Orange County Hunt. Within hours of Jackie's departure, Mimi Beardsley arrived at the White House with her overnight bag—just in time for the crisis to take another dark turn.

That evening, Beardsley waited upstairs while JFK met with ExComm members. He managed to come up to the residence for a quick drink but "his expression was grave," Mimi said. "Even his quips had a half-hearted, funereal tone." After returning from one meeting, he told the college sophomore, "I'd rather my children be red than dead." She concluded that "these were the words of a father who adored his children and couldn't bear them being hurt."

That night, Jack did not join Mimi upstairs. Instead, he and Dave Powers unwound in the White House theater watching one of JFK's favorite films, 1953's *Roman Holiday*. Given Jack's fondness for action movies and westerns, the romantic comedy starring Gregory Peck and Audrey Hepburn seemed out of character. Kennedy had briefly dated Hepburn before he was married, but apparently that wasn't the main reason he screened *Roman Holiday* again and again. In her Oscar-winning American screen debut, the saucer-eyed, winsome Hepburn played a headstrong young princess who falls for an American reporter (Peck) during her one day of freedom in Rome. During another screening of the movie, Jack leaned over to Cassini and whispered, "Doesn't she remind you of Jackie?"

ONCE THE CRISIS WAS OVER, Jack searched for a way to thank the ExComm members and other advisers—Bundy, McNamara, Rusk, Gilpatric, Salinger, and so on—for going without sleep for days on end as they searched for a solution. JFK wanted them to know," he told Jackie, "how much it meant to have them stick by me." He decided on a sterling silver calendar showing the month of October with the recipient's initials and "J.F.K." in script at the top. The thirteen perilous days—October 16 through October 28—were highlighted.

Tish Baldrige took JFK's hand-drawn design to her old boss, Tiffany chairman Walter Hoving, who then went ahead and produced forty of the calendars. However, he refused JFK's request for a discount. "Never!" Hoving protested. "Abraham Lincoln tried to get a discount from Tiffany on a pearl necklace for his wife and we wouldn't do it. We never give discounts to presidents."

After the predictable blowup ("What? You tell that bastard Hoving . . ."), Jack paid for the calendars out of his own pocket. On the day they arrived Jackie discovered Jack had ordered one for her as well. Completely taken by surprise, she unwrapped it, placed it on the desk she had inherited from her father—and burst into tears.

In the wake of the Cuban Missile Crisis, Jack's popularity soared to an impressive 76 percent in the polls—enough to ensure a solid showing for the Democrats in the 1962 midterm elections. Among the six new Democratic senators: thirty-four-year-old Teddy Kennedy, who despite having no political experience and a tarnished past (he was expelled from Harvard for cheating), sailed to a lopsided two-to-one victory in Massachusetts.

With one son in the White House, another serving as U.S. attorney general, and now another in the U.S. Senate, Papa Joe's dreams of dynastic glory were being realized. Yet at the series of small get-togethers the Kennedys hosted to celebrate JFK's triumphs on both the world and domestic stages, Kennedy himself refused to gloat. Over dinner with the Bradlees, Jack downplayed the significance of his so-called victory over the Soviets. He predicted that a misstep between the two superpowers would inevitably lead to a war that would "wipe out all of us at this table and our children."

"Jack could make these grim statements with a twinkle in his eye," the Kennedys' friend George Plimpton said. "He meant what he was saying, but he also wasn't going to let it get in the way of his enjoyment of life."

Not even when it came to predicting the possible circumstances of his own death, which he did frequently. JFK believed assassination was "not unlikely," and that if it were to happen he would be shot "while riding in an open car through a downtown street, with all the people and the noise."

One Sunday JFK's Hyannis Port neighbor Larry Newman was sitting next to the president at Mass. Gesturing to the people sitting around him, Kennedy leaned over to Newman and asked nonchalantly, "Do you think if somebody tried to take a shot at me, they'd get one of you first?"

Newman swallowed hard. "No, Mr. President," he replied. "But now that I think of it, I won't be sitting with you next Sunday!"

"That's okay," JFK said with a grin, turning to look at the reporters seated just a few rows behind him. "I still have the press right behind me for protection."

Humor, Pierre Salinger said, was the Kennedys' "secret

weapon. The things they had already gone through could have made them both bitter, but they were as far from bitter as you can be. They both loved to laugh, and got a special kick out of kidding each other."

The first lady had a thin skin when it came to satire, however. Released that November, *The First Family*, comedian Vaughn Meader's send-up of the Kennedys, sold a breathtaking 7.5 million copies, making it the biggest comedy album of all time. Jackie hated *The First Family* because she thought it mocked her children, but Jack loved it, cracking at a press conference that he thought Meader's impersonation of his clipped Boston accent sounded "more like Teddy."

Nonetheless, Jackie took special pleasure in teasing her husband—friends knew this was about to happen when she started calling him "Bunny"—and was never more satisfied than when she could prick his often overinflated ego. "Where's that famous Kennedy wit I keep hearing so much about?" she asked. "We certainly don't see any of it around here."

In reality, the Kennedy wit was most in evidence when they were able to unwind in the company of their closest friends—the Bartletts, the Spaldings, the Radziwills, the Bradlees, Billings, Cassini, Walton, Smathers, Plimpton, and one or two others. This core group was essential because, Jackie explained, "being in the White House does make friendships difficult. Nobody feels the same. Jack's even more isolated than I am, so I do try to have a few friends for dinner as often as possible."

Letting their hair down, the Kennedys felt free, for example, to discuss the eighty-six positions of the *Kama Sutra* with Cassini. The designer and the president also talked "quite a lot about what makes a great lover, and how romantic personalities are different from erotic personalities."

"Well," JFK asked, "which am I?"

"Oh, you're definitely erotic," Cassini replied. "You could be right up there with the greats in history, like Don Juan and Casanova, because you have the physical attributes, and also the charm to seduce. The only thing you lack is the time. And of course, you're married."

JFK laughed. Jackie, seated just a few feet away, pretended not to hear.

Another game Jack and Oleg liked to play involved "zoomorphizing" the people they knew. Cassini was a Siamese cat, Bobby a basset hound, Joe an owl, a lawyer they knew "a complete toad." The president was a golden retriever or an Irish setter, and Jackie a fawn.

Gossip was the lifeblood of these cozy evenings, and both Jack and Jackie hung on every delicious morsel of scandal brought to them from the outside world. "Jack loved to hear what was going on in New York—who was going out with whom, the real gossip," said Spalding. One evening Spalding was perched on JFK's bathtub, rattling off one salacious tidbit after another while the president shaved.

Spalding was in the middle of one of his stories when, suddenly, Jack looked at him and put his index finger to his lips. "Then he reaches around the door," Spalding said, "and who does he pull in but Jackie."

"We had a deal," the president told her. "We wouldn't open each other's mail, we wouldn't listen in on each other's phone conversations, and we wouldn't eavesdrop on each other!"

Jackie, unchastened, simply looked them up and down. "Two

excited little schoolboys jabbering away about what's going on in New York," she said with a sigh. "It's pathetic."

"She's jealous," Jack told Chuck as Jackie waltzed off, "because I'm getting all the hot gossip *first*."

The first lady could be withering in her assessments of people, skewering journalists, social lions, and world leaders alike. She described Germany's revered postwar chancellor Konrad Adenauer as *un peu gaga* to André Malraux, derided Lyndon and Lady Bird Johnson as "Col. Cornpone and his little pork chop," pulled down her cheeks to imitate the droopy, basset countenance of British prime minister Harold Macmillan, and offered up devastating impersonations of Eleanor Roosevelt, Pat Nixon ("with her little frizzy permanent"), Richard Nixon ("poor, poor Dick"), Indira Gandhi ("a real prune—bitter, kind of pushy, just a horrible woman"), Dean Rusk ("such a timid man"), Hubert Humphrey, and J. Edgar Hoover—to name just a few. De Gaulle, whom she had once worshiped from afar, was now simply "that *egomaniac*." Even minor figures she encountered while traveling were not exempt: "Did you see Khrushchev's daughter in Vienna? She looked like some Wehrmacht blonde who ran a concentration camp!"

Gore Vidal, for one, couldn't have been more pleased. Jackie was, he recalled, "very malicious—but in the most enchanting, life-enhancing way. She had a very black humor. She hardly had anything good to say about anyone. Jack was very much the same way." Unwinding with their tight circle of friends, Vidal added, "the two of them were just *devastating* about everyone else, and when you left the room, you knew they'd be doing it to you, too. That was one of the reasons I liked them so much."

Baldrige agreed that, contrary to her ladylike persona, the first lady was a "natural comic" whose impersonations of world leaders in particular were uncannily accurate. "Imagine," Tish mused, "if any of her little performances ever got out at the time." Like Vidal, she had no delusions of immunity. "Are you kidding?" laughed the irrepressibly good-natured Tish. "I was one of their favorite targets!"

Their favorite targets, in fact, were each other. "She loved to needle him," Smathers said, "and he was pretty good at it, too." Whenever he could, Jack ribbed his wife about her friends ("those snobby bitches on Park Avenue"), her love of riding ("a sport that appeals to some awfully dull people") and of the Virginia horse country ("I love Camp David, Jackie, because it's *not* in Virginia!"), and her own social airs. ("Come off your high horse every once in a while, kid. You might like it down here with the rest of us.")

Jackie's digs often dealt with her husband's ego ("Tell the Marine Band to play 'Hail to the Chief.' He never gets tired of that"), his vanity ("I think Liberace looks in the mirror less often than Jack does"), and the Boston pols he had known for years ("Oh, there's Patsy 'the China Doll' Mulkern, who got his name because he was a boxer with a glass jaw, and 'Onions' Burke, and Jack's driver 'Muggsy' O'Leary, and 'Juicy' Grenara. . . . Gosh, Jack, are we living in a production of *Guys and Dolls*?").

Occasionally, she zeroed in on Jack's frat-boy obsession with the opposite sex. "Jack and I would be talking about how great some gal looked in a tight dress," Smathers remembered, "and sure enough Jackie would pop up out of nowhere." There would be the inevitable awkward attempt to change the subject, but Jackie just laughed. "I know what you were talking about," she'd say. "You guys will never grow up!"

Less good-natured were the spats Jackie and Jack had over

money. Each month Jackie's secretary, Mary Gallagher, handed over the first lady's bills to the president—and waited for him to explode. By the time the Bradlees sat down with the Kennedys for dinner in November 1962, Jackie was spending more than $120,000 a year (the equivalent of more than $1 million today)—a third of that on clothes.

Jackie's spending had her husband "boiling," said Ben Bradlee, who cringed with the Kennedys' other dinner guests while their hosts quarreled. Jack was "not so much mad, but amazed and indignant."

"Jackie, this has got to stop," he told her. "You're spending me into the poorhouse!"

Jackie argued, rather convincingly, that a U.S. ambassador's wife had an expense allowance paid for by the government, but the first lady had none. "At state dinners and when I travel, Jack, you want me to look good, don't you?" countered Jackie, who pointed out that Joe was still gladly paying for her Oleg Cassini wardrobe. "I mean, I am representing our country."

Much to the amusement of those who knew him, the president groused constantly about money—even though he had such little need for his $100,000 presidential salary that he donated the entire amount to charity. His $10 million personal fortune (roughly equal to $80 million today) meant he could easily afford to indulge Jackie's extravagant tastes. But from the onset of his administration, the press had zeroed in on Jackie's spending. "It was the Marie Antoinette thing," Plimpton said. "Jack really didn't know much about money because he never had to worry about it. But he did know about politics, and being perceived as having a rich wife who threw money around was going to cost him votes in the next election."

Of course, Jackie's fondness for haute couture wasn't the only problem. Perhaps to compensate for growing up as a poor relation of the Auchinclosses, Jackie also spent thousands each month on art and antiques. "If Jackie liked something," Mary Gallagher recalled, "she ordered it and coped with the bills later."

In the fall of 1962 there was something brand new for Jack to complain about. The lease on Glen Ora was up and the owners wanted to move back in—but only after the Kennedys paid to have Jackie's pricey redecorating job undone and the place restored to its original state of shabby chic.

Now Jackie was building her own hunt country retreat in Atoka, Virginia, on a secluded forty-acre parcel that abutted 1,400 acres owned by her wealthy friends Paul Mellon and Hubert Phipps. The actual site was called Rattlesnake Mountain, which struck Jackie as odd because, as she told Pierre Salinger, "there are no rattlesnakes and there's no mountain."

Jackie sketched out the design herself on drafting paper: a modest 3,500-square-foot ranch-style house of yellow stucco and fieldstone, with seven bedrooms, five and a half bathrooms, stables, a swimming pool, a small pond—and a sweeping view of the Blue Ridge Mountains.

At first, Jack was convinced that Wexford—the house was named after the Kennedy family seat in Ireland—could be brought in at or near the original $45,000 budget. By the time it was actually finished in November 1963, Wexford cost well over $100,000 to build.

As usual, Jackie pledged to curtail her spendthrift habits, and her husband retreated. "It was a little dance they did every now and then," Spalding said. "He'd blow up, make his point, then she'd apologize and he'd back down. If he didn't, Jack knew Jackie would sulk and he couldn't stand that."

IN THE WAKE OF THE Cuban Missile Crisis, Thanksgiving at Hyannis Port took on added meaning. "This was one of the Ambassador's favorite holidays," said Ham Brown, the Secret Service agent assigned to protect Papa Joe. At gatherings like this, the rest of the family—especially Jack—relied on what they believed was Brown's ability to interpret what Joe's "no no no's" meant. "Hell, I had no more idea of what Joe was saying than the man in the moon," Brown admitted. But when he had the chance, Brown usually told Jack and his brothers that the old man was looking forward to seeing them for dinner the next day. "Of course every father," Brown explained, "wants to have his family around for dinner."

Back at the Executive Mansion, children's birthday parties—Caroline's fifth and John's second—provided a welcome distraction the last week in November. At both events, Caroline and John blew out the candles on their birthday cakes with some help from Mom, and then tore into their presents. The Marine Band provided entertainment, and at one point John grabbed a pair of maracas and joined in. Once they finished playing with the toys, dolls, and coloring books they'd been given, everybody filed into the White House movie theater for an afternoon of cartoons.

The post-crisis euphoria spilled over into the Christmas season. The president and first lady went through all the motions in Washington—hosting a series of White House Christmas parties, lighting the national tree, sending out thousands of Christmas cards with a photo of Jackie, Caroline, and John on a sleigh drawn by Macaroni. But the family was eager to celebrate the holidays as they always had, in the warm Florida sunshine.

As they had the previous year, Jack and Jackie were renting the C. Michael Paul villa a mile up the road from Joe. While Jackie took the kids to see Santa Claus at Burdine's department store (Caroline asked for a talking Chatty Cathy doll, John for a toy helicopter), their father stayed up north and tended to some end-of-the-year business.

As he operated solo in Washington, much of what Jack was called on to do as the year wore down was ceremonial, and often fun. The day after Caroline's birthday party, he welcomed two of his more high-profile supporters in Hollywood, Judy Garland and Danny Kaye, to the White House. Garland, right at home, lit up a cigarette and posed for pictures perching on the corner of JFK's Oval Office desk. Two days later, the president attended the Army-Navy Game at Philadelphia's Municipal Stadium, sitting on the Navy side of the field and then, at halftime and with considerable fanfare, walking across the field to sit with the Army—all by way of showing the old Navy man's theoretical objectivity as commander in chief.

On December 15, 1962, the president sat down in the Oval Office for an unprecedented interview with correspondents for the three national networks—NBC, CBS, and ABC. Three days later, Jack and British prime minister Harold Macmillan were in the Bahamas, hashing out the merits of various nuclear weapons systems. For three days, the two allies were locked in tense negotiations. But Jack had his distractions—namely, Mimi Beardsley, ensconced by Dave Powers in her own luxurious villa at the exclusive Lyford Cay Club.

Four days before Christmas, Jackie took Caroline and John to surprise their father when he finally arrived back in Palm Beach aboard Air Force One. Just as JFK was about to climb into the presidential limousine, they jumped out of their hiding place and ran toward him shouting "Daddy! Daddy!" Grinning broadly, he took them both in his arms and they smothered him with kisses.

As usual, what followed were lazy days spent cruising aboard the *Honey Fitz*, sunbathing by the pool, Christmas shopping on Worth Avenue, and lunching with friends. There was one major difference this time: Jackie declined to give any of her usual daredevil water-ski exhibitions. In fact, for reasons that later became clear, she didn't water-ski at all.

On Christmas Eve, the Kennedys were joined by Lee and Stas (pronounced "Stash") Radziwill and their children, who all sat on the living room floor playing with Clipper the German shepherd and Charlie the wire-haired Welsh terrier while Jack carefully hung up everyone's stockings—nine in all—on the fireplace mantel. "It was like any family scene in any home in America on Christmas Eve," said White House photographer Cecil Stoughton, who captured it all on film. "The President and Mrs. Kennedy were so happy to be with the kids, and Caroline and John were like kids anywhere. It is painful to think that this was their last Christmas all together."

The next morning, everyone tore through the wrapping on their presents with abandon. Jack, in particular, made a point of ripping open presents with unvarnished glee and he instructed the children to do likewise. "It's half the fun," he once told Baldrige, who had her own methodical approach to unwrapping gifts. "Jesus, Tish," he complained as he watched her gently open gifts at an impromptu office party, "you're not disarming a bomb."

What was inside those packages, in the Kennedys' case, was usually something rare—and costly. When buying gifts for each other, Jackie and Jack took great care to come up with something unique. That Christmas, she had commissioned Milton Delano—a distant cousin of FDR—to etch a sperm whale's nine-inch molar with the presidential seal. This became the centerpiece of Jack's scrimshaw collection, proudly displayed in the Oval Office.

The president devoted just as much time and energy to finding the perfect gifts for his wife: a Renoir drawing of two nudes, and a painting by post-Impressionist master Maurice Prendergast titled *Summer Day in the Park*. As soon as they returned to Washington, Jackie hung the Prendergast in her bedroom.

The Cuban Missile Crisis had left Jack with one important piece of unfinished business. In return for the Soviets' withdrawing their missiles, JFK had promised not to invade Cuba. As part of the grand bargain, the United States would pay a ransom of $53 million in humanitarian aid for the safe return of the 1,113 Bay of Pigs fighters imprisoned by Castro.

Two days after Christmas, JFK invited five newly released leaders of the invasion force known as Brigade 2506 to the Paul mansion in Palm Beach. Jackie, in particular, was eager to have the children meet the "brave fighting men" she believed the United States had abandoned twenty months earlier.

On December 29, 1962, the president and first lady helicoptered to Miami Beach's Orange Bowl to join forty thousand Cuban exiles in welcoming home the freed soldiers. Jackie, who at this stage might have shied away from such a big event, had instead insisted on accompanying her husband. JFK had planned to read a carefully crafted, somewhat restrained speech, but when a Bay of Pigs veteran proudly presented him with Brigade 2506's battle-worn flag—hidden by a prisoner during his thirty months in captivity—JFK suddenly became emotional. "I can assure you," he told the cheering crowd, "that this flag will be returned to this brigade in a free Havana!"

Translating her husband's stirring words into flawless Spanish, Jackie once again had the crowd hanging on her every word. Then, speaking without notes, she added heartfelt remarks of her own. "It is an honor to stand here today," she began in Spanish, "with some of the bravest men in the world—and to share in the joy of their families who have hoped and prayed and waited so long . . ." When she was done, the spectators, many of whom were openly weeping, burst into cheers and thunderous applause.

The first couple then climbed into a white Lincoln convertible and waved to the throng as they drove out of the stadium. "You were wonderful, Jackie," the president told her. "They loved you. Your remarks were just perfect."

JACKIE SCORED ANOTHER INTERNATIONAL TRIUMPH less than two weeks later, when the most famous painting in the world, the 460-year-old *Mona Lisa,* was unveiled at Washington's National Gallery of Art. Thanks to Jackie's warm relationship with both de Gaulle and French minister of culture André Malraux, the French government was allowing Leonardo da Vinci's masterpiece to leave the Louvre on one condition—that it be loaned not to an American museum, but personally to the president.

Shipped in a climate-controlled, bulletproof crate and occupying its own stateroom aboard the luxury liner SS *France,* *La Gioconda* had arrived in the United States in late December. On January 8, after attending a dinner for one hundred at the

French Embassy, JFK and Jackie joined some 1,200 invited guests at the National Gallery. When the elevator to the second floor of the gallery got stuck, Jackie, dressed in a Cassini strapless mauve silk chiffon gown glistening with crystal beads, could only make it up the stairs with an uncomfortable Clint Hill holding her short train—like, the Secret Service agent recalled, "an attendant at a wedding."

Once the president and first lady arrived, the reception quickly devolved into chaos. In the crush of guests and photographers, it became evident that Jackie—not the *Mona Lisa* or even JFK—was the real star of the evening.

Three days after upstaging Leonardo, Jackie was in the middle of dictating a letter to her secretary, Mary Gallagher, when she came to an abrupt halt. She wanted to know if Gallagher thought she'd done enough as first lady. She needn't have waited for an answer; even with her frequent absences from the White House to spend time with her horses and her children, Jackie already ranked as one of the most activist first ladies in U.S. history.

Jackie called Tish Baldrige to the West Sitting Room and declared, "I am taking the veil!" From now on, she was going to cut back dramatically on her official duties and devote more time to her family. "Semi-official" trips abroad, ship launchings, press luncheons were to be back-burnered. And while Jackie claimed she would only perform those official duties her husband deemed essential, Baldrige knew that meant "she was going to do what she wanted to do. The President, bless his heart, really couldn't force her to do anything if she didn't want to."

Neither Gallagher nor Baldrige knew the reasons behind Jackie's decision to scale back her workload, although Provi the maid had already guessed: Jackie was pregnant. The baby was due the first week in September, and she intended to keep her pregnancy under wraps as long as possible.

Her self-described "declaration of independence" aside, Jackie's schedule was more packed than ever in the early months of 1963. In the span of a few weeks, she and Jack dined at the Washington homes of Franklin Roosevelt Jr., the Douglas Dillons, and the Joe Alsops, then went to New York to catch the hit satirical revue *Beyond the Fringe* and attend parties thrown in their honor by Adlai Stevenson and former U.S. ambassador to Cuba Earl Smith. (Smith's wife, former model turned society queen bee Florence Pritchett, had dated JFK when he was a young senator and remained one of Jack's closest female friends.)

Flush with the excitement of having another child on the way, Jackie and JFK took full advantage of their weekend in New York. Trailed by their Secret Service detail, they strode up and down Park Avenue on their way to and from favorite haunts like Voisin and Le Pavillon. With the Carlyle as their base, Jackie and Caroline had managed to walk up and down the streets of Manhattan's Upper East Side without drawing a crowd. Even the president was able to take his daughter on a stroll through Central Park. Rather than using the Carlyle's front entrance, they sneaked out a service door on East Seventy-seventh Street, directly opposite the tony Finch College for Women (which Richard Nixon's daughter Tricia would soon be attending). Unnoticed, JFK and Caroline were then able to enjoy a rare treat, laughing and chatting as they walked hand in hand through one of the world's most famous public spaces.

Caroline's parents cherished such stolen moments of privacy.

But they remained the exception to the pomp- and ceremony-filled rule. To a state dinner honoring Lyndon Johnson and Chief Justice Earl Warren on January 21, Jackie wore a citron yellow chiffon-and-satin gown inspired, she said, by the turbans she had seen on her trip to India. Weeks later, it was black silk chiffon and pearls for a state dinner honoring Venezuelan president Rómulo Betancourt.

From the moment they learned she was pregnant, both Jackie and the president were understandably concerned that, once again, she might lose the baby. There were now days when, overcome with exhaustion, she would lie down for a nap and sleep for twelve hours straight. As the first lady entered her third month, only a handful of people—Joe and Rose Kennedy, Clint Hill and one or two other key Secret Service agents—were let in on the secret. Jackie's own mother, the talkative Janet Auchincloss, was not.

Jackie had already given up water-skiing and riding, replacing her workouts astride Sardar, Bit of Irish, and Rufus with long, brisk walks. Nothing too taxing, of course—and nothing like the torture her husband had in mind for their friends.

Even before he was sworn in as president, Jack railed in speeches and articles against the new "generation of spectators" who had replaced strenuous exercise with long hours spent staring at the television set. To get these "soft Americans" back on the road to fitness—literally—he resurrected a 1908 memo from then-president Theodore Roosevelt to his Marine Corps commandant instructing corps officers to stay in shape by periodically hiking fifty miles in less than twenty hours.

Soon Americans everywhere were taking the president and TR up on the challenge. JFK himself was in no condition to do any such thing; his back pain in early 1963 was so excruciating he told the Bradlees he'd prefer the pain of childbirth. But he still wanted a member of his administration to march alongside the Marines. "Unfortunately," said the rotund, cigar-smoking Pierre Salinger, "he kept looking at *my* waistline."

Salinger played along for a while, until finally bowing out on the grounds that, as he put it, "if I went I would be dead—serious!" The man closest to JFK had already proven himself up to the task. While Jackie and Jack were traipsing around Manhattan, Bobby Kennedy hiked fifty miles up the Chesapeake & Ohio Canal straight to Camp David—and in only eighteen hours.

The previous Christmas, JFK had bet Stas Radziwill and Chuck Spalding a thousand dollars they could never finish the hike. Jack's sister Eunice Shriver upped the ante by another thousand, with everyone agreeing that the winners would donate the money to charity. Now that Bobby had successfully completed the hike, Jack was more determined than ever to have his band of hikers follow through.

Sibling rivalry, Kennedy-style, was now in play as Radziwill and Spalding began their hike along the new Sunshine Parkway from Palm Beach to Miami at 2 a.m. on February 23. To ensure their safety, Clint Hill was enlisted to hike alongside them. "Bobby had hiked through the woods," Spalding said, "and Jack didn't want to be shown up by his little brother." The event quickly took on a life of its own, and soon Radziwill and Spalding were inundated with sneakers sent to them by well-meaning strangers from around the country.

Although it was going to cost him and his sister two thousand dollars, JFK was determined that his friends beat Bobby's time. To ensure that, he sent along Dr. Max Jacobson—whose Constructive Research Foundation stood to get the money if Stas and Chuck won—to look after the middle-aged hikers. In addition to oxygen, Jacobson was, said Spalding, "giving us shots all over the place."

Jackie and Lee drove out periodically to check on their progress, and the president interrupted a cruise aboard the *Honey Fitz* to rendezvous with his hikers when they reached Pompano Beach—the thirty-five-mile mark. While Stas and Chuck sprawled on the grass, the president drove up in his white Lincoln Continental to deliver a "pep talk. Mainly," Spalding said, "Jack was worried about Stas having a heart attack and told him he could quit if he wanted to." Radziwill declined, and the trio made it to the finish line in Fort Lauderdale at 9:35 p.m.—fifteen minutes ahead of Bobby's time.

Along the way, they weren't exactly roughing it. All three men took frequent smoking breaks, and whenever the mood struck them they called for the Secret Service to deliver ice, steaks, and even champagne and orange juice to make mimosas. Once it was over, a limousine picked them all up and drove them to Palm Beach, "where," Spalding said, "Jack had a big buffet waiting for us and champagne, and the jukebox was playing 'Bei Mir Bist Du Schoen' by the Andrews Sisters."

"Congratulations!" Jack said as he hung a "medal" made of purple construction paper around each hiker's neck. These medallions were inscribed with a personal message from JFK, who boasted with a wink that he had even drawn a presidential seal on each one "to make it official." (Back at the White House, Salinger gleefully accepted an award from his press office staff for *not* hiking fifty miles.)

The fifty-mile hike down Florida's Sunshine Parkway made front-page news across the country, but it seemed doubtful that it could have been accomplished without the help of Dr. Max. "What people didn't know," Spalding said, "was that with all that speed we could've walked all the way to Rio, we were so hyped up!"

Spalding also noticed during this time in Palm Beach what he called a "sea change" in the outward relationship between the president and his wife. "They were as happy as I'd ever seen them," he said, "and they were much more affectionate toward each other. We couldn't put our finger on what was up exactly . . . because none of us knew at the time that Jackie was pregnant."

There were other, subtle signs that changes might be afoot. On March 8, 1963, Jackie and Jack gave what would be the last of their now-famous White House dinner dances—this one for World Bank chief Eugene Black. With music provided by society bandleader Lester Lanin in the softly lit Blue Room and fireplaces roaring in the Green Room and the Red Room, the Executive Mansion was, recalled Tish Baldrige, "everything I believed Jackie ever hoped it could be when she first set foot inside—an elegant, inviting home brimming over with life."

Perhaps a little too much life. As with many of the Kennedys' bashes, this one had its bacchanalian moments. The girlfriend of JFK's Air Force aide, General Godfrey McHugh, reportedly took a dip in the White House pool and then went upstairs to the residence to jump on Abraham Lincoln's bed. When word reached the president the next day, he was not amused. "Get after McHugh," he told Jackie, who had actually dated McHugh before she met Jack.

The March 8, 1963, dinner dance was memorable for more than just hijinks. One of the guests that night was Mary Meyer, who by late 1962 had become a fixture at the White House. "She was almost part of the furniture," recalled White House counsel Myer Feldman. "I would see her in the Oval Office or over in the residence. There wasn't any attempt to hide her the way there was with some of the other women."

For over a year, Meyer had occupied a special place in the hierarchy of Jack's women. "He was certainly smitten by her," Charlie Bartlett allowed. "Heavily smitten." Yet the same bohemian spirit that made Meyer irresistible to him also gave Jack pause. "Mary would be rough to live with," he suggested to Ben Bradlee more than once, and, more than once, Bradlee agreed.

At one point at the last dinner dance, Jack looked out over the sea of beautiful women on the dance floor, turned to Bradlee, and sighed, "If you and I could only run wild, Benjy." Bradlee, who claimed to be unaware of JFK's shenanigans at the time, took that as nothing more than a nostalgic reference to their bachelor days. In retrospect, George Plimpton later theorized, "Jack was admitting that he couldn't 'run wild' any more and risk hurting Jackie. And certainly not while she was pregnant. They were both terrified she'd lose the baby, and of course he would do anything to keep that from happening."

LATER THAT EVENING, JACK CORNERED Mary and they disappeared together for a heart-to-heart conversation. Despite the freezing temperatures outside, she had chosen to wear a frilly chiffon summer dress that had belonged to her great-grandmother, instantly setting herself apart from the other women in the room. When she and the president were finished talking, an anguished Meyer wandered out onto the snow-covered South Lawn in her flimsy dress, then fled the party on the verge of tears.

It is unlikely that Jackie had delivered an ultimatum to her husband, demanding that he break off his relationship with Meyer—

since Marilyn Monroe's death, the only "other woman" Jack seemed to have any real feelings for. There was no need. Jackie's pregnancy had changed everything.

That same evening at the White House, she turned to Adlai Stevenson and, without revealing that she was expecting, hinted that things might be different inside her marriage. "I don't care how many girls Jack has," she told the stunned Adlai, "as long as I know *he* knows it's wrong, and I think he does now. Anyway," Jackie added, looking across the crowded room at her husband, "that's all over, for the present."

⚹

I know my husband was devoted to me. I know he was proud of me.
It took a very long time for us to work everything out, but we did.

—JACKIE

⚹

9

❧

"*You're* My Ideal, Jacqueline"

"John, slow down now. You've got to behave. Watch where you're going, John!" Maud Shaw's pleas fell on deaf ears as the headstrong two-year-old darted at his customary break-neck speed across the lawn toward Daddy's office. The nanny reached out, but before she could grab him, the boy stumbled and banged his mouth on a concrete step. A bloody tooth went flying, and John collapsed on the grass in tears. Nanny Shaw finally managed to calm the toddler down when, suddenly, John jumped up and dove into the bushes. He emerged holding the incisor, which he then proudly showed off—along with his new gap-toothed grin—to Secret Service agents, cabinet members, and anyone else he came across that day.

John had to wait until his father got home before he could show him the wayward baby tooth; when all the commotion occurred outside his office, the president was busy delivering his third State of the Union speech to a joint session of Congress. History re-peated itself just two weeks later when John broke another tooth while playing in the Kennedy children's treehouse. This time Jack was in the Oval Office and rushed outside to comfort the boy.

As he looked forward to the birth of another child, Jack seemed more besotted than ever with the two he already had. He was so eager to communicate with John, for example, that when the boy was only ten months old his father demanded to know why it was taking him so long to learn to talk.

"Oh, but he does talk, Mr. President," Maud Shaw answered. "It's just that you can't understand him."

"That's right, Daddy," Caroline chimed in. "He does talk to me." JFK decided that, from then on, Caroline would serve as the president's official interpreter of John-speak.

The Kennedys' dinner guests often availed themselves of Caroline's services. "John-John has a big thing about coming up to you and whispering a lot of gibberish in your ear," Ben Bradlee said at the time. "If you throw your head back and act surprised, John-John roars with laughter until he drools."

Bradlee was impressed with the way "John-John and JFK quite simply just break each other up. Kennedy likes to laugh and likes to make people laugh, and his son is the perfect foil for him."

Jack couldn't resist teasing the boy. "So how're you doing, Sam?" he would ask John-John nonchalantly when he toddled into the room.

"I'm not Sam, I'm John."

"What was that, Sam?"

"No, no, no," John answered. "I'm not Sam. I'm John. John, John, JOHN!"

"Oh, sorry, Sam."

Vacations in Palm Beach, at Hyannis Port, and at Hammersmith Farm gave father and son even more opportunities for mischief. A favorite spot to swim near Hammersmith Farm was the swimming pool at Bailey's Beach in Newport. There, according to Jamie Auchincloss, his two-year-old nephew often jumped off the low diving board into the deep end with no one there to catch him—sending suited-up members of the Kiddie Detail scrambling to pull him out. Other times, John would ask for help to climb up the ladder to the high diving board, and go "racing off the board to ten feet of free fall. His father was often there to catch him."

As John climbed up the ladder one day, the president reached up and yanked his swim trunks down, exposing the boy's derriere.

"Daddy," John protested as he pulled his swimsuit up. "You are a bad man!"

John turned and resumed his climb up the stairs, only to have his father pull down his trunks a second time. "Daddy," said the toddler, now seething with righteous indignation, "you are a poo-poo head!"

Feigning outrage, JFK lowered his voice. "John," he said, "no one calls the President of the United States a poo-poo head."

Father and son were "really great pals," White House photographer Cecil Stoughton said. "Little John was so endearing. His father couldn't get enough of him."

It was typical for John to wander in and out of the West Wing, and the president "really didn't try very hard to get rid of him," Salinger said. "He liked having John around." George Smathers believed his friend JFK "could not deny that boy anything. If the President was having a cabinet meeting or talking to some head of state, it didn't matter—he'd stop everything if John came skipping into the Oval Office."

Ted Sorensen remembered John lingering at one breakfast meeting attended by Pierre Salinger, Arthur Schlesinger, and Mc-George Bundy. "After shaking hands and bowing all around, John took over a proffered chair and very nearly took over the meeting," Sorensen said. "His father's suggestions to leave, accompanied by bribes to take him to the office later, were loudly resisted. Deciding to ignore him, the President opened his request for questions with the usual, 'What have we got today?' "

John answered immediately. "I've got a glass of water," he proclaimed.

On those rare occasions when John was barred from the Oval Office, he didn't handle it well. While JFK tried to pin down Soviet foreign minister Andrei Gromyko on such critical issues as Cuba and the Berlin Wall, a frustrated John stood outside the door shouting "Gromyko! Gromyko!" until he was led away by Maud Shaw.

To the White House press corps, there was no more familiar sight than John waiting impatiently on the South Lawn for his father's helicopter to land. The president would then climb down the helicopter steps and stretch out his arms to greet his son—only to have John dash straight past him toward the chopper.

By early 1963, whenever Marine One landed to whisk the president away, John would plead, "Daddy, please don't leave me." It wasn't long before Jack started taking the boy with him to Andrews Air Force Base, then kissing him goodbye before he was choppered back to the White House.

There were times when Jack couldn't take the boy along to Andrews, and on one of those occasions the president reached into his pocket and pulled out a tiny plastic plane. "Here's a toy airplane for you until I get back," he told John. "You fly this one, son, and as soon as you grow up Daddy's going to buy you a real one."

As much as John liked his plastic plane, his favorite plaything was the toy helicopter he got for Christmas. White House photographer Cecil Stoughton guided John's hand as the boy wrote his name on the toy. "It was," Stoughton said decades later, "his first autograph."

Even when there were no helicopters around, John amused himself by pretending to be one. Arms extended and imitating the sound of a rotor, the boy spun around until he toppled over, giggling, from dizziness. Soon the president had a new nickname for his frisky son: Helicopter Head.

There were quieter, more private moments between JFK and his son. Jack would take John to the hangar where Marine One was parked and, said Maud Shaw, sit "patiently inside the helicopter, putting the helmet on John and showing him how things work, moving gadgets for him just like a big boy." Soon "Captain John" was in the pilot's seat, confidently issuing orders to the president—orders that JFK convincingly pretended to obey.

On the afternoon of March 28, 1963, Jack summoned Stoughton to the West Wing. When Stoughton arrived, his boss was already on the terrace outside the Oval Office. Caroline and John, wearing the matching red winter outfits their mother had picked out for them, were dashing between Daddy's legs, "laughing and giggling," Stoughton recalled. "Nothing got to John and Caroline like the Tunnel Game. The President would squeeze his knees together and trap them, then give them a pat on their behinds as they squirmed through. They were in hysterics by the time he was finished with them."

Later JFK sat on the steps with his son for a few minutes, playing with a toy palomino pony John had been given for Christmas. Then the president walked Caroline and John back toward his office. Before they went inside, the trio turned around and posed for Stoughton. Jack, clutching both children's hands, grinned broadly.

Suddenly Stoughton's job—and those of photographers like Jacques Lowe and Stanley Tretick—had gotten a little easier. "Mrs. Kennedy seemed a little more relaxed about having the children photographed," said Stoughton, whose photographs captured a father clearly besotted with his children. "He really came to understand them and he played with them in that marvelous way that some people have and others don't." To Stoughton, it seemed JFK "was enjoying them even more now, if that was possible. Obviously, he was excited about the new baby, although at the time none of us knew about it."

Jackie knew that her husband was hoping for another boy, although he would never admit it. Certainly his bond with Caroline was stronger than it had ever been. He also was counting on her to help Maud Shaw keep John in line. "Now, Buttons," JFK told Caroline, "you're the big sister. You outrank John, so don't let him forget who's boss."

It wasn't easy. "A lot of the time," Evelyn Lincoln recalled, Caroline "talked about her brother misbehaving. That was a favorite topic of hers." Rose Kennedy's secretary, Barbara Gibson, recalled that Caroline was "always after him, 'John, do this' and 'You're not supposed to do that, John.' " After one particular sleigh ride at the White House, Caroline dashed off a note to Grandma Rose complaining that her brother was a "bad, squeaky boy who tries to spit in his mother's Coca-Cola and who has a very bad temper."

☙

THAT TEMPER WAS IN EVIDENCE whenever John, who had a tough time pronouncing "Caroline," felt he was being upstaged by "Cannon." One week Caroline pestered half the White House staff with the riddles she had learned from friends at school. It was only a matter of time before John piped up with, "Miss Shaw, I know a riddle, too."

"Yes, John," she said, "and what's your riddle?"

John thought for a moment before shouting, "Um . . . apples, giraffes, and alligators!"

Miss Shaw gave it some thought. "I'm afraid you've stumped me," she answered. Delighted, John ran to tell Caroline the news.

Only one thing troubled JFK about his son's upbringing at this point. The saga of PT-109 and Kennedy's own World War II exploits notwithstanding, he told Stoughton he was worried about what impact all the parades, wreath-layings, color guards, and twenty-one-gun salutes were having on his son. "I'm concerned about John's fascination with military things," JFK said. "He's right there when he sees guns, swords, or anyone wearing a uniform."

"Why don't you just stop letting him watch the parades?" Stoughton asked.

That, of course, was not about to happen. "I guess we all go through that phase," the president mused. "John just sees more of the real thing."

This sudden concern on JFK's part may have been a direct result of his staring down the barrel at Armageddon during the Cuban Missile Crisis. "Like a lot of men of his generation who had been to war," journalist Theodore White observed, "Kennedy hated to see it glorified." Ironically, it was Jackie who made sure John got a ringside seat for the marches and military ceremonies. "She'd come outside and stand behind the bushes and hold him up," Baldrige said, "just so he could get a clear view."

NOW THAT SHE WAS WELL into her second trimester, Jackie cut her official schedule down to only one evening event for the entire month of March 1963—a state dinner on March 27 for thirty-three-year-old King Hassan II of Morocco. Hassan, who wore his white dress uniform, presented JFK with a gold sword encrusted with diamonds. Jackie, dressed for the occasion in a floor-length white silk gown embroidered with colored gemstones, was enthralled with the dashing monarch and would later write a five-page letter to him in French promising to visit Morocco.

In the meantime, the Kennedys provided their visitors with one of the more memorable evenings at the White House. At dinner JFK pointed out in his toast that Morocco was the first country to recognize the United States, and he read George Washington's thank-you letter to Morocco's ruler.

JFK's Harvard classmate and friend Alan Jay Lerner had imported the entire cast of his hit Broadway musical *Brigadoon* to entertain that evening, and Tish Baldrige had prepared for every eventuality. Because of the limited space in the East Room, taped music was used in lieu of the Marine Band. When the president expressed concern that the tape might break, Tish reassured him that a backup tape would be running at the same time.

All went smoothly until the halfway mark, when an extra spotlight was turned on and blew a fuse, thrusting the East Room into total darkness. A dozen Secret Service agents drew their guns and rushed to every exit and window. The president, unable to see his hand in front of his face, leaned in the direction of his guest of honor. "Your Majesty," he whispered reassuringly, "it's part of the show, you know."

Once the lights came back on two minutes later, the first lady glanced over at her husband—and winked. She knew it wasn't the first time the president had been called upon to calm his guests. The year before, Metropolitan Opera singers were performing Mozart's *Così Fan Tutte* for the children of diplomats when the feathered turban worn by one of the stars touched a wall sconce and burst into what Baldrige described as a "towering mass of flame." A fire extinguisher took care of the problem within seconds, but even though the president threw his arms around the terrified children, they kept crying. So, Baldrige said, JFK "burst out laughing . . . [and] with the sight of the President laughing and laughing, well, they started laughing too, and soon the whole room was laughing."

By April 1, the Kennedys had moved out of Glen Ora, and Wexford, their new Virginia hideaway at Rattlesnake Mountain, was nearing completion. Her supply of large yellow legal pads always at the ready, Jackie spent the next few weeks jotting notes about everything from plumbing fixtures and doorknobs to room colors, draperies, furniture, and landscaping. From this point on, Jackie, aware that the name "Rattlesnake Mountain" might give her husband's detractors some ammunition in the coming 1964 elections, called the site Atoka after the hamlet where it was situated.

While construction continued apace in Virginia, Jackie looked around for another spot secluded enough to serve as a weekend retreat. For whatever reason, Jackie and Jack had both shied away from using FDR's old Navy-operated refuge, Shangri-La—which Dwight Eisenhower later renamed Camp David after his grandson—convinced that the 125-acre compound would not be to their liking. "Jack always said, 'It's the most depressing-looking place,' " Jackie recalled, "which it is—from the outside."

For two years, JFK's naval aide Taz Shepard kept "pestering and pestering him to go there," Jackie said. "And Tish used to say to me, 'The Navy's so hurt and demoralized he won't go there.' " Another strong advocate for Camp David was Clint Hill, who tried for years to persuade Jackie to give Camp David a try.

On the spur of the moment in March 1963, they finally went— and Jackie was surprised to discover Camp David offered everything they had been looking for in the way of a family retreat. Laced with hiking and riding trails winding through the scenic Catoctin Mountains, Camp David boasted a swimming pool, a bowling alley, skeet-shooting facilities, and both a driving range and a putting green.

The main residence, a rambling timber-and-stone structure called Aspen Lodge, was surrounded by several luxuriously appointed guest cabins with names like Hickory, Rosebud, and Dogwood. Once Jackie explored the premises, she was pleased—and perhaps a little embarrassed—to discover that, without her having to ask, new stables had been constructed specifically for Macaroni and Sardar.

Through the spring of 1963, as they waited for Wexford to be completed, the first family spent nearly every available weekend at Camp David. From this point seventy miles northwest of Washington, the inveterate history buffs embarked with Caroline and John on tours of great Civil War battlefields. One weekend, they piled in Jack's white Lincoln convertible and drove to Gettysburg. The next, they were off to Antietam by helicopter.

Sticking to her decision to stay off horses during her pregnancy, Jackie spent the first week of April with her husband and children at the White House. On April Fools' Day, the president took a break from hammering out the details of a proposed Nuclear Test Ban Treaty with the Russians and went looking for his children on the White House grounds. He wandered down to the children's playground and found Caroline and John picnicking in the noonday sun. Three days later, with the orange-red tulips outside the South Lawn already in bloom, Jackie invited several children from the White House School to swim with Caroline and John in the South Lawn fountain. When John refused to come out, the first lady kicked off her shoes and waded into the fountain to retrieve him.

Such happy family scenes were repeated in Palm Beach, where the Kennedys would once again spend the Easter holiday. Jackie flew out first, and when JFK arrived in Florida the next day aboard Air Force One she rushed up to greet him with hugs and kisses. "She thought they were way out of camera range, so it wasn't for our benefit," said one reporter. "There was obviously a genuine warmth between them that we hadn't seen that often before—they were such private people. . . . A lot of us got the feeling something was up."

Wearing the sleeveless Lily Pulitzer dresses JFK had bought for them on Worth Avenue, Jackie and Caroline showed John how to color Easter eggs; Mom and Maud Shaw stashed the eggs around the house for the children to find. Later, the first family was photographed coming out of Easter services at vine-covered St. Edward's Church. But for the second time since the family patriarch suffered a stroke, they also attended a private Mass with Joe at the ambassador's estate, La Guerida.

The president never attended one of the famous Easter egg

rolls on the White House lawn, but he and Jackie did take their children to an Easter egg hunt at the Wrightsman estate that morning. John found a gold egg, which he proceeded to carry around with him for the rest of the day.

That afternoon, JFK was relaxing on the deck of the *Honey Fitz* with Red Fay when they spotted a catamaran with *Pattycake* emblazoned across its stern. "Let's have some fun," he told Fay. Ten minutes later the president was at the tiller, steering the catamaran into open water while *Pattycake*'s beaming owner looked on.

Jackie's pregnancy remained a tightly guarded secret, but she was starting to make coy remarks here and there: "My bust is bigger than yours, but then so is my waist," she told a bewildered Tony Bradlee over dinner. At the same dinner party, Jackie abruptly switched gears and began teasing her husband about his fondness for Ben Bradlee's wife. "Oh, Jack, you know you always say Tony is your ideal." The president went along with the joke— "Yes, that's true"—before looking into his wife's eyes and suddenly turning serious. "*You're* my ideal, Jacqueline," he said.

The occasional obtuse hint aside, Jackie managed, in every sense of the word, to keep her condition under wraps. So it came as a jarring surprise to the Washington press corps and to the nation when Jackie made the official announcement from Palm Beach on April 15, the day after Easter. A simultaneous statement from Pierre Salinger further explained that, on the advice of her doctors, Jackie was canceling her official schedule.

Only once before—when Grover Cleveland's daughter Esther was born in 1893—had the wife of a president given birth while her husband was still in office. (Esther retained the honor of being the only baby actually born *in* the White House.) Esther Cleveland was now sixty-eight years old, married to a retired

British army officer and living in Yorkshire. The press wasted no time hunting the hapless woman down and peppering her with questions.

One of the first congratulatory notes Jackie read in Palm Beach was from Roswell Gilpatric, the patrician New York lawyer who now served as defense secretary Robert McNamara's deputy. The first lady made no effort to conceal her affection for the fifty-seven-year-old, Yale-educated Gilpatric, and their flirtatious behavior over the past two years had not gone unnoticed by the president or by Madelin Gilpatric, the third of Ros's five wives. "They were certainly very, very close," said Madelin, who would file for divorce in 1970 over her husband's unflagging devotion to Jackie. "Just say it was a particularly close, warm, long-lasting relationship."

NOW THAT SHE WAS CLEARING her calendar ("No more ladies' lunches!"), Jackie looked forward to a few more days in Palm Beach before moving on to spend the summer in Hyannis. She went ahead with plans to be at the White House for the state visit of Luxembourg's Grand Duchess Charlotte, in part because Caroline had been teaching her brother how to bow for their royal visitor.

To guarantee success, Maud Shaw promised both children cookies and ginger ale as a reward after they greeted the grand duchess. Unfortunately, just as Jackie was introducing her son to Grand Duchess Charlotte, John threw a major tantrum. He fell to the floor and remained there, motionless.

"John," Jackie said, "get up this minute."

The boy refused to budge.

Jackie turned to an aide. "Would you ask Miss Shaw to come in?" she sighed.

The chagrined nanny came to Jackie's rescue, scooping John up and whisking him away. "Now what on earth did you do that for?" she asked John. "That's not being my big boy, is it?"

"But Miss Shaw," he tried to explain, "they didn't give me my cookie."

Caroline, in the meantime, rolled her eyes with mortification, then executed a perfect curtsy. Later, she enjoyed her reward in front of her brother. "You were very naughty, John," Caroline said with a wag of her finger. "*That's* why you don't get a cookie."

Nureyev and Fonteyn almost put JFK to sleep, but he was eager to see the dance recital Caroline's White House kindergarten class staged that May. Caroline's mom came up with the concept—a tribute to White House chef René Verdon—and even designed the costumes: paper toques blanches and leotards. Jack's "Buttons" stepped boldly out front while a chorus line of youngsters danced holding serving trays from the pantry. For part of the show, Jackie rested her head on the president's shoulder. When the curtain came down, he led the packed house in a standing ovation.

Jackie had plenty of time to devote to her children, but she stuck to her pledge to sharply curtail her schedule. The fact that she was not the only pregnant Kennedy further complicated matters for Tish Baldrige. When a thousand Sacred Heart alumnae showed up for a White House tour, Tish scrambled to find someone to greet them.

"I promised them a Kennedy wife," she told JFK over the phone. Ethel was eight months pregnant (again) and felt too uncomfortable to leave Hickory Hill. When Jack suggested Joan, Tish reminded him that she, too, was pregnant—"two months along and suffering from morning sickness."

With Ethel, Jackie, and Joan all pregnant at the same time, the president had no choice but to do the job himself. "I know you wanted to meet one of the Kennedy wives," he explained, "but they're all expecting babies, as you may know. . . . My sisters may all be expecting as well," he cracked, "I don't know. Don't quote me on that."

Around the same time, Alan Jay Lerner and singer Eddie Fisher (both fellow patients of Max Jacobson) teamed up to produce a forty-sixth birthday extravaganza for their friend the president. Like the previous year's memorable Madison Square Garden party, this one at New York's Waldorf-Astoria was a celebrity-packed Democratic Party fund-raiser. Unlike the previous year, Jackie was there.

A markedly more tame affair, the gala featured Ed Sullivan and famed trial lawyer Louis Nizer dancing in a chorus line, as well as appearances by boxing legend Sugar Ray Robinson, *The Music Man* star Robert Preston, and actor Tony Randall. With Marilyn Monroe's forty-fifth-birthday rendition of "Happy Birthday" still fresh in the public's mind, everyone breathed a sigh of relief when the unfailingly classy Audrey Hepburn serenaded the president. (It would be decades before it was revealed that Hepburn had also briefly been one of JFK's lovers, before he married Jacqueline Bouvier.)

Before anyone had the chance to get too comfortable, Fisher's then-girlfriend, Ann-Margret, took the stage. The redheaded bombshell had just bounced and slithered her way through the film version of her Broadway hit *Bye Bye Birdie,* and now that she was only a few feet away from JFK she was determined to out-Marilyn Marilyn. "Ann-Margret did this provocative dance right in front of Kennedy,"

Fisher recalled. "People remember Marilyn's incredibly suggestive song, but Ann-Margret just buried that. She was so bold."

As for the first lady: "Jackie was sitting right next to the President, smiling," Fisher said, "but I don't think she meant it." There was an important difference this time: Ann-Margret was not having an affair with JFK.

On his actual birthday, Jack proudly received the George Washington Medal as Father of the Year in the Oval Office. Coincidentally, May 29, 1963, was also Tish Baldrige's last day on the job.

The social secretary's decision to leave had been a long time coming, spurred on by Jackie's refusal to cooperate. To be sure, Jackie did agree to attend a dinner for Indian president Sarvepalli Radhakrishnan the first week in June. But in the meantime, she skipped a number of commitments, including the annual congressional wives' brunch in early May. Doctor's orders, Jackie claimed, although the morning papers were filled with photos of her attending a ballet performance at New York's Metropolitan Opera the night before.

It had all proven too much for the self-deprecating, outgoing, unpretentious Tish Baldrige, who had used up her own credibility with the Washington press corps to run interference for Jackie. She couldn't always shield the first lady from her obligations, and that meant there were times when Tish told Jackie bluntly, "You just have to do this." Even then, Jackie seldom cooperated. "I don't *have* to do anything," she often answered, storming off to complain to Jack.

Baldrige chalked up her boss's recalcitrance to a "lapse of selfishness going back to her school days of doing what she wanted, being independent, and stamping her foot." In the end a burnt-out Baldrige, who often had to scramble to find a last-minute replacement for Jackie, confessed that she was in "a most unfortunate position, being both someone who worked for her and an old friend."

Jackie quickly replaced Tish with another old friend—arguably her closest—Nancy Tuckerman. The two women had known each other since they were nine-year-olds at New York's Chapin School, and had been roommates at Miss Porter's in Farmington. "Tucky" seemed to be everything Tish was not—shy, somewhat drab, and not in the least bit interested in forcing Jackie to do anything she didn't want to.

At about the same time JFK was being pinned with his Father of the Year medal, Jackie threw a farewell party for Tish in the White House China Room, where the walls are lined with china services from previous administrations. The champagne flowed freely, and there were gifts—most notably a table Jackie had specially made that was inlaid with the autographs of White House senior staff and the first family, including a doodle from John. Then, while the Marine Band played, the staff sang "Arrivederci, Tish" to the tune of "Arrivederci Roma," with lyrics Jackie had written for the occasion.

Baldrige was touched at the warm send-off, but also a little mystified by what she would take as a backhanded compliment from the president when he said goodbye to her in the Oval Office. "Tish," JFK told her, "you are the most emotional woman I have ever known."

A few hours later, the White House staff threw another surprise party—this one for the president's birthday—held downstairs in the no-frills Navy Mess. JFK gamely opened one gag gift after another: a copy of "Debate Rules" from Richard Nixon, boxing gloves "to deal with Congress," a Lilliputian rocking chair, and Jackie's gift—a basket of dead grass from the "White House Historical Society, genuine antique grass from the antique Rose Garden." The dead grass, poking fun at Jackie's own ongoing crusade to fill the White House with antiques, drew the biggest laugh.

That night, Jackie went ahead with plans of her own for Jack's birthday—a cruise down the Potomac toward Mount Vernon aboard the *Sequoia.* Jack let it be known that he preferred the *Honey Fitz,* but he was told "the boat's got rotting stern timbers— like the rest of us, I guess."

The invitation called for "yachting clothes" and instructed everyone to be on time for an 8:01 departure. It was a dismal, rainy evening, but the yacht embarked anyway with a full complement of guests: Lem Billings, the Bradlees, the Shrivers, the Smatherses, Bobby and Ethel, Teddy, the Bartletts, the Fays, actor David Niven and his wife Hjordis, Bill Walton, an old Boston pol named Clem Norton, Mary Meyer, and one or two others.

With thunder and lightning crashing all around, drinks were served on the covered fantail, followed by a dinner of roast filet of beef in the elegant, mahogany-paneled main cabin. As the 1955 Dom Perignon flowed, toasts were delivered and the laughter grew louder. Everyone was having too good a time to notice the storm raging outside.

ALTHOUGH BY NOW THE TWIST was decidedly passé, it remained Jack's favorite piece of dance music. On orders from their commander in chief, the three-piece Marine Band aboard the *Sequoia* played the tune over and over again until it was finally time for JFK to unwrap his presents.

Sitting in one of his padded rockers, Jack ripped through the presents as he always did, reacting to each with unalloyed glee. As he held each gift aloft for the others to see, Jackie gave a running commentary—until a soused Clem Norton stumbled and put his foot right through the rare engraving of a scene from the War of 1812 that had been Jackie's gift to her husband.

It took a moment for the gasps to subside. "That's really too bad, isn't it, Jackie?" Jack said as he reached for the next gift. "Oh, that's all right," she said, disappointed but determined not to put a damper on the proceedings. "I can get it fixed." Although Tony Bradlee knew from Jackie's expression that she was "distressed," Ben Bradlee was impressed by how "unemotional" Jackie and Jack were. "They both so rarely show any emotion," he observed, "except by laughter."

At JFK's request, the *Sequoia* sailed downriver and back again a total of five times. By the time the captain finally docked the yacht at 1:23 a.m., most of the guests were drunk, Teddy had somehow managed to rip the left leg of his trousers completely off, and JFK—with Jackie *and* Mary Meyer right there—got caught up in the moment and chased Tony Bradlee around the boat while crew members roared with laughter. The episode, which apparently went unnoticed by Jackie, left Tony feeling "flattered, and appalled too."

By the next morning the storms had rolled away, leaving behind warm temperatures and a cloudless sky. JFK, none the worse for the wear, marked Memorial Day by laying a wreath at the Tomb of the Unknown Soldier in Arlington National Cemetery. Instead of immediately returning to the White House, he decided to take a stroll in the sunshine with Caroline on the cemetery's well-tended grounds. This had long been one of Jack's favorite spots, and he took care to point out Arlington's spectacular views of the Potomac and the monuments of Washington, D.C. beyond.

Caroline was particularly struck by the stately hilltop mansion overlooking the cemetery. "Who lives there, Daddy?" she asked.

"That's the Custis-Lee Mansion," he answered. "A very famous Civil War general named Robert E. Lee lived there a long time ago."

From this day forward, Caroline would scan the horizon for the mansion whenever she was being driven through Washington. "When Caroline was very little," Jackie said, "the mansion was one of the first things she learned to recognize."

The sudden arrival of spring and the breathtaking views also had a profound impact on Caroline's father. "You know, Buttons," he told her as they stared out over the capital, "I could stay here forever."

That afternoon, the Kennedys boarded a helicopter on the South Lawn and headed for Camp David with the Bradlees and the Nivens. Jack, decked out in white pants, a sky-blue polo shirt, and tasseled loafers, drove everyone in his Lincoln convertible to a skeet-shooting range, where David Niven cracked everyone up by pretending to be an expert marksman ("It's all in your tone of voice when you say 'pull!' ")—and then missing every shot.

Later, when the group went for a swim in Camp David's heated outdoor pool, JFK lent the British actor his swim trunks; the president wound up in the pool wearing only his white cotton boxers. It was obvious to everyone that Jack's back pain was even worse than usual. Niven and Bradlee were surprised when JFK took off his shirt to swim to see that he was wearing his back brace (which French ambassador Hervé Alphand described as "his peculiar little white corset"). Jack kept it on even for the short walk from the dressing room to the pool.

Before lunch, everyone gathered on the terrace to sip Bloody Marys while the president opened more presents that had somehow survived the mayhem of the night before. Again, Jack tore through the pile, paying equal attention to expensive gifts from close friends and inexpensive items that had been sent to the White House by total strangers. Bill Walton's elegant framed drawings of Lafayette Square were a hit with Jackie. JFK's favorite was a scrapbook from Ethel parodying the White House tours by substituting her own Hickory Hill "madhouse," overridden with untamed children, for the Executive Mansion.

AFTER ENDURING A MISCARRIAGE, A stillbirth, and two difficult pregnancies, Jackie looked forward to a relaxing summer in Hyannis Port. Once again, they had rented a house on Squaw Island that was close enough to the Kennedy compound but afforded Jackie the peace and privacy she craved.

It was also important to her that, while JFK's children were allowed to play with their rambunctious and often ill-behaved Kennedy cousins, Caroline and John should always follow her strict rules of conduct. Keeping the Bouvier-Kennedys a healthy distance from Ethel's wild brood would be an essential part of Jackie's plan to raise two well-mannered kids. "Jackie didn't want Caroline and John *inhaled* into that frenzied macho world of the Kennedys," her friend David Halberstam, the Pulitzer Prize-winning journalist, later remarked. Another longtime acquaintance, Peter Duchin, said the influence of the wild Kennedy cousins was something Jackie "worried about all the time."

Nestled in the woods at the end of a narrow gravel road, "Brambletyde" was a sprawling gray-shingled house that offered glorious ocean views from the rear and a broad private beach. It was also more luxurious, more secluded, and infinitely quieter than the houses that made up the Kennedy homestead. The plan was to set up house there on June 27, then move on to Hammersmith Farm for the baby's anticipated arrival in September.

Before she settled into Brambletyde at the end of June, the first lady put the finishing touches on Wexford. The house did have panoramic windows that offered jaw-dropping Blue Ridge Mountain views, but it was otherwise unremarkable. Jackie sought to change that with the décor, filling the rooms with brass tables, carved elephants, camel saddles, tapestries, and other exotic mementos of her travels through India and Pakistan.

Jackie was perhaps proudest of her Mogul miniatures—scenes from the *Kama Sutra*—which she displayed prominently in the dining room. Clint Hill had his own theory as to why Jackie hung the erotic works in the dining room as opposed to the bedroom, which Gallagher deemed more appropriate. "Shock value," Hill wrote in his excellent memoir. "Pure and simple." It turned out that Jack was even more impressed with the green, red, and orange paisley wallpaper that covered every square inch of the guest room—walls, doors, even the ceiling. "It looks," the president said, "like the inside of a Persian whorehouse."

After all Jackie's hard work, she made a startling decision after spending just one night at Wexford that spring: she and Jack would lease the place out from June to October at $1,000 a month ($8,000 a month in 2013 dollars). JFK was especially pleased, since he was once again on the warpath about Jackie's spending, and this was one way to offset the cost of renting Brambletyde. "The President wasn't too thrilled about spending money on the Squaw Island rental," Larry Newman said, "when they had a beautiful home at the compound." But in the end, Oleg Cassini said, "he wanted her to be happy at all costs, especially with the baby coming."

The first week in June, Jack headed west to address graduates of the U.S. Air Force Academy in Colorado Springs, Colorado, observe missiles being launched in White Sands, New Mexico, and watch a display of America's military might from the flight deck of the aircraft carrier *Kitty Hawk* off the California coast. He also spoke with the nation's mayors in Honolulu, attended party fund-raisers in Los Angeles—and met with Lyndon Johnson and Texas governor John Connally about a campaign trip to Dallas tentatively planned for November.

Jackie, meanwhile, amused herself by spending a day at the Maryland farm of Ros Gilpatric—"the second most attractive man in the Defense Department" (next to Secretary of Defense Robert McNamara). Gilpatric was returning to his law practice in New York, and Jackie was crestfallen. In Jack's absence, Gilpatric, whose own romantic entanglements had provided grist for the New York and Washington rumor mills for years, had provided a sympathetic ear. He had also provided her husband with sound advice that led JFK to make the right decisions during the Cuban Missile Crisis.

The following Thursday, Jackie sat down at her desk in the White House and wrote Gilpatric an emotional farewell letter. "I loved my day in Maryland," she said. "It made me happy for one whole week . . . I always push unpleasant things out of my head on the theory that if you don't think about them they won't happen—but I guess your departure—which I would never let myself realize until tonight—is true."

Jackie went on to say that she pitied whoever would replace Gilpatric at the Defense Department. "They will always live in your shadow . . . and no one else will be able to have force and kindness at the same time. . . . Please know Dear Ros that I will wish you well always—thank you—Jackie."

Gilpatric conceded that he "filled a void" in the first lady's life. But by the time he left Washington he was more impressed than ever with new direction the Kennedys' marriage had taken. "They loved each other," he reflected. "If anything, I think they were growing closer toward the end."

Whatever the strains between them over the years, there was one thing Jackie never doubted about Jack: his greatness. On June 10 and June 11, she watched in awe as her husband gave back-to-back speeches that were instantly hailed as historic. In his "Peace Speech," delivered at American University's commencement in Washington, Kennedy announced that the United States was suspending aboveground nuclear testing and called for both a reduction in nuclear weapons and an across-the-board reexamination of U.S.-Soviet relations.

The next day, in the wake of segregationist Alabama governor George Wallace's vow to block the integration of the University of Alabama, JFK took to the airwaves again. In an eloquent eighteen-minute prime-time address to the nation, Kennedy argued for equal rights under the Constitution and promised to propose new laws against discrimination based on race, religion, ethnic origin, or sex.

Medgar Evers, Mississippi field secretary of the National Association for the Advancement of Colored People, was so excited by JFK's speech he rushed home from his office to tell his young children what had just happened. As he got out of his car outside his house, Evers was shot by a white racist and bled to death in front of his family. Jack was so moved by the tragedy, which further galvanized the civil rights movement, that he met with Evers's widow and their children in the Oval Office just ten days later.

Jack continued to use his wife as a sounding board, talking about the difficulties that confronted him at every turn as he grappled with the issues of the day. She downplayed her importance in this role, but it was crucial to JFK's decision-making process. "She had a keen mind and knew all the personalities involved," John Kenneth Galbraith said. "Jackie, like her husband, was also a student of history. What she thought clearly mattered a great deal to him, and she was very proud of that."

Given her delicate condition, there was no question of Jackie accompanying her husband when he embarked June 22 on a history-making two-week trip to Europe. Without Jackie there to speak to the multitudes in their native tongues, the linguistically challenged president would have to fend for himself.

The first stop was West Berlin, and he was determined to say at least a few short phrases in German. Struggling with the pronunciation as he practiced his lines for more than an hour, he finally jotted a few key lines phonetically and prayed.

More than 1.5 million people—three-fifths of Berlin's entire population—poured into the streets to hear Kennedy's rebuke of communism and the ugly wall that now divided the city. "Freedom has many difficulties, and democracy is not perfect," he told the cheering crowd, "but we have never had to put up a *wall* to keep our people in." He concluded that "all free men, wherever they may live, are citizens of Berlin, and therefore, as a free man, I take pride in the words 'Ich bin ein Berliner.' "

(Jackie, who watched the speech at the White House with Robert McNamara, called to congratulate her husband. However, she would later be told by a German-speaking friend that by inserting "ein" before "Berliner" he may have been saying something entirely different. "You were wonderful, Jack," Jackie said, "but apparently it sounded to him like you were saying 'I am a doughnut.' ")

No matter. Just hours after leaving Germany, JFK was given an equally hearty welcome in Ireland. Sixteen years earlier he had visited his ancestral homestead in County Wexford's Dunganstown, and now his distant cousins welcomed the world's most famous Irishman back with tea, cookies, hugs, and smiles. Here, in particular, people wanted to know how Jackie was doing, and they congratulated the president on their coming new addition to the family. JFK was exuberant, bounding up the stairs at the U.S. Embassy in Dublin and shouting, "They love me in Ireland!"

JFK was still in a jovial mood when he stopped over in England to compare notes on the Nuclear Test Ban Treaty with Harold Macmillan. The British prime minister later wrote that the president's disposition was "puckish"—due partly to the resounding success of his "Ich bin ein Berliner" speech but also to improved conditions on the home front, mainly Jackie's pregnancy.

From London, Jack flew on to Rome, where the Vatican was still reeling from the death of the beloved reformist pope John XXIII. "The two Johns" were often linked in praise for ushering in a new era of change, but ironically they had never met. Instead, Jack met with John XXIII's successor, Pope Paul VI, whose installation had taken place less than twenty-four hours earlier. Back home, the press held its collective breath to see if America's first Catholic president would kneel before the new pope and kiss the ring of St. Peter. As the two men came together for the first time, Jack smiled broadly, reached out, and firmly shook the pontiff's hand.

BACK AT HYANNIS PORT, JACKIE was reminded of her own precarious position when Joan suffered a miscarriage in June, just six weeks before her baby was due. She and Teddy already had a daughter and a son, but he was in a race to outdo Bobby, and Joan felt "under pressure" to reproduce. Jackie understood completely. When Ethel gave birth to her eighth child—the second of her sons to be born on the Fourth of July—Jackie invited Joan to Squaw Island. "Jackie was so wonderful," Joan said of her sister-in-law's efforts to console her. "So wonderful."

THAT SUMMER, MIMI BEARDSLEY HAD returned to the White House for a second internship, although now her services were largely restricted to supervising the staged photo shoots inside the Oval Office. When Mimi told the president that she was dating a young Williams College student, Jack the Harvard man reacted with mock indignation. "Williams!" he gasped. "How could you?" But now that Jackie was pregnant, JFK seemed more than willing to curtail his extracurricular activities. He was intent on spending every free moment with his family at Hyannis Port, and that was fine with Mimi.

Jack's customary blasé attitude about such matters was much in evidence when he returned to Washington from Europe. Mimi had invited her roommates, fellow Miss Porter's alumni Wendy Taylor and Marnie Stuart, for a swim in the White House pool when JFK suddenly walked in. After putting on his trunks and joining Mimi and her dumbstruck friends, Jack called for someone to bring down a large box and set it by the pool. Inside the box were animal pelts—fox, rabbit, squirrel, and mink. Jack asked the three bewildered coeds to pick them up and examine them carefully. Before they could get too excited, he told the young women that he was picking out a present for Jackie. "He was planning to give Mrs. Kennedy a fur throw for Christmas," Mimi said, "and wanted the opinion of three fellow Farmington girls about which fur was the softest."

Jackie spent most of July on Squaw Island painting on her second-floor sunporch, reading Kipling, and drawing up plans to convert a small guest room in the White House into a nursery. She was also mapping out her return to public life later that year. Mary Gallagher, imported for the months of July and August, met with Jackie nearly every weekday to cope with the hundreds of letters she received each day from around the world. In addition to ironing out the details of her various preservation projects (should the new guard boxes outside the White House be green or white?) Jackie bombarded J. B. West with notes on a wide range of household issues and peppered Oleg Cassini with her latest fashion ideas.

"Jackie never specifically wore maternity clothes," Cassini recalled, "and I never created anything that was a maternity dress." Jackie did, however, wear Cassini's designs throughout her last pregnancy. "Some clothes just lent themselves to being used in that way, especially the A-line or princess-line dresses. We sent quite a few air freight packages to Squaw Island that summer."

During these lazy weekdays without Jack, Jackie often walked from Brambletyde to the main Kennedy compound to spend time with her father-in-law. She read the newspapers to him, brought him up to date on what was going on in the children's lives, and shared tidbits of gossip gleaned from friends and the scandal sheets she devoured. (Throughout her life Jackie was an avid tab-loid reader, and circled in red ink all the items that were written about her.)

"Jackie and Joe were closer than ever that summer," said Secret Service agent Ham Brown. "After the stroke, she went right on talking to him as if nothing had changed. She never talked down to him the way some people do. He really loved her like a daugh-ter. You could see it in his eyes."

Late each Friday, Jack would arrive for the weekend with the usual fanfare. As soon as the presidential helicopter landed in the front yard of Joe Kennedy's Hyannis Port residence, a dozen or more Kennedy cousins came running with Caroline in the lead. Then Jack would jump behind the wheel of a waiting golf cart, shout "Anyone for ice cream?!" and wait for all twelve kids to climb aboard. With everyone hanging on for dear life, the president then zoomed the few blocks to the tiny news store that served ice cream and candy. "The grin on his face," Brown said, "was a mile wide."

The president was also delighted by Jackie's reaction when she opened the gift he brought back from Europe: a small two-thousand-year-old bust of a young boy. She was equally impressed with what he picked up for the Oval Office—a small rendering of Herakles (Hercules) circa 500 B.C. After Jackie teased him for having such exquisite taste, Jack confessed that he had dispatched Lem Billings to pick out the antiquities while he chatted up the new pope.

For the two or three days a week the president managed to carve out for Hyannis Port, everyone followed the usual summer routine: noontime lunch cruises aboard the *Honey Fitz*, touch football on the lawn, golf at Hyannis Country Club, maybe a short sail on his twenty-six-footer, *Victura,* and dinner with Joe when it was possible.

There was no question that the new baby was continuing to pull Jack and Jackie closer together. Squaw Island house guest Red Fay went looking for his friend and found him—lying on the bed in the master bedroom with Jackie in his arms. After a red-faced Red sputtered his apologies, Jack just laughed. "Don't worry about it," he told his mortified buddy. "We're just lying here chatting."

There were tense moments, as well. If the baby arrived on schedule in early September, Jackie intended to have it delivered by caesarean section at Walter Reed Army Medical Center. But there was also a backup plan if the baby came early. In that event, she would be taken to Otis Air Force Base Hospital, just twenty miles from Hyannis Port. JFK also asked Jackie's obstetrician, Dr. John Walsh, to spend the rest of the summer at Hyannis Port, just in case.

The third week in July, Jackie awoke feeling queasy and faint. Jack immediately sent for the doctor and then stayed by Jackie's side, holding her hand and offering words of comfort and reassurance. It was a side of Jack that their friend Jim Reed, who stayed with them that week, had seldom witnessed.

As a desperate search went on for Dr. Walsh, a more familiar side of the president emerged. Out of Jackie's earshot so as not to upset her, he demanded, "Where the hell is that Goddamned doctor? He is here for emergencies just like this. Why in the hell does he think he's up here?" Soon Walsh did appear, explaining that he had been taking a brief walk along the beach. The doctor quickly determined that it was a false alarm and Jackie was fine, and Jack's mood lightened. "In the future, Dr. Walsh," he said politely, "always tell someone where you are and how you can be reached immediately."

Jack was anything but polite when he picked up the *Washington Post* on July 25 and saw a photo of a young officer proudly posing next to an expensive new U.S. Navy project: a bedroom at Otis Air Force Base Hospital specially furnished for the first lady. According to the article, the bed, dresser, nightstand, and lamp cost a then-astounding five thousand dollars.

Angry at the expense, not to mention the potential for negative publicity, JFK promptly called Assistant Secretary of Defense Arthur Sylvester. "Five thousand for *that*?" he shouted into the phone before threatening to cut the Air Force budget. A follow-up call to his Air Force aide, General Godfrey McHugh, was even more heated. Again threatening to cut the budget "another billion dollars," the president railed against the "silly bastard" smiling in the photo. "Silly bastard!" he shouted again and again. "I wouldn't have him running a cathouse!" In the end, he also demanded that the officer "have his ass transferred out of there in about a month"—to Alaska. Searching for more expletives, JFK concluded that the whole episode was "obviously a fuckup."

ONCE HER HUSBAND AND HIS entourage departed each Monday, Jackie breathed a sigh of relief. "She loved having him there of course," Cassini said. "She missed him. But she was determined to have that baby, and she needed for things to be calm."

As she had during her previous pregnancies, Jackie continued to smoke. The surgeon general's report outlining the dangers of smoking in clinical detail had not yet been released, but the obvious deleterious effects of smoking cigarettes had been known for well over a century.

The general public was also aware that smoking was believed to cause low birth weight. In fact, many expectant mothers in the 1960s smoked for just that purpose—to keep the baby's weight down, and theoretically make delivery easier. Some mothers also saw it as a way to keep their own weight under control. Jackie had dieted to regain her figure almost immediately after the birth of Caroline and John, and this time she was planning on doing the same. Looking ahead to life after the birth of her third child, Jackie asked J. B. West if a vibrating-belt weight-loss machine could be installed for her in the White House exercise room.

In light of her previous obstetrical difficulties, Dr. Walsh strongly urged the first lady to quit smoking. So did Dr. Janet Travell, Jack's omnipresent back doctor. Jackie was so adept at concealing her nicotine habit from the world—and she would do this for the rest of her life—that perhaps they thought she did quit, or at the very least cut back.

In stark contrast to Jack's boozy *Sequoia* bash two months earlier, Jackie quietly celebrated her thirty-fourth birthday on July 28 smoking and reading aboard the *Honey Fitz,* then spending the evening with Jack and the children at Brambletyde.

On August 5, 1963, Secretary of State Dean Rusk signed the Nuclear Test Ban Treaty in Moscow—a crowning foreign policy achievement for the Kennedy administration. That night, while Jackie remained at Squaw Island, Jack dined with Mary Meyer upstairs at the White House. Their sexual relationship apparently over, JFK and Meyer nevertheless remained friends. "The test ban treaty was a major victory for President Kennedy," Pierre Salinger said, adding that at such times JFK "hated to be alone."

Two days later, at eleven in the morning, Jackie took Caroline to her riding lesson at nearby Osterville stables. They had just arrived and were walking toward the ring when Jackie turned to Secret Service agent Paul Landis and asked him to drive her back to the house—"Right *now*, Mr. Landis."

One of the agents assigned to the Kiddie Detail stayed behind at the stables while Landis helped her into the rear seat. The agent then floored the accelerator, and the car sped off down the narrow, winding country road back toward Squaw Island. With Jackie pleading with him to hurry, Landis radioed headquarters to have Dr. Walsh come to the house and ready the helicopter. Clint Hill, who was enjoying his day off, was also called. "Oh God," Hill remembered thinking. "The baby isn't due for another five weeks. She can't have the baby now, it's too early."

DR. WALSH DROVE UP TO BRAMBLETYDE just as Landis was helping Jackie out of the car. "I think I'm going to have that baby," she told him flatly. After a quick examination, Walsh confirmed she was in labor and had to be transported to the hospital immediately.

Shortly after 11 a.m., Agent Landis was walking Jackie toward the helicopter that would take her to the hospital when Dr. Travell, who was also staying at Hyannis Port that summer, arrived at the scene. "Should I notify the President?" Travell asked.

"No!" Jackie shouted as she climbed into the chopper bound for Otis Air Force Base with Dr. Walsh and Mary Gallagher at her side. Though surprised at the time, Travell believed Jackie was on some level "holding onto the slim hope" that this was another false alarm.

Clearly, that hope was fading fast. "Dr. Walsh," Jackie pleaded, "you've just got to get me to the hospital on time! I don't want anything to happen to this baby."

"We'll have you there in plenty of time," Walsh reassured her, but Jackie was far from certain. "Please hurry," she begged. "This baby mustn't be born dead!"

Nothing must happen to Patrick. I just can't bear to think of the effect it might have on Jackie.

—JACK, TO JACKIE'S MOTHER,
JANET AUCHINCLOSS

&

There had always been this wall between them, but their shared grief tore that wall down. At long last, they were truly coming closer together. But it would prove to be too late.

—THEODORE WHITE

*There was a growing tenderness. I think their marriage
was really beginning to work at the end.*

—ROSWELL GILPATRIC, FRIEND

❧

We were about to have a real life together.

—JACKIE

10

✤

"If I Ever Lost You . . ."

*A*fter ten minutes in the air, the helicopter landed at Otis Air Force Base and Jackie was whisked to the special presidential wing that had been set up to handle just such a medical emergency. Clint Hill, who had separately radioed the Secret Service Command Center and told them to notify the president, arrived at Otis by car and rushed to Jackie's side. Hill touched Jackie's arm and reassured her that everything was going to be okay, but there was no escaping the worry in her eyes.

At 12:52 p.m., Wednesday, August 7, 1963, Jackie gave birth by caesarean section to a four-pound, ten-and-a-half-ounce boy who was immediately placed in an oxygen-fed Isolette incubator. Despite Jackie's insistence that her husband not be notified, JFK was in the air and headed for the hospital even before the baby's delivery. To further complicate matters, the president was not able to fly aboard one of the large planes that usually served as Air Force One. Since he wasn't scheduled to travel until Friday, one plane was in the air on a flight check and the other was undergoing routine maintenance. Once at Andrews, JFK and his party commandeered one of the slower, eight-passenger JetStars sitting on the tarmac.

"It was obviously a tense flight," recalled Pierre Salinger, who along with Nancy Tuckerman and Pamela Turnure "dropped everything" to accompany JFK on the flight to Otis. "Nobody knew what to say, and President Kennedy spent most of the flight staring out the window, lost in his own thoughts."

The president's plane touched down at Otis at 1:35 p.m. and ten minutes later he walked into the hospital. Before leaving Washington, Jack had called his Hyannis Port friend and neighbor Larry Newman from the Oval Office and asked him to drive over to the hospital "just to be there for Jackie." Newman was sitting in the lobby when JFK walked in.

"He almost threw his arms around me, but then his natural reserve kicked in and he grabbed my hand," Newman recalled.

"Thanks for being here, Larry," he said. "It makes me feel so much better just knowing you were here."

Newman was struck by "the emotion in his eyes. We'd known each other for so long, but I'd never seen this depth of feeling before. He was very emotional, and deeply worried about Jackie."

Jackie was still in surgery when he arrived, but as soon as she regained consciousness Jack went in to see her, and then to see the baby. In the hallway outside, he conferred with Dr. Walsh. The news was not good. The baby was born with hyaline membrane disease, a severe respiratory disorder not uncommon among premature infants. It was, in fact, the same condition shared by John and his stillborn sister, Arabella. A specialist from Boston, Dr. James E. Drorbaugh, was being flown in to help decide the best course of action.

In the meantime, JFK approached Clint Hill and asked him to find the base chaplain so that the baby could be baptized immediately. Less than twenty minutes later, the baby was christened Patrick Bouvier Kennedy, after Jack's paternal grandfather and Black Jack Bouvier.

For the moment, no mention would be made of the baby's medical problems. In announcing Patrick's birth to reporters waiting outside the hospital, Salinger would only say that he was five and a half weeks premature and that "the baby's condition is described by the doctors as good, and Mrs. Kennedy's condition is described as good." In fact, Jackie was also in a weakened condition, having undergone two major blood transfusions following her caesarean.

It was agreed that Patrick should immediately be transported by ambulance to Children's Hospital in Boston, where he would get better treatment. Jack broke the news to Jackie. "Oh no, Jack," she said. "Does he have to go? I want to be with him, Jack."

"It's just a precaution, Jackie," he explained. "Apparently he's got the same lung problem John had. The doctors think it's best just to play it safe. Everything will be okay."

Jackie would never get to hold her infant son in her arms, or even touch him. But she would at least be allowed to see him once—if only for a few fleeting minutes. Jack wheeled tiny Patrick's incubator into Jackie's room so that she could say goodbye, then accompanied him to the ambulance. Mary Gallagher was standing in the hallway and got a glimpse of Patrick as he was wheeled past. "His hair was dark," she said, "his features well-formed."

At 5:55 p.m., the ambulance carrying Patrick departed for Boston with a full police escort. Jack spent a few more minutes with Jackie, then rushed to Squaw Island to spend time with Caroline and John.

AT MAUD SHAW'S URGING, CAROLINE had been praying for her mother and new baby brother. Now she and John lit up as their father walked through the front door. "Patrick has a little problem breathing and has to go to a hospital in Boston where they can make him better," he explained patiently. "Mommy is fine, everything is going to be okay."

An hour later, JFK returned to Otis to check on Jackie before flying on to Boston. He was pleased to find Louella Hennessey, the Kennedy family private nurse who had cared for Jackie after John's birth, sitting at the first lady's bedside.

At 8:45 p.m., JFK's helicopter, emblazoned with the presidential seal, lifted off from Otis. It landed at Boston's Logan Airport twenty minutes later. As his motorcade made its way through downtown Boston, crowds lining the streets waved and cheered.

JFK was soon shuttling between a suite at the Ritz-Carlton Hotel and Children's Hospital, where a team of Harvard-trained specialists worked feverishly to keep the president's son alive. Jack also flew in an expert of his own—Dr. Sam Levine from New York's Cornell Medical Center, the doctor who had treated Lee Radziwill's daughter just two years earlier.

After ninety minutes quizzing doctors and watching his tiny

son struggle for every breath, Jack returned to the Ritz-Carlton. The crowds this time were even larger and more enthusiastic, and larger still when he made the short trip back to Children's Hospital the next day. At 10:40 a.m. on Thursday, with thousands of cheering people lining the roadways in both directions, the president flew back to Otis Air Force Base to bolster Jackie's spirits.

He planned to check in on Caroline and John as well, but at 1:14 p.m. the doctors in Boston called with disturbing news. In a last-ditch effort to keep Patrick breathing, they were moving him to the adjacent Harvard School of Public Health and placing the newborn in a thirty-one-foot-long hyperbaric chamber.

"After consulting with the doctors," a grim-faced Salinger announced, "the President is returning to Boston immediately." This time when his motorcade sped toward the hospital, the people were still there, and in even greater numbers than before, but they were solemn. Now America and the world, transfixed by the unfolding drama, prayed for tiny Patrick's recovery.

Jackie, meanwhile, drifted in and out of consciousness. The president and her doctors agreed that, in the interest of her recovery, she not be told everything. "What's the point?" Jack asked Hennessey rhetorically. "I don't see the point . . ."

JFK wound up checking on Patrick four times that day, and was joined at one point by Janet, the baby's grandmother. "Nothing must happen to Patrick," he told her. "I just can't bear to think of the effect it might have on Jackie." Reporters swarmed around Jackie's mother when she left the hospital, peppering her with questions about Patrick's condition. "He's doing very well," she replied unconvincingly. "Although maintaining her poise," one paper reported, "Mrs. Auchincloss appeared somewhat distressed."

That night, Jack refused to leave the hospital. Instead, he and Dave Powers moved into a vacant room five floors above the basement oxygen chamber where Patrick battled for his life. To make the modest room more suitable for their important guest, the hospital furnished it with a desk, multiple phone lines—and a padded rocker.

At 2 a.m. Friday, Powers awakened the president to tell him Patrick had taken a turn for the worse. He was now in critical condition. On the way to the elevator that would take them downstairs, JFK and Powers passed the room of a severely burned child. Jack stopped the night nurse and asked about the child, then dashed off a heartfelt note of encouragement to the mother. "There he was, with his own baby dying downstairs," Powers said, "but he had to take the time to write a note to that poor woman, asking her to keep her courage up."

Just outside the door to the chamber, JFK and Powers were given surgical gowns, masks, and caps. They would not be allowed inside the chamber—that required a far more elaborate pressurized bodysuit and helmet—but they could observe what was happening through a small window in the door. For the next ninety minutes, JFK paced in the corridor, stopping every now and then to look inside at the doctors in their Buck Rogers outfits bending over Patrick's incubator.

It was no use. There was nothing more the elite medical team could do. The door opened, and the baby was wheeled out into the hallway. One of the doctors lifted Patrick out of the incubator, and, after telling Jack the baby had only a few more minutes to live, gently handed him to the president.

At 4:04 on Friday morning, April 9, Patrick Bouvier Kennedy died of cardiac arrest in his father's arms. He had lived thirty-nine hours and twelve minutes. Back at Otis Air Force Base, Jackie had been restless all night long, tossing and turning and unable to find a moment's peace. At the same moment Patrick passed away, the night nurse noticed something strange. As if a switch had been flipped, Jackie abruptly stopped stirring and fell into a deep, peaceful sleep.

"He put up quite a fight," Jack told Powers. "He was a beautiful baby." Then the president returned to the vacant room upstairs, closed the door behind him, sat on the edge of the bed, and wept. Jack was too proud to let anyone see him crying, Powers said, "so he asked me to go outside and telephone Teddy."

JFK felt John Walsh was best equipped to break the news to Jackie. When the doctor arrived to tell her the tragic news at 6:25 a.m., he tried to avoid the red-rimmed eyes of nurses, orderlies, Secret Service agents, and Air Force officers. "It was a national tragedy," Salinger said. "Did I cry? You bet I did. Anybody with a pulse cried, especially if you knew them. It was just terribly, terribly sad."

After Dr. Walsh left, Jackie's quiet sobs were nonetheless audible in the hallway. "If you weren't weeping before," Dr. Travell said, "you were now." It took more than an hour for Jackie to pull herself together with tissues, some makeup, and Mary Gallagher's help. She knew Jack was as devastated as she was, but she was determined to put on a brave face for him. "How terrible Jack must feel," said Jackie, who seemed to focus on the pain of others as a way of coping with her own. "This is such a heartbreak for him."

But when Jack walked in the door of her hospital room, they broke down together. "Oh, Jack, oh, Jack," she sobbed. "There's only one thing I could not bear now—if I ever lost you."

At the house on Squaw Island, Maud Shaw was handed the unenviable task of telling the children. She was crushed by the news of Patrick's death, and asked that someone less emotional—one of the Secret Service agents, perhaps—break the news to Caroline and John.

After hours of hemming and hawing, Shaw finally screwed up her courage and asked the children to sit down at the kitchen table. This was not going to be easy. The arrival of a baby brother had been eagerly anticipated by both children, but especially by Caroline. In her bossy big-sister way, she had taken care to lecture John on the care, feeding, and sleeping habits of infants.

"I have some bad news, children," Shaw said. "Do you remember what your daddy said about Patrick not being able to breathe? Well, the doctors tried to help little Patrick, but it was just too hard for him. He's with the angels now."

Caroline thought for a moment. "Miss Shaw," she said, "Patrick is still my baby brother, right?"

"Yes," the nanny answered. "He is still your baby brother."

"Then I think," she said, folding her hands in prayer, "we should ask God to take care of him in heaven."

Shaw was in awe of the little girl JFK called Buttons. "Caroline was so quiet, so composed," Shaw said. "And the rest of us all had red eyes from crying."

Jackie spent a full week recovering from her ordeal, and was too exhausted to attend Patrick's funeral. She did have one special request, however—that the tiny coffin be completely covered in flowers as her father's had been.

On Saturday, JFK, New York's Francis Cardinal Spellman, Bobby and Ethel, Teddy and Joan, Lee Radziwill, and Jamie and Janet Auchincloss were among the few who heard Richard Cardinal Cushing celebrate a "Mass of the Angels" at the chapel inside his Boston residence. Once it was over, Jack stepped forward and placed the gold St. Christopher medal Jackie had given him as a wedding present inside the tiny white casket.

As the family filed out of the chapel, Jack was crying "copious tears," Cushing recalled. The president was the last of the mourners to leave, with Cushing following right behind. The casket was in a white marble case, and at one point, the cardinal recalled, "the President was so overwhelmed with grief that he literally put his arms around that casket as though he was carrying it out."

"Come on, Jack," Cushing said, putting his arm around JFK. "Let's go. God is good."

The burial took place at Holyhood Cemetery in Brookline, not far from JFK's birthplace; sadly, baby Patrick was the first Kennedy laid to rest in the large family plot purchased by Joe Kennedy. A grief-stricken Jack reached out to touch the tiny coffin as it was lowered into the ground. "Goodbye," said Patrick's father, tears streaming down his cheeks. "It's awfully lonely down there."

After the funeral, JFK went straight to the hospital to check on Jackie. He reported to her that the service was beautiful, and that Patrick's casket had been covered with a blanket of flowers as she requested. Within minutes, Dave Powers recalled, they were both crying.

Powers returned to the Squaw Island house to keep Jack company the night of the funeral, and shortly after dinner the two men were joined by Joan. Having just suffered a late-term miscarriage, JFK's sister-in-law understood the pain they were going through.

"Why would God let a child die? An innocent child?" It was a question he began asking when Patrick was still alive, and for the moment he felt compelled to pose it again and again. Joan answered that she didn't know if things happened for a reason, as Cardinal Cushing had said. But she knew that bad things happen, and that "when they happen we just have to go on somehow, and know that we have the strength to carry on." More than anyone she knew, Joan told him, Jack had the courage and the strength to cope with tragedy—even the loss of a child.

According to Powers, Jack was "deeply moved" by what Joan had to say. "She was there the next night and the next, and the President was grateful."

JACK WAS NO LONGER THE kind of husband who could happily cruise the Mediterranean while his wife coped with the loss of a child. This time his grief was palpable, and his concern for Jackie paramount. He visited her at least twice a day, and just two days after Patrick's death brought Caroline along. Jackie lit up when she saw Caroline holding on tightly to a bouquet of black-eyed Susans. She wore a paisley sundress and sneakers, and her blond hair was pulled back in a ponytail.

Still, Jack worried that Jackie might sink deeper into a well of depression. "The President was very concerned about her," Arthur Schlesinger said. "He tried to think of ways to cheer her up."

Knowing how fond she was of Adlai Stevenson, he wanted Schlesinger to ask if Adlai would drop her a note at the hospital. "It would mean a lot to her," JFK said. Jackie was, Schlesinger said, "deeply touched" when Stevenson's letter arrived. Jackie never suspected that her husband was behind it. "He was just happy to see her smile."

The White House was swamped with thousands of phone calls and letters of condolence—touching expressions of sympathy from common people and world leaders alike. Later, at Squaw Island, the president showed several to Bill Walton. "He'd read them and then pass them over to me to look at," Walton recalled, "and he'd say, 'Look at what the pope said,' or 'How am I going to answer that one?' "

Back in Washington, Jack gave Mimi Beardsley her first "real lesson in grief" when he asked her to sit with him on the Truman Balcony while he pored over the heartfelt notes of sympathy from both friends and strangers. Mimi recalled tears "rolling down his cheeks" as JFK would periodically scrawl a reply in the margin. "But mostly he just read them and cried," she added. "I did too."

Patrick's death was also a "crucial signpost" in her relationship with the president, filling him "not only with grief but with an aggrieved sense of responsibility to his wife and family." Looking back, it dawned on Beardsley that even though they saw each other countless times in the Oval Office that summer of 1963, the president had been "winding down" the physical part of their relationship for some time. Now, even when she accompanied him on trips, there was no hanky-panky. She believed he was finally "obeying some private code that trumped his reckless desire for sex" and "shutting down our sexual relationship"—just as he had done with Mary Meyer.

Jackie put up a brave front when she left the hospital, presenting each doctor and nurse with a framed lithograph of the White House that she had signed. "You've been so wonderful to me," she told the nurses, "that I'm coming back here next year to have another baby."

As they walked outside, the president and first lady held hands—a rare open display of their affection for one another. Both somehow managed a smile for the cameras. Behind the façade, the first lady was "destroyed. To lose another child that way," Schlesinger said, "was bad enough. But for it to be such a public spectacle magnified the pain a thousand fold."

As Jackie became more depressed, Janet Auchincloss confided in Jack that she feared for his wife's mental health. "I'm afraid Jackie will have a nervous breakdown," she told him. Jack worried, too, but he also understood. "It is so hard for Jackie," he told Red Fay. "After all the difficulties she has in bearing a child, to lose him is doubly hard."

JFK did not only have Jackie to be anxious about. "He knew how sad Caroline was going to be," Jamie said, "and he wanted to try and offset that in some way." So, before their mother returned home from the hospital, Jack showed up with a cocker spaniel puppy.

The day JFK escorted their mother home from the hospital, the kids ran outside to greet her. "Look, Mommy!" Caroline shouted, holding up the newest member of their canine family. "The puppy's name is Shannon!" The others—Clipper, Charlie, and Pushinka's puppies White Tips, Blackie, Streaker, and Butterfly—barked and wagged for attention.

For the rest of the summer Jack tried to be there for his wife as much as he could, adding quick midweek overnights to Cape Cod along with the usual long weekends. While Jackie recuperated, JFK swam off the *Honey Fitz* with the children, drove Caroline to her riding lessons, and, when it was time to depart for Washington, let them both ride with him to Otis Air Force Base in the presidential chopper.

During this period Jackie also counted on her sister for moral support. Only days before, Lee Radziwill had boarded a Boston-bound flight in Athens thinking Patrick was going to be just fine.

Now she was on Squaw Island doing whatever she could to help Jackie get over the death of her son.

"It was obviously tough, very tough," said Chuck Spalding, the first person outside the family to visit. "We golfed late in the day—I thought it would be good to get Jack's mind off things—but it didn't matter. He and Jackie were just crushed, and there was no way of getting around it."

Spalding, like the others, witnessed a heightened intimacy between his hosts. "They folded into each other on the couch," he said. "You couldn't tell where one ended and the other began." Once Spalding saw Jackie beginning to get emotional. Before Spalding could do or say anything, Jack was "at her side with a tissue, wiping her tears and holding her. They didn't seem interested in hiding their feelings anymore." At private moments like this, "you almost felt you were intruding. There were times when I had to look away."

"She hung on to him and he held her in his arms," said Bill Walton, who also spent the weekend with them. This was "something nobody ever saw at any other time because they were very private people." It was Jack, Theodore White said, who finally saw the light. "They were both shattered by Patrick's death," White observed, "and for the first time, Jack reached out to her as he had never done before, had never been *capable* of doing before."

Caroline noticed the difference. "There was a tenderness between her parents that she really hadn't seen before," Salinger said. "It made an impression on her." As she watched her parents embrace in front of others "you could see the little gears in her head turning."

Lee Radziwill's gears were turning as well. After spending time with Jackie at Squaw Island, she returned to Europe in mid-August convinced that her sister was headed for a nervous collapse if something wasn't done—and soon. The two Bouvier women had always been close. They both adored their father Black Jack, who called Jackie "Jacks" and Lee "Pekes," and barely tolerated their social-climbing mother. At social events, Jackie and Lee could invariably be spotted gossiping in a far corner—a scene that was repeated so often Truman Capote dubbed them the "Whispering Sisters."

Cruising the Aegean with Aristotle Onassis and his longtime mistress, the opera diva Maria Callas, Lee talked movingly of her sister's anguish. "If only there was some way I could help cheer her up," Lee said. "She really needs to just get away for a while . . ." Onassis took the bait, inviting both the president and Jackie to join them aboard the *Christina*.

Lee's own affair with the notorious Greek shipping tycoon had been going on for months, and there were rumors that Lee intended to divorce Stas Radziwill and marry Onassis. Knowing that Jack and her sister were now more deeply in love than ever, she certainly did not see Jackie as potential competition for Onassis's affections—or his millions. She jumped at the chance to invite them both.

Jackie had fallen in love with Greece during her trip there in 1961 and wanted desperately to return. She knew Jack couldn't go, of course, but she needed to escape—to "experience life just for the sake of living," she told Cassini, before being "swallowed up by Washington."

True, there was no political fallout eight years earlier when then-senator Kennedy and his wife met Winston Churchill aboard the *Christina*. But now that he was president—and facing reelection—Jack balked at the idea. Onassis's notoriety extended far beyond the $7 million fine he paid for illegally operating U.S. surplus warships. Since World War II, his connections with fascist dictators, his nearly successful attempt to secure a shipping monopoly on Saudi oil, and his slaughter of undersize sperm whales in violation of international law had all made him a target of the FBI.

Onassis had also purchased a 52 percent interest in Monte Carlo's Société des Bains de Mer (Sea Bathing Society, SBM for short). SBM owned Monaco's famed casino, the Yacht Club, the Hôtel de Paris, and about 34 percent of Monaco itself. The purchase in effect gave Onassis economic dominion over the tiny principality. For years Onassis, who also maintained ties to organized crime, battled fiercely with Prince Rainier—husband of the Kennedys' old friend Grace Kelly—for total control of Monaco.

"I don't want you to go, Jackie," JFK said. "Onassis is a pirate. That's not just a turn of phrase. He is a *real* pirate." JFK called Spalding and complained that if Jackie was photographed in Greece cavorting with Onassis, "it's not going to look good—all those jet-set types, Americans don't like them." More specifically, he believed Onassis to be "a real crook," and that Jackie's association with him was going to cost him votes in the upcoming election. "That Onassis is trouble," he told Spalding. "Jackie's playing with fire, only it's my ass that's going to get burned."

On Squaw Island, Martha Bartlett was surprised when the president literally dropped to one knee and "begged" his wife not to accept Onassis's invitation. Jackie was unmoved. "She wanted to go," Evelyn Lincoln said, "and that was that. Nobody told Jackie what to do, not even the President." Tish Baldrige described this as "typical Jackie behavior. If you really wanted her to do something, then you told her *not* to do it. In this case, that's where President Kennedy went wrong."

Since he couldn't dissuade Jackie from going, JFK scrambled for someone who might go along and lend the trip an air of respectability. Jackie suggested their friends Franklin and Sue Roosevelt. Now undersecretary of commerce, FDR Jr. boasted impeccable credentials and an unassailable surname, but he was also worldly and fun-loving. "Jackie knew," Evelyn Lincoln said, "that he wasn't going to get in the way of her having a good time."

In the end, all JFK could do was make it look as if the trip had been his idea all along. "Well, I think it will be good for Jackie," JFK told Pam Turnure when she raised concerns about the election. "And that's what counts." (Later, Jackie gave full credit to Jack. "He sent me to Greece," she told Arthur Schlesinger Jr., "you know, for a sad reason this year, but he thought I was getting depressed after losing Patrick . . .")

As it turned out, even Onassis was aware of the potential for embarrassment and offered to get off the *Christina* as soon as Jackie arrived. "I could not accept his generous hospitality and then not let him come along," Jackie said. "It would have been too cruel."

Excited about her upcoming trip, Jackie began to contemplate her return to Washington. She wasn't quite yet up to hosting the state dinner for Afghanistan's King Mohammad Zahir Shah on September 5—Jack's sister Eunice filled in for her instead—but Jackie did oversee every last detail by phone from Squaw Island.

The president had a rare treat in store for his guests when, on his command, the Jefferson Memorial was illuminated for the first time. The evening also marked the first fireworks display at a state dinner, although problems arose when JFK asked that the eight-minute display over the White House be squeezed into four minutes. The resulting barrage was so unexpected, Secret Service rushed toward the king and the president to shield them. Within minutes, the Washington, D.C. police department switchboard was overwhelmed with calls from citizens wanting to know if an airliner had gone down or the capital was under attack.

The next day JFK was back with Jackie in Hyannis Port, this time to attend Joe's seventy-fifth birthday. It was the usual raucous Kennedy family affair, with children dashing about, party favors and gag gifts, horseplay, cake, and song parodies.

The birthday boy, presiding over the festivities wearing a red, white, and blue party hat, appeared to be having the time of his life—until the president launched into his favorite tune, "September Song." With its bittersweet message of time slipping away, Jack's heartfelt rendition of the melancholy Kurt Weill–Maxwell Anderson ballad suddenly had half the room near tears.

"It was all part of his elegant fatalism," said Oleg Cassini, who heard JFK sing "September Song" several times. "It expressed what Jack felt about himself, that he wouldn't be around very long. It was a surprise to many people that he sang it so beautifully."

ON SEPTEMBER 12, THE KENNEDYS' movable feast relocated to Hammersmith Farm, where the president and his wife celebrated their tenth anniversary with—appropriately—a candlelit dinner for ten. Ben and Tony Bradlee rode up with Jack on the presidential helicopter, and the moment they landed in Newport they were struck by the new closeness between the Kennedys.

"This was the first time we had seen Jackie since the death of little Patrick," Ben recalled, "and she greeted JFK with by far the most affectionate embrace we had ever seen them give each other. . . . They are the most remote and independent people, so when their emotions do surface it is especially moving."

Before they sat down to dinner, Jackie and JFK exchanged gifts. She gave him a set of brass blazer buttons emblazoned with the insignia of the Irish Brigade, the famous infantry unit made up predominantly of Irish-Americans that fought on the Union side during the Civil War, and a scrapbook of before-and-after photos illustrating the restoration of the White House Rose Garden—a project that made them both especially proud.

The room grew silent when, as a poignant reminder of the baby they just lost, Jackie gave Jack a gold St. Christopher medal to replace the one he had placed in Patrick's coffin. He, in turn, gave her a small gold ring with emerald chips—a reference to Patrick's Irish heritage—that she wore on her little finger.

Then Provi the maid walked in with an armload of small boxes. Two contained drawings by Fragonard and Degas from the Wildenstein Gallery in New York. The rest were from a New York antiques dealer, J. J. Klejman, and contained an assortment of antiquities—mostly Greek, Roman, and Etruscan objets d'art and jewelry—along with catalog descriptions and a price list. "You can have any one you want, Jackie," Jack said, "but remember, you can only pick one."

While she examined each item, Jack read aloud the catalog description but refrained from stating the price. Several times, however, his eyes widened when he saw what he'd have to pay for the more expensive items. "Oops—got to steer her away from that one," he muttered, only half joking, under his breath.

"I could see the present he wanted me to choose most was this Alexandrian bracelet," recalled Jackie, who more than anything wanted to please her husband. "It's terribly simple, gold, sort of a snake. I could see how he loved it. He'd just hold it in his hand. . . . He wouldn't say which one he wanted to give me, but I could tell so I chose it." (Jack was also rooting for an Assyrian horse bit until one of their guests that night, Jackie's Vassar classmate Sylvia Whitehouse Blake, nixed the idea. "I do think we might have something a bit more sentimental for your tenth anniversary," Blake laughed. Jack agreed, but he still wanted to try the ancient horse bit out on Macaroni "to see if it really works.")

"I can't think of two people who packed more into ten years of marriage than they had," Janet later mused, adding that "all their strains and stresses, which any sensitive people have in a marriage, had eased." Now, she believed, "they were very, very, very close to each other and understood each other wonderfully. He appreciated her gifts and she worshiped him."

Jack and Jackie made a valiant effort to be merry that evening, but there were moments when the couple's despair bubbled to the surface. "Just before we retired," Ben Bradlee remembered, "Jackie drew me aside, her eyes glistening with tears, to announce, 'You two really are our best friends.' It was a forlorn remark, almost like a lost and lonely child in desperate need of any kind of friend."

The Bradlees stayed on at Hammersmith Farm for the next few days, golfing, swimming, and cruising on Narragansett Bay aboard the *Honey Fitz*. Every day, Jackie told them the same thing. "Jack and I were so touched by your letters when Patrick died," she said. "Your words meant so much to us . . ." Bradlee had been so shell-shocked by Patrick's death and the suicide just days before of their mutual friend, *Washington Post* publisher Phil Graham, that he couldn't remember what he'd written. In a masterpiece of understatement, Bradlee concluded, "It had been a bad summer for our friends."

AS SEPTEMBER DREW TO A close, Jackie seemed to be turning a corner. When Red and Anita Fay arrived on September 20 to spend the weekend, she seemed "exuberant," according to Fay. No sooner had longtime Kennedy friend Vivian Crespi joined the party than Jack announced that he was in the mood for something entirely different.

"He called me over," recalled White House photographer Robert Knudsen, "and said they wanted to have some fun and shoot a movie. The President wrote the script and he didn't want anyone to know about it."

Unknown to JFK, reporters on a distant hill had their binoculars trained on the action. In the key scene JFK gets off the *Honey Fitz* and is walking down Hammersmith Farm's long private pier when he suddenly clutches his chest and falls to the ground.

First Crespi and her small son, Marcantonio, get off the boat and nonchalantly step over Jack on their way to the shore. Jackie is next, taking dainty steps over the president's body as if it isn't there. But when it's Red Fay's turn, he trips over the body and a gush of ketchup surges out of JFK's chest, covering the front of his shirt.

Other scenes directed by JFK would have Fay in his underwear, chasing after a bikini-clad Crespi, pouncing on her in the rosebushes, then also winding up a bloody corpse. But obviously, it was the memory of the president acting out his own death just nine weeks before the actual event that came to haunt Knudsen and the others involved in the film. "I wondered if it was a premonition he had," said the photographer, "or a quirk of fate."

Mortified to learn that reporters had been watching their shenanigans all along, JFK instructed Knudsen to keep the only copy of the film under lock and key. "Anyone who knew Jack knew he was fascinated with death," Chuck Spalding said. "That he wanted to actually act out his own on film, even in a silly way, was his way of facing it."

Jack had always had the habit of abruptly turning to his friends and asking, "How would you like to die?" Whenever someone asked the same question of him in return, for years Kennedy answered "poison." Now, he simply said, "Airplane." Why? "Quick."

Knowing that she would soon be off on her Greek adventure, Jackie returned to the White House on September 23 after a three-month absence. She wanted to be on hand that week when Caroline started first grade. Jackie also made Caroline's religious instruction a top priority, motivated in part by the cosmic questions—Why would God let a baby die? Will we see Patrick in heaven someday?—she had been posing since her baby brother's death.

Jackie, who at this point was markedly more devout than the president, had actually started the search for a suitable catechism school months before their tragic summer. The previous May she had dispatched Alice Grimes, headmistress of Caroline's little White House School, to the Georgetown Visitation Academy—a cloistered convent—to see if it might take on Caroline and her six Roman Catholic classmates.

Sister Joanne Frey of the Mission Helpers of the Sacred Heart was Caroline's catechism teacher at Georgetown Visitation. Although parents were invited to observe the first day of class, Frey was somewhat relieved when it appeared Jackie wouldn't be able to make it. But Jackie did show—fifteen minutes late. "I went to the wrong side of the church," Jackie said. "It's so stupid of me, and now I'm disrupting your class . . ."

"SHE WAS QUITE FLUSTERED, QUITE apologetic," Sister Joanne remembered. " 'I'm just so sorry,' she said. 'Would you mind if I stay for class?' Of course I was just looking at her and thinking, 'Oh God . . .' "

Caroline "would have stood out even if she wasn't the President's daughter," Sister Joanne said. "She was exceptionally well spoken for someone her age, and completely unspoiled." When Frey asked students to draw the creation, the other kids drew animals and Adam and Eve. Caroline covered her paper in black crayon, then held it up to reveal she had punched out holes for the stars and a crescent moon. "And then there was light," she said.

After class, Jackie went up to Sister Joanne. "If I had had religion taught to me in that way," she said, "it would have been a much happier experience for me. Would you mind if I take the drawing home to show to the President?"

Another time, Sister Joanne asked her pupils to tell a story using pictures cut out of magazines. Caroline proudly showed Frey a picture of a woman cradling an infant and a child of five or six. "This is Mommy, this is me," she said, "and this would have been Patrick, my baby brother. He's in heaven."

These moments of innocence "really kind of took your breath away," Sister Joanne said. "Everyone had gone through the tragedy of Patrick's death. The experience was still fresh in people's minds. What could you say?"

IN THE END, JACKIE MADE frequent trips to Caroline's catechism class, the existence of which remained unknown to the public for the full eight months she attended them. Sometimes she brought John along as well. One day in October 1963 John marched nois- ily into class with his make-believe rifle—a stick—over his shoul- der. "He thinks he's a soldier," Caroline sighed, "and he doesn't even know how to salute." She had no way of knowing that, within a matter of weeks, little John would snap off the most famous sa- lute in history.

I should have guessed that it would be too much to grow old with him and see our children grow up together. So now he is a legend, when he would have preferred to be a man.

—JACKIE

11

⚬

"They Had Been Through
So Much Together"

On October 1, Jackie was scheduled to depart from New York's Idlewild Airport aboard a TWA flight bound for Rome. Before she did, however, she wanted to join her husband in welcoming Ethiopian emperor Haile Selassie at Washington's Union Station. It would be her first public appearance since Patrick's death.

The diminutive seventy-one-year-old monarch had been a revered figure on the world stage for more than forty years, and while Jackie would not be hosting the state dinner for him that night, she wanted to meet the man she had admired since childhood.

Met with a royal fanfare, Selassie stepped off the train and bowed his head when Jackie, wearing a trim-fitting black wool suit and clutching two dozen red roses, extended her gloved hand.

The two hit it off instantly, later chatting away in French over tea in the West Sitting Room. There were presents for his hosts: a carved ivory soldier for John, a doll and a gold medallion on a chain for Caroline, and—the pièce de résistance—a full-length leopard coat for Jackie. "Je suis comblée!" ("I am overcome"), she said, wasting no time jettisoning her wool jacket and trying the coat on. She wore the coat as they strolled into the Rose Garden. "See, Jack," she said. "He brought it to me! He brought it to me!"

On October 4, Jackie and her entourage boarded the *Christina* bound for Istanbul. A great believer in keeping up appearances ("You do not stand a chance of becoming rich unless you *look* rich in the first place"), Onassis splurged on penthouses, limousines, helicopters, even his own airline—Olympic Airways. None of his other toys could compare, however, to the converted 325-foot frigate he had christened after his adored only daughter in 1954. The *Christina* featured an Olympic-size saltwater swimming pool, several bars, a ballroom, Baccarat crystal chandeliers, lapis lazuli balustrades, gold-plated bathroom fixtures, allegorical friezes of nude nymphs representing the four seasons in the dining room, a grand piano in the glass-walled sitting room, a private screening room, an El Greco hanging in the formal study (next to crossed swords in gold scabbards that were a gift from Saudi King Ibn Saud), and mosaic floors throughout depicting scenes from Greek mythology.

A jewel-encrusted Buddha that Ari bought in 1960 for $300,000 ($2.4 million today) sat on a bureau in his four-room master suite. Ari's bathtub was of blue Sienna marble with mosaic dolphins and flying fish inspired by King Minos's palace at Knossos. The children's playroom was decorated by Jackie's old friend (and *Madeline* creator) Ludwig Bemelmans, and the canopied beds were piled with dolls dressed by Dior.

For excursions off the ship, the *Christina* carried on board four motorboats (including two mahogany-hulled Hacker speedboats), two kayaks, a small sailboat, three dinghies, a glass-bottom boat, a small car, a helicopter, and a five-passenger Piaggio seaplane.

Ari (friends stopped calling him "Aristo" when he turned forty) took special pride in one of the yacht's more curious features. Located on the main deck was a circular bar made from the timbers of a sunken Spanish galleon. But what made the bar unique were the stools with seats covered in the foreskins of white whales. "Madame," he announced to the reclusive screen legend Greta Garbo, "you are sitting on the biggest penis in the world!" Garbo became a regular aboard the *Christina*—along with the likes of Cary Grant, John Wayne, Princess Grace, Richard Burton and Elizabeth Taylor, Humphrey Bogart and Lauren Bacall, Clark Gable, Gary Cooper, Judy Garland, Frank Sinatra, and of course his prize catch—Winston Churchill.

Not exactly Jackie's style, to be sure. But then, even the first lady had not been pampered to quite this extent. As a black-sweatered crew of sixty (not counting the dance band) catered to the passengers' every need, the Dom Perignon flowed freely and no fewer than eight varieties of caviar were served. When Jackie wasn't exploring the cobblestone streets of Crete, Ithaca, and Lesbos, she and her fellow guests were dining on lobster and foie gras or cutting loose to bouzouki music on the yacht's mosaic-tiled dance floor.

As they island-hopped across the Aegean, Jackie kept in touch with JFK by ship-to-shore phone, and more than once dashed off a flowery letter saying how much she wished he could have come along. Yet she clearly seemed happier than she had been in months. With Lee giggling in the background, Jackie called to report that the *Christina* was now in the hands of pirates. "I told you so," Jack deadpanned.

Stateside, newspapers were soon filled with pictures of Jackie sunbathing on board the *Christina* in a bikini. When the yacht docked in Istanbul so that Jackie could visit the Blue Mosque and see the magnificent jewels housed in the Topkapi Palace, tourists pressed in to catch a glimpse of her. To Jack, it was all beginning to look like a replay of Jackie's *la dolce vita* romp with Gianni Agnelli.

Jack, meanwhile, was planning a trip of his own, although he doubted Jackie would be willing to tag along. Texas Governor John Connally invited JFK to visit Texas at the end of November. An ongoing feud between liberal Senator Ralph Yarborough and conservative Connally, an LBJ ally, threatened to cleave the state's party right down the middle. If JFK wanted to hold on to the Lone Star State in 1964—not to mention bolster his flagging popularity with white voters in the South—then some serious fence-mending was in order, Connally warned.

The two-day swing through Texas was to include fund-raising events in San Antonio, Houston, Fort Worth, and Dallas. Then the Kennedys were invited to spend the weekend at Lyndon Johnson's ranch on the Pedernales River. Jackie hadn't campaigned for her husband since the 1960 primaries, and she wasn't scheduled to resume her duties as first lady until January 1964. It seemed unlikely that she'd be willing to visit Texas, but Connally was adamant. "Well," JFK told the governor, "we'll just have to wait to see what she says when she gets back." With Salinger, he felt free to say what he really thought. "There's no way in hell," he told his press secretary, "that Jackie is going to agree to go to Texas."

As the Aegean cruise progressed, Onassis started to lavish more and more attention on Jackie. By the time they reached Ari's private island of Skorpios, Lee was seething. When Onassis gave Jackie a spectacular ruby-and-diamond necklace, Lee wrote to Jack in mock indignation, "All I've got is three dinky little bracelets that Caroline wouldn't wear to her own birthday party!"

Inevitably, tongues began to wag about the nature of Jackie's relationship with the swarthy Greek tycoon. Their shipmates, however, insisted nothing inappropriate was going on between Onassis and the first lady at the time. There was "definitely a relationship between Lee and Ari," FDR Jr. said. But Jackie "was there simply for the rest." Moreover, Onassis was "very conscious of his image. He didn't want to do anything to embarrass the President's wife."

No one back home dared suggest that the first lady was cheating on her husband. But once again stories about high-living Jackie and her jet-set pals filled the papers, providing Jack's critics with plenty of ammunition. "Does this sort of behavior," asked the *Boston Globe*, "seem fitting for a woman in mourning?"

Jackie may have had a "twinge" or two of guilt, Roosevelt conceded, but certainly not enough to make her suddenly turn around and fly home. Indeed, instead of cutting her trip short, Jackie extended it so she could visit Morocco. Earlier, she had teased Jack that if given a choice between Morocco and Ireland, she'd much rather spend time in Morocco. Besides, King Hassan II was eager to repay the Kennedys for the hospitality they had shown him seven months earlier.

Desert tribeswomen greeted Jackie with their shrill, warbling call as she and Lee were driven to Hassan's Bahia Palace overlooking the Atlas Mountains. Coincidentally, King Hassan II's firstborn son, Prince Mohammed, had been born on August 21. In keeping with Muslim tradition, the entire country was celebrating his first forty days of life. Everyone was concerned that this might bring back painful memories for Jackie, but her attitude remained upbeat. She told Clint Hill that she felt it was "wonderful" that they could celebrate their infant son's future. "The President and I," she said, "had similar hopes and dreams for Patrick."

As part of the national celebration, Berber warriors put on a dazzling display of their prowess on horseback, firing rifles into the air and whooping as they galloped across a field. Jackie covered her eyes with both hands to avoid seeing Secret Service agent Paul Landis, who was on the field taking snapshots, narrowly escape from being trampled to death.

While Jackie seemed to be climbing out of her depression, Jack appeared to be diving deeper into his. "Everyone was so concerned about Jackie," Cassini said, "they seemed to forget that Jack was suffering too." Pierre Salinger noted that his boss "seemed a little deflated, a little distracted." Instead of pounding on his desk and shouting down the phone lines about the negative press Jackie's trip was generating, the president "more or less shrugged it off. He wasn't happy about it, but he was more disappointed than angry."

Arthur Schlesinger had a fairly simple explanation for JFK's solemn mood, beyond the heavy burden of his office: "They had just lost a child. They were still feeling it. . . . He missed her."

The state dinner for Irish Prime Minister Seán Lemass on October 15 certainly did help matters. With his sister Jean Smith substituting for Jackie, JFK presided over what Gene Kelly dubbed a "four handkerchief evening" of groaning bagpipes, Irish fiddlers, and melancholy Irish tunes.

After the dinner, fifteen guests were invited upstairs for more of the same. Everyone laughed and clapped as Kelly danced an Irish jig, then brushed away a tear while Teddy belted out "An Irish Lullaby" ("Too-ra-loo-ra-loo-ra") and family friend Dorothy Tubridy sang the mournful "Boys of Wexford."

Through it all, Jim Reed couldn't take his eyes off Jack. "The President had the sweetest and saddest kind of look on his face," Reed recalled. "He was standing by himself, leaning against the doorway, and just seemed transported."

The Kennedy children, however, could still be counted on to provide comic relief. One of John's bigger faux pas occurred while he stood on the Truman Balcony watching a welcoming parade for Yugoslavia's president, Marshal Tito. As the Marine Band played, John stood waving two toy pistols and shouting "We want Kennedy! We want Kennedy!" One of the guns went flying over the railing, landing at Tito's feet. "John has grown up," the president sighed to Kenny O'Donnell, "to develop a colorful personality."

The same day her son was threatening to cause an international incident, Jackie prepared to leave Marrakech aboard the king's private plane, bound for Paris. She hadn't realized that, when she first arrived, Hassan II had instructed his minions to acquire any object in the kingdom that seemed to catch her fancy. Once she got to the airport, Jackie was surprised to see uniformed guards loading three carloads of gifts onto her plane.

Jack, Caroline, and John-John were at Dulles International Airport to greet Jackie when she finally returned on October 17,

1963. "Oh, Jack," she said, throwing her arms around him, "I'm so glad to be home!" On the ride to the White House, Caroline squeezed between her parents while John nuzzled up to Mommy. Jackie, still wearing her white gloves, tickled John until he was squealing with laughter.

"Be careful, Mommy," Caroline said. "He just had something to drink."

For all the homecoming hugs and kisses, Mommy and Daddy went their separate ways the next day. Jackie headed to Wexford for a weekend of riding, and Jack to Boston for a football game and a fund-raiser.

Neither, it quickly became clear, had fully come to terms with Patrick's death. Bronzed and healthy-looking but emotionally spent, Jackie finally found the release she needed riding Sardar through the fields and valleys surrounding Wexford.

In Boston, the president was watching a Harvard-Columbia football game when he suddenly turned to Kenny O'Donnell and Dave Powers. "I want to visit Patrick's grave," he said. "Right now. Alone."

The president's party somehow managed to duck out, elude the press, and drive to Holyhood Cemetery in Brookline without being followed. With Powers, O'Donnell, and his Secret Service detail keeping a respectful distance, the president walked slowly up to the headstone marked, simply, KENNEDY. "He seems," Jack said, "so alone here."

JACKIE HAD BEEN HOME LESS than a week when JFK sprang the Texas trip on her over dinner with the Bradlees. Jackie was feeling "a little remorseful," Ben Bradlee recalled, "about all the publicity" generated by her cruise with Onassis, "including a *News-week* story she felt went a little heavy on the hijinks." But, she said, "Jack is being really nice and understanding about everything."

"So Jackie's guilt feelings may work to my advantage," JFK said with a smile. "Maybe now you'll come with us to Texas next month."

"Sure I will, Jack," she answered. JFK was right—Jackie was feeling guilty. She knew Jack had desperately wanted another son. "He felt the loss of the baby in the house," she said, "as much as I did." Jackie also knew that her ongoing depression over Patrick only made it that much harder on Jack. "I was melancholy after the death of our baby," she confessed to Catholic priest Richard T. McSorley after Dallas, "and I stayed away longer than I needed to."

Jack's advisers were amazed to hear that the first lady was willing to hit the campaign trail. "I almost fell over when he told me Jackie was coming with us," O'Donnell said.

"You know how I hate that sort of thing," she told friends. "But if he wants me there, then that's all that matters. It's a tiny sacrifice on my part for something he feels is very important to him."

Caught up in the moment, Jackie instructed Pam Turnure to issue a press release stating that this was only the first of many campaign trips she intended to make on her husband's behalf. She intended to let the American people know that she would do whatever she could to ensure Jack's reelection.

Before the White House could make a formal announcement, however, an ugly incident was already giving Jackie second thoughts. On October 24, an angry anti–United Nations mob attacked Adlai Stevenson after he gave a speech celebrating world peace in Dallas. The illustrious UN ambassador was jeered, spat upon, pelted with eggs, and struck in the head with a placard. City fathers were mortified, issuing an immediate apology, but the episode left Stevenson shaken and Jackie wondering if going was such a good idea.

Over dinner at the White House the following night, FDR Jr. and his wife, Sue, expressed their misgivings. The next morning, Jackie told her husband that she had changed her mind; she would bow out on the advice of her doctors. When he got wind of this, Connally exploded. The first lady was well liked in Texas—more popular than several politicians who came to mind—and she simply had to be there.

Jackie stayed on the fence for days. Right after the dinner with the Roosevelts, she sought the advice of Clint Hill. The first lady trusted her loyal Secret Service agent implicitly; he was her friend as well as her guardian. When he told her she should feel "perfectly safe going to Texas with the President," Jackie understandably felt reassured. "You always know exactly the right thing to say," she told him.

On November 7, Salinger made the official announcement: "Mrs. Kennedy will accompany the President on the entire Texas trip." Asked if, as in the past, ill health might force Jackie to cancel at the last minute, Salinger hedged. "She will help in every way she can," he said, "consistent with other obligations and continuing good health."

Even after the official announcement, Bobby and Senator J. William Fulbright, a longtime Kennedy ally, stepped forward to voice concern. They understood that the president felt he had to go, but they saw no reason for Jackie to subject herself to jeers and catcalls. But by mid-November, Jackie was committed. "If Jack wants me," she said, "I'll go anywhere."

Ben and Tony Bradlee were the Kennedys' most frequent guests and at one point were invited over for dinner followed by a movie in the White House theater. During the cocktail hour, Jackie put on records of Moroccan music and demonstrated some of the hip-swiveling belly-dance moves she had observed on her trip before dissolving in laughter.

That night's movie was the latest James Bond offering, *From Russia with Love,* and Bradlee felt Jack "seemed to enjoy the cool and the sex and the brutality of it." Jackie, meantime, had just done her new weekly stint as one of the mother-helpers at the White House School and allowed that she was "appalled" at having to help the little boys go to the bathroom.

On November 10, the Kennedys invited the Bradlees to join them for the weekend at Wexford. The four friends perched on the stone wall surrounding the main house, sipping Bloody Marys while they took in the last of Virginia's brilliant fall foliage. John ran around playing soldier in a plastic army helmet, and Jackie and Caroline both showed off their skills on horseback.

The weekend's most memorable moment came while Tony and JFK were sitting on the ground chatting. As Jackie and Ben looked on, Macaroni walked up to JFK and began nibbling his head. Tony's attempts to pull the horse away failed, and Kennedy rolled on the ground laughing. "Keep shooting, Captain," he told White House photographer Cecil Stoughton, who captured the scene on film. "You are about to see a president being eaten by a horse."

The last time the Bradlees saw JFK was the next day, Veterans Day, as he helicoptered off to Arlington to lay a wreath at the Tomb of the Unknown Soldier. At the cemetery, with hundreds of spectators watching, John managed to bolt from the Kiddie

Detail and join his grinning father in the parade. The president's left-handed son loved to salute, but it had taken the combined efforts of the Secret Service and the U.S. Army to get John to switch hands. This time, as soon as the president placed the wreath on the tomb, John joined the color guard in saluting his father on cue—this time the proper way, with his right hand.

It was only a matter of time before John, hypnotized by the fluttering flags and the colorful uniforms, drifted away again. The president looked out over the thousands of headstones and markers rolling up and down the hillsides. "Go get John," he ordered a Secret Service agent. "I think he'll be lonely out there."

On November 13, 1963, General Maxwell Taylor stood in full dress uniform on the White House balcony with the children, waiting for the president and first lady to arrive. Bundled up against the cold, Caroline and John sipped tea poured for them by White House butlers. Once Jack and Jackie appeared, the 1,700 underprivileged children and their families who had gathered on the South Lawn to hear the kilted Black Watch pipers burst into applause.

John squirmed in his mother's lap, then jumped up to peer over the wrought-iron railing. Caroline, meantime, was content to snuggle up against her father, her arms around his shoulders.

JFK had always loved the plaintive wail of bagpipes, and of all the pipers, Scotland's famous Black Watch Regiment was his favorite. "They're wonderful, aren't they, Buttons?" he asked.

"Yes, Daddy," she answered, "and very loud."

This was the last time the Kennedys and their children—America's most celebrated first family—would be seen together in public.

Dinner that night at the White House had the touch of the

surreal, with Greta Garbo as the guest of honor. Garbo brought along her lover, George Schlee, and her best friend—Schlee's wife, Valentina. The president seemed less interested in Garbo's storied film career than he was in her open arrangement with the Schlees.

Also among the guests was Lem Billings, who had become friendly with Garbo the previous summer while they both cruised the Mediterranean aboard movie producer Sam Spiegel's yacht. Jack decided to play a trick on his friend, and asked Garbo to pretend she didn't know him. When Garbo walked into the dining room with Jackie, Billings rushed up to greet her. "Greta!" he said.

The Great Garbo held him at arm's length. "I have never seen this man before," she insisted. For the next hour—straight through to the second course—everyone managed to keep up the charade, and no one was enjoying Billings's pained reaction more than the president. "I just don't understand it. Are you sure, Lem? Maybe it was just someone who *looked* like Garbo."

"It was a lovely, intimate dinner," Garbo recalled. "President Kennedy did not smoke and drank only water. I felt like one of the damned when I lit a cigarette." After dinner, Garbo was given a tour of the White House by her hosts, and at one point took off her shoes to climb onto Lincoln's bed.

The tour moved on to the Oval Office. When Garbo commented on his scrimshaw collection, Jack impulsively gave her a prized piece—one with a tall ship carved on it. It had been, he neglected to mention, a birthday gift from his wife. "He never gave *me* a whale's tooth," Jackie joked, although it was obvious to Billings and the others that her feelings were hurt.

Jack invited Garbo to stay the night, but by this time she felt she may have overstayed her welcome. "I must go," she announced. "I think I am getting intoxicated."

"I think she is," Jackie muttered as Garbo left with the Schlees.

In her thank-you note to Jackie, Garbo thanked the Kennedys for a "really fascinating and enchanting evening. I might believe it was a dream if I did not have in my possession the President's 'tooth' facing me. I shall forever cherish the memory of you, the President, and the evening."

THE NEXT DAY JACK FLEW to New York to give a speech, opting this time to dispense with what he called the "fuss and feathers" of a motorcycle escort from the airport into Manhattan. At one of the ten midtown lights that stopped the presidential limousine as it made its way to the Carlyle, a woman bolted from the sidewalk and ran up to the car, firing off a flashbulb in the startled president's face. "She might well have been an assassin," a New York police official told *Time* magazine in an issue that was actually on the stands the week *before* Dallas. The incident, *Time* said in its eerily prescient piece, "aged the Secret Service detail ten years."

That evening, Jack sneaked out the side door of the Carlyle to attend a small party at the Fifth Avenue apartment of Stephen and Jean Smith. Over dinner, Adlai Stevenson described in harrowing detail what it was like to be spat upon and threatened by a Dallas mob. He urged the president not to go—with or without Jackie. "It is simply too dangerous, Mr. President," said the man who had been the Democratic nominee for president in 1952 and 1956. "There's something very ugly going on down there."

Oleg Cassini was at the party that night, and listened while Stevenson spoke. "Adlai Stevenson had been in politics his entire life. He was not a fearful man, and he was certainly accustomed to facing hostile crowds," Cassini said. "He was telling the President that this was different, that he might be placing himself in danger."

As they stood in the hallway saying their goodbyes to the Smiths, Cassini turned to Jack and asked, "Why do you go? Your own people are saying you should not go." Jack shrugged and smiled. "We shook hands and I thought nothing of it," Cassini said. "I was always asking why he did this, and didn't do that. It was a comment made *en passant.*" It was the last time Cassini saw the president.

While Jackie returned that weekend to ride her beloved Sardar at Wexford, her husband headed down to Florida to watch the launch of a Polaris missile and review troops at Tampa's MacDill Air Force Base before flying on to Palm Beach. Once back at his father's estate with Dave Powers and a few other old friends—Kenny O'Donnell, Harvard classmate Torbert Macdonald, Smathers—Jack took a late-afternoon swim and then sat back to watch the Navy–Duke football game on television.

That night after dinner, Jack settled into a padded rocking chair, lit up a cigar, and talked politics with the old gang. Although he was still concerned about the "ugly mood" in Texas, the president was looking forward to the coming campaign and confident of reelection. Once again, he sang "September Song"—this time, Powers said, with even more emotion than usual.

That Sunday, Jack and his friends watched TV coverage of the Green Bay Packers–Chicago Bears game, then screened the ribald new movie *Tom Jones,* starring Albert Finney. The period farce quickly bored the president, and after twenty minutes he headed for La Guerida's saltwater pool. While sunbathing with Powers on the terrace, he talked about the ambitious plans he and Jackie had for the summer of 1964. Between the house on Squaw Island and the new lease they just signed on a large property abutting Hammersmith Farm—not to mention Wexford—there would be lots of opportunity for relaxation and fun during breaks in his campaign schedule. "I can't wait," he said. "Can't wait."

On the way back to Washington the next day aboard Air Force One, Jack let Smathers know that he still had misgivings about the upcoming trip. He was especially disappointed that Vice President Johnson hadn't been able to handle the squabble between Governor Connally and Senator Yarborough himself. "Damn it to hell," JFK told his friend half jokingly, "I've got to go out to Texas. Your friend Lyndon is causing me trouble."

"Lyndon Johnson helped you get elected," Smathers replied. "You owe a lot to him."

"How do I get out of it?" JFK asked.

"You can't get out of it, Mr. President," Smathers stressed. "You've got to go. You're doing the right thing."

Jack grudgingly agreed, but went on to say that he just wished "we had this thing over with." Smathers never forgot what his friend said next, although it was a phrase he had heard Jack utter dozens of times over the years. "You've got to live every day like it's your last day on earth and it damn well may be!"

Looking back on the day he urged JFK to go ahead with his fateful trip to Texas, Smathers admitted, "I wish to God I hadn't said it." He was not alone. Less than forty-eight hours before the Kennedys left Washington, Pierre Salinger was getting ready for his own trip to Japan with Secretary of State Dean Rusk. "I wish I weren't going to Texas," the president told his press secretary.

Salinger had just finished reading a letter from a woman in

Dallas imploring him to tell JFK to cancel the trip. "I'm worried about him," the letter read. "I think something terrible will happen to him."

Salinger said nothing to the president about the letter; instead he brushed aside Kennedy's concerns. "Don't worry about it," he reassured JFK without a moment's hesitation. "It's going to be great and you're going to draw the biggest crowds ever. Going with Mrs. Kennedy will be terrific."

On the eve of their departure for Dallas, the first couple hosted a reception for the U.S. Supreme Court justices and seven hundred other members of the judicial branch. Jackie had spent the morning riding in Virginia, and as usual supervised every detail of the evening with Nancy Tuckerman—right down to the music—over the phone. True to form, she also tried to weasel out of going at the last minute.

This time, the president said no. "You're not getting out of this one, Jackie," he said, reminding Jackie that the attorney general and his wife, Ethel, were also going to be there to greet the justices and would be "very disappointed" if she didn't show. In fact, he went on, it was Bobby's thirty-eighth birthday, and he and Ethel would be there for the judicial reception even if it meant RFK would be late for his own party later that night.

Shortly after Clint Hill deposited Jackie back at the White House that afternoon, he met with fellow Secret Service agents Roy Kellerman and Floyd Boring to discuss the upcoming Texas trip. All three men were surprised Jackie was going but, Hill later wrote, they were also convinced "that the President and Mrs. Kennedy seemed so much closer since Patrick died, and we felt it might actually be beneficial for her to get out in public." Still, Hill worried that such an exhausting trip might trigger a relapse.

Jackie, he thought at the time, "had only just started laughing again."

Wearing a claret silk velvet two-piece evening suit over a white silk charmeuse shirt, Jackie joined Jack in welcoming Chief Justice Earl Warren and other Supreme Court justices in the Yellow Oval Room before proceeding downstairs. As the first lady mingled with their distinguished guests in the Blue, Red, and Green rooms, it quickly became clear she was the main attraction. Jackie had been away for months, and many of the guests literally tripped over each other welcoming her back. This was, in fact, Jackie's first official appearance at a formal White House function since Patrick's death.

The president and first lady stayed for less than forty-five minutes; Bobby and Ethel left not long after for Hickory Hill. With the judges and their spouses still downstairs waltzing to the strains of Lerner and Loewe's *Camelot*—each number chosen by the first lady—Jack and Jackie packed for the next morning's flight to San Antonio, the first stop on their Texas trip. Jackie packed several suits and dresses by Cassini, but the president insisted she wear one outfit in particular, and that she wear it in Dallas: a double-breasted pink wool Chanel suit with gold buttons, a navy blue collar, and matching pink pillbox hat.

At around 10:40 the next morning, Marine One landed on the South Lawn to pick up the president and his party. John was along for the ride as far as Andrews Air Force Base; Jack and Jackie had already said goodbye to Caroline before she went off to her little school in the White House solarium.

Once they got to Andrews, the president got off the helicopter, turned, and bent down to say goodbye to his son, who was still strapped into his seat. John often protested at times like these, and this was no different. "I want to come!" he cried. "I want to come!"

Mommy leaned over, kissed her little boy, and reminded him that when they got back it would be his birthday. John would have none of it. Squirming and wailing, arms outstretched, he was simply inconsolable. Secret Service agent Bob Foster took over from here, trying to distract the indignant toddler while his parents walked up the gangway to Air Force One.

As they boarded the plane, Jack turned to O'Donnell and smiled. "I feel great," he said. "My back feels better than it's felt in years." Their takeoff had been delayed slightly; true to form, the first lady, despite getting up at 6 a.m. to have her hair done by the celebrity stylist Kenneth, was running a little late.

No longer anxious about the trip, Jackie and Jack spent much of the flight gossiping with Powers and O'Donnell about Bobby's wild birthday party the previous night at Hickory Hill. The only sour note on the flight had to do with the weather. The advance report Jack had been handed failed to predict the heat wave that was sweeping across Texas. The president now worried that Jackie's pastel wool suits, especially the pink Chanel number he had picked out for Dallas, would be uncomfortably warm.

Before the plane touched down in Texas, Jackie changed into one of Cassini's lightweight designs—a white, short-sleeved suit with a cowl collar, worn with a narrow black belt, long white gloves, and a black beret. Despite the heat, the first lady knew she needed some way to keep her hairstyle from being obliterated as they drove through the streets with the top down.

As soon as the president and his wife stepped out of the rear door of Air Force One, a roar went up from the five thousand people waiting to greet them at San Antonio Airport. Jack headed straight for the crowd to shake hands, while someone handed the first lady a bouquet of yellow roses—the first of many. It was a repeat of that day in 1960 when Jack had returned to Hyannis Port after winning the nomination, only this time Jackie wasn't going to be left behind. She followed her husband to the fence. Jackie, noted CBS correspondent Bob Pierpoint, looked like someone "who was very much in love with her husband and even in love with the fact that he's a politician."

More than 125,000 people lined the motorcade route, cheering wildly and waving signs that read BIENVENIDO MR. AND MRS. PRESIDENT, JACKIE COME WATERSKIING IN TEXAS, WELCOME JACK AND JACKIE, and simply WE LOVE YOU, JACKIE! "See," Jack told her as they waved to the crowds, "you do make a difference."

The first stop was Brooks Air Force Base, where Jack spoke at the dedication of the new School of Aerospace Medicine. As he was being shown the facilities, JFK lingered at the school's oxygen chamber before turning to one of the scientists. "Is it possible," he asked, "that space medicine might improve treatment for premature infants like my son Patrick?"

From San Antonio, they moved on to Houston, where they drew even bigger and more enthusiastic crowds. It was obvious to everyone why. "Mr. President, your crowd here today was about the same as last year's," Powers told his boss, "but a hundred thousand more people came out to cheer for Jackie." As far as this fence-mending operation was concerned, said longtime JFK political aide Larry O'Brien, "Jackie is a pretty good carpenter."

♂

TO BE SURE, SHE WAS again proving herself to be a huge asset on the stump. Speaking to the League of United Latin-American Citizens in relatively effortless Spanish (midway through she stumbled over the word *Massachusetts*), a radiant Jackie charmed not only her Hispanic audience but old Texas hands like Lyndon Johnson and John Connally. Immediately following Jackie at the lectern, LBJ admitted that anything he could say was "anticlimactic" and praised her as the president's "lovely, gracious lady."

At a testimonial dinner in the Houston Coliseum that night for Texas congressman Albert Thomas, all eyes remained on the first lady—a fact that clearly delighted JFK. "The people just love that gal," LBJ remarked to his aide Jack Valenti. "They sure do."

On the flight to Fort Worth, it was obvious that the packed schedule of motorcades, dedications, and testimonial dinners was beginning to take its toll. Jackie smoked her way through half a pack of Newport menthol cigarettes (she had recently switched from L&M's) and, for the first time in weeks, the tremor in Jack's hands was back, triggered by nervous exhaustion. "He'd had it for years," noted Jamie Auchincloss. "That's why he often had his hand tucked in his blazer pocket—to hide the trembling."

They arrived shortly before 1 a.m. at their three-bedroom suite on the eighth floor of Fort Worth's Texas Hotel. Normally, Jackie would have noticed that wealthy local art collectors had covered the walls with Picassos, Van Goghs, and Monets in honor of their distinguished guests, but not tonight. They were both simply wrung out.

This last night of JFK's life, Jackie went to Jack's bedroom to spend the night with him, but he told her it probably wasn't a good idea. The stomach cramps that had plagued him for years were back with a vengeance—another nervous reaction, he surmised, to their grueling schedule. "You were great today," Jack told her as they fell into each other's arms. In that moment, Jackie later said, they were both so tired it was as if they were holding each other up. They kissed, and she returned to her separate room for the night.

The next morning, they awoke to the sound of a crowd gathered in a parking lot across from the hotel. Thousands of people had waited in the rain for hours to see the president and Mrs. Kennedy, and they were far from satisfied when only Jack came out to address them.

"Where's Jackie? Where's Jackie?" the crowd demanded.

Jackie was, in fact, upstairs with Mary Gallagher, digging through her luggage for makeup that had already been packed away for Dallas. She had taken a close look in the mirror and decided she needed a touch-up for the tough day ahead. "One day in a campaign," she sighed to her secretary, "can age a person thirty years."

All of which left the president downstairs in the parking lot, trying to explain to the crowd why she wasn't coming down to see them. "Mrs. Kennedy is organizing herself," he told them. "It takes a little longer, but of course, she looks better than us when she does it."

From there, the president went to the hotel's grand ballroom, where he was guest of honor at a Chamber of Commerce breakfast. According to their schedule, Jackie was not supposed to attend this event, either. Now that the crowds in the parking lot were clamoring for her, he told the Secret Service to bring her down to the breakfast—and fast.

With Mary Gallagher's help, she buttoned up her short white kid gloves and then took one last look in the mirror. "Oh Mary," she said wistfully, "I've found another wrinkle." When she finally made her entrance a half hour after the breakfast started, the ballroom erupted in hoots and cheers; men *and* women climbed up onto chairs to applaud.

JFK watched as Jackie was guided to the dais and seated at the head table. "Two years ago," he told the euphoric crowd, "I introduced myself by saying I was the man who accompanied Mrs. Kennedy to Paris. I am getting somewhat that same sensation as I travel around Texas." Then, glancing over at Jackie in the pink Chanel suit he had picked out for her to wear in Dallas, he asked, "Why is it nobody wonders what Lyndon and I will wear?"

Thrilled at their reception that morning, the president and Jackie returned to their hotel suite to relax before boarding Air Force One for Dallas. They took a few minutes to appreciate the masterpieces that were hanging on their walls, and quickly placed a call to one of the donors to say they were "touched" by the gesture.

Jack was also touched by his wife's willingness to campaign with him; he always knew that together they were a potent force, but assumed she would sit this election out as she did in 1960. It was just another sign, their friends agreed, of the strengthening of their marriage.

"They had been through so much together in the last few years," Spalding said, "particularly the baby's death. I think by the time they got to Dallas she saw herself as a full partner."

At 10:35 a.m., Kenny O'Donnell knocked on their hotel room door and told them it was time to depart for Dallas. As they walked out the door, Jackie said to Jack, "I'll go anywhere with you this year."

He wasted no time taking her up on the unexpected offer. "How about California in two weeks?" he asked.

"I'll be there," she grinned.

The president looked at O'Donnell, eyes wide in mock disbelief. "Did you hear *that?*" he asked.

On the thirteen-minute flight to Dallas, someone handed Jack a copy of that morning's *Dallas News,* containing a black-bordered full-page ad paid for by the "American Fact-finding Committee." The ad slammed Kennedy's "ultra-leftist" policies and branded him "fifty times a fool" for signing the Nuclear Test Ban Treaty.

Jack showed his wife the ad and shook his head. "We're heading into nut country today," he told her. Then he made the kind of comment she had heard so often, it no longer had any impact. "But Jackie," he said, "if somebody wants to shoot me from a window with a rifle, nobody can stop it, so why worry about it?"

By the time Air Force One touched down at Dallas's Love Field, the rain had been replaced by blue skies and sunshine. The president and Mrs. Kennedy stepped out into the broiling heat and were once again welcomed with wild cheers and applause.

Someone thrust another bouquet in her arms, and then she and Jack headed for the fence to shake hands. It was then that she realized the roses she clutched weren't the yellow roses of Texas she had been handed in San Antonio and Houston and Fort Worth. They were red.

AS THE PRESIDENT'S LIMOUSINE LEFT Love Field at 11:55 a.m., Secret Service agent Roy Kellerman radioed to all units "Lancer and Lace departing." With them were Governor Connally, who sat on the pull-out jumpseat in front of Jack while Nellie Connally sat in front of Jackie. The motorcade was bound downtown for the Dallas Trade Mart, where 2,600 people were waiting to have lunch with the president and his wife.

To everyone's surprise, the reception in Dallas was the friendliest yet. Thousands of cheering, placard-waving Texans lined the streets, in some spots thirteen people deep. Elated, the president stopped the motorcade twice—first to shake hands with a group of awestruck schoolchildren and then to say hello to a group of nuns.

Making small talk along the route, Jack asked Nellie Connally how she would respond if someone booed her husband. "If I'd get close," Nellie answered, "I'd scratch their eyes out." Kennedy laughed but kept right on waving. "Mr. President," she said as the car made a hard left turn from Houston Street onto Elm Street, "you certainly can't say Dallas doesn't love you."

"No," he replied, "you certainly can't."

Sweltering in her wool suit and squinting in the brilliant sun—Jack had asked her not to wear sunglasses so the crowd could see her face—Jackie prayed they would reach their destination soon.

Nellie Connally pointed to an overpass ahead.

"We're almost through," she said. "The Trade Mart's beyond that."

"Good," Jackie thought to herself as she and Jack exchanged a fleeting glance. "It will be so cool in that tunnel . . ."

WHAT HAPPENED NEXT WAS SAID to be the catalyst for an era of turmoil, discord, and bloodshed. Vietnam, campus unrest, the assassinations of Martin Luther King and Robert Kennedy, race riots, the rise of the counterculture and a surge in drug abuse, even the toxic political climate that gave rise to Watergate—all seemed to flow from the wellspring of shock and despair that was tapped in Dallas on November 22, 1963.

Serious historians and conspiracy theory crackpots alike have spent a half century dissecting the events of that day and analyzing how an assassin's bullets changed the trajectory of history. Along the way, dark secrets were unearthed and the Camelot myth that Jackie had so painstakingly nurtured shattered beyond repair. For all this, we seem no closer to the truth about JFK's murder (Was it a lone gunman? The Mafia? Fidel Castro? The CIA?) or what Kennedy might have done—particularly whether he would have sent American troops to fight in Vietnam.

One simple fact, however, has never been disputed—that Jackie's strength and natural sense of dignity in the days following her husband's death were the glue that held a stunned nation together. Only those closest to her knew that for months after the assassination Jackie was consumed with grief.

"I cry all day and all night until I'm so exhausted I can't function," she told her friend Kitty Carlisle Hart. "Then I drink." Jackie wrote Ben and Tony Bradlee telling them that there was "one thing you must know. I consider that my life is over, and I will spend the rest of it waiting for it really to be over." She confessed to her friend Roswell Gilpatric that, for a time, she had even considered suicide. "I have enough sleeping pills to do it," she told him. "But of course she wouldn't," Gilpatric said, "because of the children."

On her own, Jackie would for decades continue her reign as one of the most talked-about, written-about, and speculated-about people in the world—the most celebrated American woman of the twentieth century. Not even her decision to marry Aristotle Onassis just months after Bobby Kennedy's assassination—so shocking to a world more comfortable thinking of her as the beloved widow of a martyred president—would tarnish Jackie's image for long. "She would have preferred to be herself," her brother-in-law Ted Kennedy remarked, paraphrasing a remark she had made about Jack. "But the world insisted that she be a legend, too."

When Jackie succumbed to lymphoma on May 19, 1994 at the age of 64 with John Jr., Caroline, and her longtime companion Maurice Tempelsman at her bedside, there was a spontaneous outpouring of emotion from world leaders and common folk alike. Many Americans, taken by surprise, were both stunned and saddened by the passing of someone who had been part of the national landscape for more than thirty years. They contemplated what their world would be like without this living, breathing reminder of a man and an era of political idealism that—for all its shortcomings—seemed at one time to hold so much promise.

In the end, it all came back to the electrifying young couple in the White House that held the world spellbound for a thousand days. Was their marriage deeply flawed? Without a doubt. Complicated, even frustratingly so? No question. Infidelity, recklessness, and deceit were part of their imperfect union. But so, too, were courage, loyalty, wit, faith, fortitude, and a true, abiding affection.

After a decade of tragedies, triumphs, betrayals and reconciliations, the president and his wife were dealt the most devastating blow any couple could endure—the loss of a child. In that brief period of time between Patrick's death and Dallas—not quite four months—Jackie and Jack grew closer together than they had ever been. Too late to make up for all the pain that had gone before? Perhaps. But not too late for Jack to fulfill the promise to Jackie he made every time he got up to sing "September Song":

And these few precious days I'll spend with you
These precious days, I'll spend with you.

Acknowledgments

&

They wanted to talk. No, they *needed* to talk, to set the record straight, to tell the story of these two remarkable people as they knew it—and before it was too late. Some of their names instantly conjure up images of John F. Kennedy's bold New Frontier and of the Camelot myth Jackie so carefully nurtured: Theodore Sorensen, Arthur Schlesinger Jr., Pierre Salinger, John Kenneth Galbraith, Evelyn Lincoln, Letitia Baldrige, to name but a few. Other noted personalities like Gore Vidal, Oleg Cassini, Clare Boothe Luce, and George Plimpton had no official role but veered in and out of the Kennedys' orbit. Then there were the confidants virtually unknown to the public—people like Chuck and Betty Spalding, Charles and Martha Bartlett, and William Walton—whom Jack and Jackie turned to more than anyone for solace, advice, and companionship.

In the course of writing four bestselling books on JFK's tight-knit little family over the past twenty years, I was honored to interview not only the people above—all but two of whom have since died—but hundreds of others: family members, friends, classmates, colleagues, neighbors, political allies and enemies, doctors, servants, staff members, Jack's former girlfriends, Jackie's ex-fiancé, and the journalists and photographers who covered the Kennedy White House. Only a few of these asked not to be identified, and I respected their wishes.

It should come as no surprise that so many of these people are no longer with us. It has, after all, been a half century since that fateful day in Dallas. But as I played the tapes and combed through the notes of my interviews with these eyewitnesses to history, the story of Jackie and Jack's last few precious days as man and wife struck me as more compelling, heartbreaking, and inspiring than ever.

Once again, I am indebted to my editor, Mitchell Ivers, for his talent, insight, and commitment to bringing this bittersweet tale to life on the page. Mitchell is just one of the many fine people at Simon & Schuster and Gallery Books to whom I owe a debt of gratitude, most notably Louise Burke, Jen Bergstrom, Carolyn Reidy, Jennifer Robinson, Natasha Simons, Paul O'Halloran, Kelly Roberts, Lisa Rivlin, Eric Rayman, Felice Javit, Tom Pitoniak, Carly Sommerstein, Ruth Lee-Mui, and Janet Perr.

My agent, Ellen Levine, will be tired of hearing this for the thirtieth time in as many years and as many books, but she is simply the best agent and advocate an author could ever hope to have—and, more important, a treasured friend. I am also grateful to all of Ellen's talented colleagues at Trident Media Group, particularly Claire Roberts, Monika Woods, Alexa Stark, Alexander Slater, and Meredith Miller.

My wife, Valerie, who has put up with me for more than forty-one years, knows there are no words to express how I feel about her. Our beautiful and gifted daughters, Kate and Kelly, have always contributed much to the process, joined now by Kate's husband, Brooke Brower, and the newest member of our team to whom this book is dedicated, Graham Andersen Brower.

Historian Michael Foster was my original guide in tapping the vast store of information available at the John F. Kennedy Presidential Library, and I must also thank author Laurence Leamer and Northeastern University professor Ray Robinson for introducing me to him. My thanks as well to the library's Maryrose Grossman, James Hill, Maura Porter, Megan Desnoyers, William Johnson, Ron Whealen, and June Payne. I am also grateful to noted British television producer Charles Furneaux and American documentary filmmaker Robert Drew for their kindness and generous assistance when I first began writing about this complicated, fascinating couple nearly twenty years ago.

My thanks again to Pierre Salinger, Arthur Schlesinger Jr., Theodore Sorensen, Letitia Baldrige, John Kenneth Galbraith, Oleg Cassini, Gore Vidal, Paul "Red" Fay, George Plimpton, Roswell Gilpatric, Nancy Dickerson Whitehead, George Smathers, Evelyn Lincoln, Jacques Lowe, Hugh D. "Yusha" Auchincloss, Jamie Auchincloss, Chuck Spalding, Charles Bartlett, Theodore H. White, John Husted, Ham Brown, Helen Thomas, Angier Biddle Duke, Godfrey McHugh, Betty Beale, Clare Boothe Luce, Peter Duchin, Larry Newman, Priscilla Johnson McMillan, Sister Joanne Frey, Drew Middleton, Martha Bartlett, David Halberstam, John Davis, Cecil Stoughton, Charles Collingwood, Patricia Lawford, Tony Bradlee, Dr. Janet Travell, William vanden Heuvel, Jack Anderson, Gloria Swanson, Alfred Eisenstaedt, Dorothy Schoenbrun, Aileen Mehle, Dorothy Oliger, Marta Sgubin, Bette Davis, Vincent Russo, James E. O'Neal, Charles Whitehouse, Kitty Carlisle Hart, Charles Damore, Jack Valenti, Bertram S. Brown, Terry L. Birdwhistell, Otto Fuerbringer, Cleveland Amory, Henry Grunwald, John Bryson, Charles Furneaux, Roy Cohn, Wendy Leigh, Linus Pauling, Fred Friendly, Doris Lilly, Stephen Corsaro, Jesse Birnbaum, Richard Clurman, Richard B. Stolley, Ronald Grele, Barry Schenck, Rosemary McClure, Cranston Jones, Halston, Steve Michaud, David McGough, Paula Dranov, James Hill, John Marion, Dale Sider, Diane Tucker, Earl Blackwell, Tom Freeman, Perri Peltz, Jeanette

Peterson, William S. Paley, Albert V. Concordia, the Countess of Roma-nones, James Bacon, Willard K. Rice, Dudley Freeman, John Perry Barlow, John Sargent, Laurence Leamer, Anne Vanderhoop, Betsy Loth, Bob Thomas, Larry Lorenzo, Brad Darrach, Maryrose Grossman, Shirley Clur-man, Sandy Richardson, Farris L. Rookstool III, Janet Lizop, Yvette Reyes, Marybeth Whelan, and Corrie Novak.

This book could also not have been written without the help of the staffs of the John F. Kennedy Presidential Library and Museum, the Houghton Library at Harvard University, the Seeley G. Mudd Manuscript Library at Princeton University, the Columbia University Oral History Project, the Butler Library at Columbia University and Columbia Univer-sity's Rare Book and Manuscript Library, the Robert Drew Archive, the Boston University Library, the Stanford University Archives, the University of Kentucky Library, the Library of Congress, the United States Secret Ser-vice, the Federal Bureau of Investigation, the Lyndon Baines Johnson Li-brary, the Choate School Archives, the Redwood Library and Athenaeum of Newport, Rhode Island, the Barnstable Public Library, Miss Porter's School, the Boston Public Library, the Archdiocese of Boston, the *New Bedford Standard Times,* the Georgetown University Library, Vassar College Library, Winterthur Museum, the Gunn Memorial Library, the Bancroft Library at the University of California, Berkeley, the Silas Bronson Library, the Carlyle Hotel, the Associated Press, Reuters, Globe Photos, Corbis.

Sources and Chapter Notes

✑

The following chapter notes have been compiled to give an overview of the sources drawn upon in preparing *These Few Precious Days*, but they are by no means all-inclusive. I have respected the wishes of those few interview subjects who asked to remain anonymous, and accordingly I have not listed them here or elsewhere in the text. The archives and oral history collections of many institutions—including but not limited to the John F. Kennedy Presidential Library and Museum, the Lyndon Baines Johnson Library, the Oral History Project of Columbia University, the Seeley G. Mudd Manuscript Library at Princeton University, Department of Rare Books and Special Collections, and the Houghton Library at Harvard University—yielded a wealth of information, much of it emerging in stages since the death of Jacqueline Kennedy Onassis in 1994.

Most significant, perhaps, has been the gradual release between 1993 and 2012 of more than 260 hours of taped conversations conducted in the Oval Office and in the Cabinet Room during the Kennedy administration—all part of a system the president had installed in an apparent attempt to capture history being made in real time. In 2011, Caroline Kennedy added to the excitement by authorizing the release of Arthur Schlesinger's historic series of conversations with Jackie that took place in 1964 but had remained under lock and key ever since. In my own series of interviews with Schlesinger, he made reference to the contents of these tapes and predicted that they would not be released until 2044 if at all. Fortunately for us, he was wrong. The eight and a half hours of conversation between Schlesinger and Jackie shed important new light on life in the Kennedy White House and, more specifically, her life with JFK.

The thousands upon thousands of articles and news reports about the Kennedys that have been published over the past half century also served as source material for this and my earlier books, including press accounts in the *New York Times, Washington Post, Time, Newsweek, Life, Vanity Fair, Look, Saturday Evening Post, Wall Street Journal, Los Angeles Times, Boston Globe, Chicago Tribune,* and *New Yorker* as well as reports carried on the Associated Press, United Press International, and Reuters wires.

Chapters 1 and 2

Interview subjects included Arthur Schlesinger Jr., Pierre Salinger, Theodore Sorensen, Letitia Baldrige, Chuck Spalding, George Plimpton, Godfrey McHugh, Jacques Lowe, Hugh D. "Yusha" Auchincloss III, Charles Bartlett, Jack Valenti, Jamie Auchincloss, Ham Brown, Richard B. Stolley, Willard K. Rice, Jack Anderson, and Dr. Janet Travell. The author also drew on numerous oral histories, including those given by Jacqueline Kennedy Onassis, Robert F. Kennedy, Eunice Kennedy Shriver, Dean Rusk, Admiral George G. Burkley, Dave Powers, Robert McNamara, Pamela Turnure, Kenneth O'Donnell, Maud Shaw, Nancy Tuckerman, Janet Auchincloss, J. B. West, Lawrence O'Brien, Douglas Dillon, Walt Rostow, Peter Lawford, Paul "Red" Fay, Ted Sorensen, Hugh Sidey, Richard Cardinal Cushing, Peter Lisagor, William Walton, John Galvin, Liz Carpenter, Torbert Macdonald, Tazewell Shepard, Jacqueline Hirsh, Sarah McClendon, Isaac Avery, Cordelia Thaxton, Dorothy Tubridy, Father John C. Cavanaugh, and Arthur Krock.

National Security Agency, Secret Service, and Federal Bureau of Investigation files released through the Freedom of Information Act shed considerable light on the events of November 22, 1963, as did the Jacqueline Kennedy Onassis papers, the John Fitzgerald Kennedy papers (*Public Papers of the Presidents of the United States, John F. Kennedy, Containing the Public Messages, Statements, and Speeches of the President (1961–1963)*, the Robert F. Kennedy papers, and the papers of Dave Powers, Kenneth O'Donnell, John Kenneth Galbraith, Theodore H. White, Kirk LeMoyne "Lem" Billings, Godfrey McHugh, Paul "Red" Fay, Dean Rusk, Sir Alec Douglas-Home, Lawrence O'Brien, Dr. Janet Travell, Rose Fitzgerald Kennedy, and Joseph P. Kennedy. Teddy White's historic "Camelot" interview conducted shortly after the assassination was released in full only in 1995, one year after Jackie's death. Other published sources consulted: William Manchester, *The Death of a President* (New York: Harper & Row, 1967); *The Warren Commission Report* (Washington, D.C.: U.S. Government Printing Office, 1964); Arthur Schlesinger Jr., *A Thousand Days* (Boston: Houghton Mifflin, 1965); Jim Bishop, *The Day Kennedy Was Shot* (New York: Funk & Wagnalls, 1968); Kenneth P. O'Donnell and David F. Powers with Joe McCarthy, *"Johnny, We Hardly Knew Ye"* (Boston: Little, Brown, 1970); Theodore Sorensen, *Kennedy* (New York: Harper & Row, 1965); "The Assassination of President Kennedy," *Life*, November 29, 1963; J. B. West, *Upstairs at the White House* (New York: Coward, McCann & Geoghegan, 1973); Ben Bradlee, *A Good Life* (New York: Simon & Schuster, 1995); Mary Barelli Gallagher, *My Life with Jacqueline Kennedy* (New York: David McKay, 1969); Maud Shaw, *White House Nanny: My Years with Caroline and John Kennedy, Jr.* (New York: New American Library, 1965); Lady Bird Johnson, *A White House Diary* (New York: Holt, Rinehart & Winston, 1970); Clint Hill with

Lisa McCubbin, *Mrs. Kennedy and Me* (New York: Gallery Books, 2012); Robert Sam Anson, *They've Killed the President! The Search for the Murderers of John F. Kennedy* (New York: Bantam, 1975); Ben Bradlee, *Conversations with Kennedy* (New York: Norton, 1975).

Chapters 3–5

These chapters were based in part on conversations with Theodore Sorensen, Jacques Lowe, Pierre Salinger, Gore Vidal, Letitia Baldrige, Arthur Schlesinger Jr., Chuck Spalding, Charles Bartlett, John Husted, Larry Newman, Nancy Dickerson Whitehead, Martha Bartlett, Hugh D. "Yusha" Auchincloss; William S. Paley, Priscilla Johnson McMillan, Robert Drew, Jamie Auchincloss, Clare Boothe Luce, Shirley MacLaine, Bette Davis, and Evelyn Lincoln.

The Laura Bergquist Knebel Papers at Boston University, oral histories: Claiborne Pell, Leverett Saltonstall, Sargent Shriver, Thomas "Tip" O'Neill, John W. McCormack, John F. Dempsey, Hale Boggs, Dean Acheson, John Sherman Cooper, James MacGregor Burns, Leonard Bernstein, Mark Shaw, Peter Lawford, Sister Parish, Patrick Mulkern, Dory Shary, Torbert Macdonald, J. B. West, Fletcher Knebel, Ralph Horton, Patrick Munroe, Joseph Alsop, Harold S. Ulen, James Farrell, William O. Douglas, Edward M. Gallagher, Francis X. Morrissey, Foster Furcolo, John Kelso, Helen Lempart, Jean McGonigle Mannix, Joanne Barbosa, Peter Cloherty, Mark Dalton, Joseph Casey, William F. Kelly, Harold Tinker, John J. Droney, Hugh Fraser, Howard Fitzpatrick, Joseph Russo, Garrett Byrne, Anthony Gallucio, Andrew Dazzi, James M. Murphy, Joseph Degugliemo, Mary Colbert, William DeMarco, Maurice Donahue, Roland Evans Jr. Some material regarding Max Jacobson's relationship with the Kennedys comes from Jacobson's unpublished memoir. Father John C. Cavanaugh's oral history can be found in the Andrew Mellon Library Oral History Collection of the Choate School and in the JFK Library's oral history collection.

Articles and other published sources for this period included Eleanor Harris, "The Senator Is in a Hurry," *McCall's*, August 1957; Herbert Parmet, *Jack: The Struggles of John F. Kennedy* (New York: Dial Press, 1980); "The Senate's Gay Young Bachelor," *Saturday Evening Post*, June 13, 1953; "How to Be a Presidential Candidate," *New York Times Magazine*, July 13, 1958; "Behind the Scenes," *Time*, May 5, 1958; Luella R. Hennessey, "Bringing Up the Kennedys," *Good Housekeeping*, August 1961; "Joe Kennedy's Feelings About His Son," *Life*, December 19, 1960; Susan Sheehan, "The Happy Jackie, the Sad Jackie, the Bad Jackie, the Good Jackie," *New York Times Magazine*, May 31, 1970; "This Is John Fitzgerald Kennedy," *Newsweek*, June 23, 1958; "Most Talked-About Candidate for 1960," *U.S. News & World Report*, November 8, 1957; Mary Van Rensselaer Thayer, *Jacqueline*

Bouvier Kennedy (Garden City, N.Y.: Doubleday, 1961); John H. David, *The Bouviers: Portrait of an American Family* (New York: Farrar, Straus & Giroux, 1969); Thomas C. Reeves, *A Question of Character* (New York: Free Press, 1991); "Jackie Kennedy: First Lady at 30?" *U.S. News & World Report*, September 1960; Mary Van Rensselaer Thayer, "First Years of the First Lady," *Ladies' Home Journal*, February 1961; Dave Powers, "I Have Never Met Anyone Like Her," *Life*, August 1995.

Chapters 6–8

For these chapters, the author drew on conversations with John Kenneth Galbraith, Oleg Cassini, Arthur Schlesinger Jr., George Smathers, Roswell Gilpatric, Pierre Salinger, Theodore Sorensen, Jacques Lowe, Angier Biddle Duke, Linus Pauling, Charles Bartlett, Letitia Baldrige, Tony Bradlee, Helen Thomas, Betty Beale, Chuck Spalding, Larry Newman, Pat Lawford, Alan Jay Lerner, Ham Brown, Halston, Nancy Tuckerman, Hugh D. "Yusha" Auchincloss III, Charles Collingwood, Dorothy Schoenbrun, Dorothy Oliger, Mollie Fosburgh, Harry Winston, Charles Furneaux, Shana Alexander, Fred Friendly, and Alfred Eisenstaedt. Jacqueline Kennedy Onassis's oral history was done by Terry L. Birdwhistell in New York on May 13, 1981, as part of the John Sherman Cooper Oral History Project at the University of Kentucky Library. Other oral histories that proved helpful include Pope Paul VI, Hubert H. Humphrey, Averell Harriman, Katharine Graham, Claiborne Pell, Nicholas Katzenbach, Lorraine Cooper, Albert Gore, Admiral George Burkley, Lucius Clay, William Walton, Walt Rostow, Jacob Javits, Dave Powers, Pamela Turnure, Laura Knebel, Clement Norton, Gloria Sitrin, Kay Halle, Traphes Bryant, Myer Feldman, Joseph Karatis, Chris Camp, James Young, Barbara Gamarekian, and Kenneth Burke. The Katharine Graham and Liz Carpenter Oral Histories are available at the Lyndon Baines Johnson Library. Published sources include Hugh Sidey, "The First Lady Brings History and Beauty to the White House," *Life*, September 1, 1961; *Jacqueline Kennedy: Historic Conversations on Life with John F. Kennedy* (New York: Hyperion, 2011); Anne Taylor Fleming, "The Kennedy Mystique," *New York Times Magazine*, June 17, 1979; Phillip Nobile and Ron Rosenblum, "The Curious Aftermath of JFK's Best and Brightest Affair," *New Times* magazine, July 9, 1976; "Queen of America," *Time*, March 23, 1962; Gerri Hirshey, "The Last Act of Judith Exner," *Vanity Fair*, April 1990; Mimi Alford, *Once Upon a Secret: My Affair with John F. Kennedy and Its Aftermath* (New York: Random House, 2012); Kitty Kelley, *Capturing Camelot* (New York: A Thomas Dunne Book/ St. Martin's Press, 2012); Thomas Maier, *The Kennedys: America's Emerald Kings* (New York: Basic Books, 2004).

Chapters 9 and 10

Information for these chapters was based in part on conversations with Arthur Schlesinger Jr., George Plimpton, Letitia Baldrige, Pierre Salinger, Oleg Cassini, Charles Bartlett, Chuck Spalding, John Kenneth Galbraith, Martha Bartlett, Richard B. Stolley, Dr. Janet Travell, Peter Duchin, Paul "Red" Fay, Hugh D. "Yusha" Auchincloss III, Evelyn Lincoln, David Halberstam, George Smathers, Theodore Sorensen, Jack Valenti, Jacques Lowe, Godfrey McHugh, William S. Paley, Sandy Richardson, Jamie Auchincloss, John Bryson, Paula Dranov, Cranston Jones, Clare Boothe Luce, and Roswell Gilpatric. The author also drew on numerous oral histories, including Dave Powers, Kenneth P. O'Donnell, Lawrence O'Brien, Luella Hennessey, Hervé Alphand, James Reed, Burke Marshall, Dean Rusk, Robert McNamara, Pierre Salinger, Walt Rostow, Janet Auchincloss, Joseph Alsop, August Heckscher, Lorraine Cooper, Lem Billings, John Sherman Cooper, and Richard Cardinal Cushing. Among the published sources: Jacqueline Kennedy, "How He Really Was," *Life,* May 29, 1964; Robert Ajemian, "A Man's Week to Reckon," *Life,* July 3, 1964; Theodore Sorensen, "If Kennedy Had Lived," *Look,* October 19, 1965; Jack Anderson, *Washington Expose* (Washington, D.C.: Public Affairs Press, 1967); Lawrence K. Altman and Todd S. Purdum, "In J.F.K. File, Hidden Illness, Pain and Pills," *New York Times,* November 17, 2002; Ted Widmer, *Listening In: The Secret White House Recordings of John F. Kennedy* (New York: Hyperion, 2012); Sally Bedell Smith, *Grace and Power* (New York: Random House, 2004); "The Kennedys' Jesuit," *Georgetown Voice,* January 15, 2004; Helen Kennedy, "Jackie Kennedy Tapes Unveil True Feelings," New York *Daily News,* September 13, 2011; Christopher Hitchens, "Widow of Opportunity," *Vanity Fair,* December 2011; Janny Scott, "In Tapes, Candid Talk by a Young Widow," *New York Times,* September 11, 2011; Andy Soltis, "Well, That's a Tough Day," *New York Post,* January 25, 2012.

Bibliography

Acheson, Dean. *Power and Diplomacy.* Cambridge, Mass.: Harvard University Press, 1958.

Adams, Cindy, and Susan Crimp. *Iron Rose: The Story of Rose Fitzgerald Kennedy and Her Dynasty.* Beverly Hills, Calif.: Dove Books, 1995.

Alford, Mimi. *Once Upon a Secret.* New York: Random House, 2012.

Amory, Cleveland. *The Proper Bostonians.* New York: E. P. Dutton, 1947.

Andersen, Christopher. *The Day John Died.* New York: William Morrow, 2000.

———. *Jack and Jackie: Portrait of an American Marriage.* New York: William Morrow, 1996.

———. *Jackie After Jack: Portrait of the Lady.* New York: William Morrow, 1998.

———. *Sweet Caroline: Last Child of Camelot.* New York: William Morrow, 2003.

Anson, Robert Sam. *"They've Killed the President!" The Search for the Murderers of John F. Kennedy.* New York: Bantam, 1975.

Anthony, Carl Sferrazza. *As We Remember Her.* New York: HarperCollins, 1997.

———. *The Kennedy White House: Family Life & Pictures, 1961–1963.* New York: Simon & Schuster, 2001.

Baldwin, Billy. *Billy Baldwin Remembers.* New York: Harcourt Brace Jovanovich, 1974.

Baldrige, Letitia. *In the Kennedy Style: Magical Evenings in the Kennedy White House.* New York: Doubleday, 1998.

———. *A Lady First: My Life in the Kennedy White House and the American Embassies of Paris and Rome.* New York: Viking Penguin, 2001.

———. *Of Diamonds and Diplomats.* Boston: Houghton Mifflin, 1968.

Beard, Peter. *Longing for Darkness: Kamante's Tales from "Out of Africa."* San Francisco: Chronicle Books, 1990.

Beschloss, Michael R. *Kennedy and Roosevelt: The Uneasy Alliance.* New York: Norton, 1980.

———. *Taking Charge: The Johnson White House Tapes, 1963–1964.* New York: Simon & Schuster, 1997.

Birmingham, Stephen. *Jacqueline Bouvier Kennedy Onassis.* New York: Grosset & Dunlap, 1978.

———. *Real Lace: America's Irish Rich.* New York: Harper & Row, 1973.

Bishop, Jim. *The Day Kennedy Was Shot.* New York: Funk & Wagnalls, 1968.

Blaine, Gerald, with Lisa McCubbin. *The Kennedy Detail.* Gallery Books, 2010.

Blair, Joan, and Clay Blair Jr. *The Search for JFK.* New York: Berkley, 1976.

Bouvier, Jacqueline, and Lee Bouvier. *One Special Summer.* New York: Delacorte Press, 1974.

Bouvier, Kathleen. *To Jack with Love, Black Jack Bouvier: A Remembrance.* New York: Kensington,1979.

Braden, Joan. *Just Enough Rope.* New York: Villard, 1989.

Bradlee, Ben. *Conversations with Kennedy.* New York: Norton, 1975.

———. *A Good Life.* New York: Simon & Schuster, 1995.

Brady, Frank. *Onassis.* Englewood Cliffs, N.J.: Prentice-Hall, 1977.

Brando, Marlon, with Robert Lindsey. *Songs My Mother Taught Me.* New York: Random House, 1995.

Bryant, Traphes, and Frances Spatz Leighton. *Dog Days at the White House.* New York: Macmillan, 1975.

Buck, Pearl S. *The Kennedy Women: A Personal Appraisal.* New York: Harcourt, 1969.

Burke, Richard E. *My Ten Years with Ted Kennedy.* New York: St. Martin's Press, 1992.

Burns, James MacGregor. *Edward Kennedy and the Camelot Legacy.* New York: Norton, 1976.

———. *John Kennedy: A Political Profile.* New York: Harcourt, 1960.

Cameron, Gail. *Rose: A Biography of Rose Fitzgerald Kennedy.* New York: Putnam, 1971.

Cassini, Oleg. *In My Own Fashion: An Autobiography.* New York: Simon & Schuster, 1987.

———. *A Thousand Days of Magic.* New York: Rizzoli, 1995.

Cheshire, Maxine. *Maxine Cheshire, Reporter.* Boston: Houghton Mifflin, 1978.

Clarke, Gerald. *Capote.* New York: Simon & Schuster, 1988.

Cohn, Roy. *McCarthy.* New York: New American Library, 1968.

Collier, Peter, and David Horowitz. *The Kennedys: An American Drama.* New York: Summit Books, 1984.

Connally, Nellie, and Mickey Herskowitz. *From Love Field: My Final Hours with President John F. Kennedy.* New York: Rugged Land, 2003.

Dallek, Robert. *An Unfinished Life: John F. Kennedy, 1917–1963.* New York: Little, Brown, 2003.

Damore, Leo. *The Cape Cod Years of John Fitzgerald Kennedy.* Englewood Cliffs, N.J.: Prentice-Hall, 1967.

Davis, John. *The Bouviers: Portrait of an American Family.* New York. Farrar, Straus, 1969.

———. *The Kennedys: Dynasty and Disaster.* New York: McGraw-Hill, 1984.

Dempster, Nigel. *Heiress: The Story of Christina Onassis.* London: Weidenfeld & Nicolson, 1989.

DuBois, Diana. *In Her Sister's Shadow: An Intimate Biography of Lee Radziwill.* Boston: Little, Brown, 1995.

Duchin, Peter. *Ghost of a Chance.* New York: Random House, 1996.

Evans, Peter. *Ari: The Life and Times of Aristotle Socrates Onassis.* New York: Summit Books, 1986.

Exner, Judith, as told to Ovid Demaris. *My Story.* New York: Grove Press, 1977.

Fay, Paul B., Jr. *The Pleasure of His Company.* New York: Harper & Row, 1966.

Fisher, Eddie. *Eddie: My Life, My Loves.* New York: Harper & Row, 1981.

Fontaine, Joan. *No Bed of Roses: An Autobiography.* New York: William Morrow, 1978.

Frank, Gerold. *Zsa Zsa Gabor: My Story.* New York: World, 1960.

Fraser, Nicolas, Philip Jacobson, Mark Ottaway, and Lewis Chester. *Aristotle Onassis.* Philadelphia: Lippincott, 1977.

Frischauer, Willi. *Jackie.* London: Michael Joseph, 1967.

———. *Onassis.* New York: Meredith Press, 1968.

Galbraith, John Kenneth. *Ambassador's Journal: A Personal Account of the Kennedy Years.* Boston: Houghton Mifflin, 1969.

Gallagher, Mary Barelli. *My Life with Jacqueline Kennedy.* New York: David McKay, 1969.

Giancana, Antoinette, and Thomas C. Renner. *Mafia Princess: Growing Up in Sam Giancana's Family.* New York: William Morrow, 1984.

Golway, Terry, and Les Krantz. *JFK: Day by Day.* Philadelphia: Running Press, 2010.

Goodwin, Doris Kearns. *The Fitzgeralds and the Kennedys: An American Saga.* New York: Simon & Schuster, 1987.

Granger, Stewart. *Sparks Fly Upward.* New York: Putnam, 1981.

Halberstam, David. *The Best and the Brightest.* New York: Random House, 1969.

Hall, Gordon Langley, and Ann Pinchot. *Jacqueline Kennedy.* New York: Frederick Fell, 1964.

Hamilton, Nigel. *JFK: Reckless Youth.* New York: Random House, 1992.

Heymann, C. David. *A Woman Named Jackie: An Intimate Biography of Jacqueline Bouvier Kennedy Onassis.* New York: A Lyle Stuart Book/Carol Communications, 1989.

Hill, Clint, with Lisa McCubbin. *Mrs. Kennedy and Me.* New York: Gallery Books, 2012.

Kelley, Kitty. *Capturing Camelot.* New York: A Thomas Dunne Book/ St. Martin's Press, 2012.

————. *His Way: The Unauthorized Biography of Frank Sinatra.* New York: Bantam, 1986.

————. *Jackie Oh!* Secaucus, N.J.: Lyle Stuart, 1979.

Kennedy, Caroline. *The Best-Loved Poems of Jacqueline Kennedy Onassis.* New York: Hyperion, 2001.

————. *Jacqueline Kennedy: Historic Conversations on Life with John F. Kennedy: Interviews with Arthur Schlesinger, Jr., 1964.* New York: Hyperion, 2011.

————. *A Patriot's Handbook: Songs, Poems, Stories, and Speeches Celebrating the Land We Love.* New York: Hyperion, 2003.

————. *Profiles in Courage for Our Time.* New York: Hyperion, 2002.

Kennedy, Caroline, and Ellen Alderman. *In Our Defense: The Bill of Rights in Action.* New York: William Morrow, 1991.

————. *The Right to Privacy.* New York: Vintage, 1997.

Kennedy, John F. *Profiles in Courage.* New York: Harper & Row, 1965.

————. *Why England Slept.* New York: Wilfred Funk, 1940.

Kennedy, Rose Fitzgerald. *Times to Remember.* New York: Doubleday, 1974.

Kessler, Ronald. *Inside the White House.* New York: Pocket Books, 1995.

Klein, Edward. *Just Jackie: Her Private Years.* New York: Ballantine Books, 1998.

Koskoff, David E. *Joseph P. Kennedy: A Life and Times.* Englewood Cliffs, N.J.: Prentice-Hall, 1974.

Krock, Arthur. *Memoirs: Sixty Years on the Firing Line.* New York: Funk & Wagnalls, 1968.

Kunhardt, Philip B., Jr., ed. *Life in Camelot.* Boston: Little, Brown, 1988.

Lash, Joseph P. *Eleanor and Franklin.* New York: Norton, 1971.

Latham, Caroline, with Jeannie Sakol. *The Kennedy Encyclopedia.* New York: New American Library, 1989.

Lawford, Patricia Seaton, with Ted Schwarz. *The Peter Lawford Story.* New York: Carroll & Graf, 1988.

Lawliss, Charles. *Jacqueline Kennedy Onassis.* New York: J. G. Press, 1994.

Leamer, Laurence. *The Kennedy Women: The Saga of an American Family.* New York: Villard, 1994.

Leigh, Wendy. *Prince Charming: The John F. Kennedy Jr. Story.* New York: Signet, 1994.

Lilly, Doris. *Those Fabulous Greeks: Onassis, Niarchos, and Livanos.* New York: Cowles, 1970.

Lowe, Jacques. *Jacqueline Kennedy Onassis: A Tribute.* New York: A Jacques Lowe Visual Arts Project, 1995.

————. *JFK Remembered.* New York: Random House, 1993.

Maier, Thomas. *The Kennedys: America's Emerald Kings.* New York: Basic Books, 2004.

Mailer, Norman. *Marilyn.* New York: Grosset & Dunlap, 1973.

———. *Of Women and Their Elegance.* New York: Simon & Schuster, 1980.

Manchester, William. *The Death of a President.* New York: Harper & Row, 1967.

———. *Portrait of a President: John F. Kennedy in Profile.* Boston: Little, Brown, 1962.

Martin, Ralph. *A Hero for Our Time.* New York: Ballantine, 1984.

McCarthy, Joe. *The Remarkable Kennedys.* New York: Dial Press, 1960.

Montgomery, Ruth. *Hail to the Chiefs: My Life and Times with Six Presidents.* New York: Coward-McCann, 1970.

Moutsatsos, Kiki Feroudi. *The Onassis Women.* New York: G. P. Putnam's Sons, 1998.

O'Connor, Edwin. *The Last Hurrah.* New York: Bantam Books, 1970.

O'Donnell, Kenneth P., and David F. Powers, with Joe McCarthy. *"Johnny, We Hardly Knew Ye."* Boston: Little, Brown, 1970.

Ogden, Christopher. *Life of the Party: The Biography of Pamela Digby Churchill Hayward Harriman.* New York: Warner Books, 1994.

O'Neill, Tip, with William Novak. *Man of the House: The Life and Political Memoirs of Speaker Tip O'Neill.* New York: Random House, 1987.

Oppenheimer, Jerry. *The Other Mrs. Kennedy.* New York: St. Martin's Press, 1994.

Parmet, Herbert S. *Jack: The Struggles of John F. Kennedy.* New York: Dial Press, 1980.

———. *J.F.K.: The Presidency of John F. Kennedy.* New York, Dial Press, 1983.

Parker, Robert. *Capitol Hill in Black and White.* New York: Dodd, Mead, 1987.

Pepitone, Lena, and William Stadiem. *Marilyn Monroe Confidential.* New York: Pocket Books, 1979.

Pottker, Jan. *Janet & Jackie.* New York: St. Martin's Press, 2001.

Reed, J. D., Kyle Smith, and Jill Smolowe. *John F. Kennedy Jr.: A Biography.* New York: People Profiles/Time, 1998.

Reeves, Richard. *President Kennedy: Profile of Power.* New York: Simon & Schuster, 1993.

Reeves, Richard, with Harvey Sawler. *Portrait of Camelot.* New York: Abrams, 2010.

Reeves, Thomas C. *A Question of Character: A Life of John F. Kennedy.* Rocklin, Calif.: Prima, 1992.

Salinger, Pierre. *P.S.: A Memoir.* New York: St. Martin's Press, 1995.

———. *With Kennedy.* Garden City, N.Y.: Doubleday, 1966.

Schlesinger, Arthur M., Jr. *A Thousand Days.* Boston: Houghton Mifflin, 1965.

Sgubin, Marta. *Cooking for Madam: Recipes and Reminiscences from the Home of Jacqueline Kennedy Onassis.* New York: A Lisa Drew Book/Scribner, 1998.

Shaw, Maud. *White House Nannie: My Years with Caroline and John Kennedy, Jr.* New York: New American Library, 1965.

Shulman, Irving. *"Jackie"! The Exploitation of a First Lady.* New York: Trident Press, 1970.

Sidey, Hugh. *John F. Kennedy, President.* New York: Atheneum, 1964.

Smith, Sally Bedell. *Grace and Power.* New York: Random House, 2004.

Sorensen, Theodore C. *Kennedy.* New York: Harper & Row, 1965.

Spada, James. *John and Caroline: Their Lives in Pictures.* New York: St. Martin's Press, 2001.

———. *Peter Lawford: The Man Who Kept the Secrets.* New York: Bantam, 1991.

Spignesi, Stephen. *The J.F.K. Jr. Scrapbook.* Secaucus, N.J.: Carol, 1997.

Stack, Robert, with Mark Evans. *Straight Shooting.* New York: Macmillan, 1980.

Storm, Tempest, with Bill Boyd. *Tempest Storm: The Lady Is a Vamp.* Atlanta: Peachtree, 1987.

Summers, Anthony. *Goddess: The Secret Lives of Marilyn Monroe.* New York: Macmillan, 1985.

Swanson, Gloria. *Swanson on Swanson.* New York: Random House, 1980.

Taraborrelli, Randy. *Jackie, Ethel, Joan.* New York: Grand Central, 2000.

ter Horst, J. F., and Ralph Albertazzie. *The Flying White House.* New York: Coward, McCann & Geoghegan, 1979.

Thayer, Mary Van Rensselaer. *Jacqueline Bouvier Kennedy.* Garden City, N.Y.: Doubleday, 1961.

Thomas, Bob. *Golden Boy: The Untold Story of William Holden.* New York: St. Martin's Press, 1983.

Thomas, Helen. *Dateline: White House.* New York: Macmillan, 1975.

Tierney, Gene, with Mickey Herskowitz. *Self-Portrait.* New York: Simon & Schuster, 1979.

Travell, Janet. *Office Hours: Day and Night.* New York: World, 1968.

Vidal, Gore. *Palimpsest: A Memoir.* New York: Random House, 1995.

Walton, William. *The Evidence of Washington.* New York: Harper & Row, 1966.

The Warren Report. New York: Associated Press, 1964.

Watney, Hedda Lyons. *Jackie.* New York: Leisure Books, 1971.

West, J. B., with Mary Lynn Kotz. *Upstairs at the White House.* New York: Coward, McCann & Geoghegan, 1973.

White, Theodore H. *In Search of History.* New York: Warner Books, 1978.

———. *The Making of the President 1960.* New York: Atheneum, 1961.

Widmer, Ted. *Listening In: The Secret White House Recordings of John F. Kennedy.* New York: Hyperion, 2012.

Wills, Garry. *The Kennedy Imprisonment.* Boston: Atlantic–Little, Brown, 1981.